Computer Accounting Essentials with Microsoft® Dynamics GP 10.0
Second Edition

Carol Yacht, MA
Software Consultant

Susan V. Crosson, MS, CPA
Santa Fe College

Joann Segovia, PhD, CPA
Winona State University

 **McGraw-Hill Irwin**

Boston   Burr Ridge, IL   Dubuque, IA   Madison, WI   New York   San Francisco   St. Louis
Bangkok   Bogotá   Caracas   Kuala Lumpur   Lisbon   London   Madrid   Mexico City
Milan   Montreal   New Delhi   Santiago   Seoul   Singapore   Sydney   Taipei   Toronto

About the Authors

Carol Yacht is a textbook author and accounting educator. Carol contributes regularly to professional journals and is the Accounting Section Editor for *Business Education Forum*, a publication of the National Business Education Association. She is the author of Microsoft Office Accounting, Dynamics-GP (Great Plains), Peachtree, QuickBooks, and Excel textbooks and Carol Yacht's General Ledger and Peachtree CD-ROMs (www.mhhe.com/yacht). In 1978, Carol started using accounting software in her classes at institutions including California State University, Los Angeles; West Los Angeles College; Yavapai College; and Beverly Hills High School.

Carol Yacht is an officer of the American Accounting Association's Two-Year College section and recipient of its Lifetime Achievement Award. She has worked for IBM Corporation as an education instruction specialist, and served on NBEA's Computer Education Task Force. Carol is a frequent speaker at state, regional, and national conventions. Carol earned her MA degree from California State University, Los Angeles; BS degree from the University of New Mexico, and AS degree from Temple University.

Susan V. Crosson is Professor and Coordinator of Accounting at Santa Fe College in Gainesville, FL. She previously taught on the faculties of University of Florida, Washington University in St. Louis, University of Oklahoma, Johnson County Community College, and Kansas City Kansas Community College. Susan is known for her innovative application of pedagogical strategies online and in the classroom. She likes to speak and write on the effective use of technology throughout the accounting curriculum. Susan is co-author of several accounting textbooks including the Computer Accounting Essentials series.

Susan serves on the AICPA's Pre-certification Education Executive Committee and on the Accounting Careers and Members in Education committee for the Florida Institute of CPAs. She is active in the American Accounting Association and has served it as a Vice President of Sections and Regions, Chair of the Membership Committee, Council Member-at-large, and Chair of the Two-Year Accounting Section. Currently, she is the co-chair of AAA's annual Conference on Teaching and Learning in Accounting. Susan has received the Outstanding Educator Award and Lifetime Achievement Award from the American Accounting Association's Two Year College Section, the Florida Association of Community Colleges Professor of the Year Award for Instructional Excellence and University of Oklahoma's Halliburton Education Award for Excellence. Susan earned her Master of Science in Accounting from Texas Tech University and her undergraduate degree in accounting and economics from Southern Methodist University. She is a CPA.

Joann Segovia will join Winona State University as Associate Professor in January, 2009. She is currently Professor at Minnesota State University Moorhead. She previously taught on the faculties of University of North Dakota and University of Minnesota Duluth. Her research and publications in various journals reflect the use of technology in the classroom. She regularly presents innovative approaches to use technologies at various accounting and technology conferences as well as using Dynamics GP throughout the accounting curriculum. Her current behavioral research includes investigating companies' responses to SOX reporting of material weaknesses. She received the Midwest American Accounting Association Best Paper Award and Creative Contribution to Accounting Education; the AIS Best Paper Award, and Minnesota State University Moorhead Academic Affairs Excellence Award in Research Activity.

Joann is active in the American Accounting Association and has served on the Midwest Steering Committee and Nominating Committee, as well as the Midwest Teaching and Curriculum Director. She also is on the Board of the Accounting Information Systems Educators and various university committees. She regularly reviews, moderates, or discusses papers within the information systems or teaching and curriculum sections for various conferences. She also prepares and reviews various instructional materials and writes CPA exam questions. Joann obtained her PhD from Texas Tech University, her MBA from Creighton University, and her BS degree in accounting from Wayne State College of Wayne, Nebraska. She is a CPA.

McGraw-Hill/Irwin Computer Accounting Titles

Supplements for Financial and Managerial Accounting, Intermediate Accounting, AIS, or Computer Accounting courses:

- *Yacht, Crosson, Segovia **Computer Accounting Essentials with Microsoft Dynamics GP 10.0**, 2e*, 007 811 0807

- *Yacht, Crosson **Computer Accounting Essentials with QuickBooks Pro 2008***, 007 337 9387

- *Yacht, Crosson **Computer Accounting Essentials with QuickBooks Online Plus**, 4e* 978 039 018 1367

- *Yacht, Crosson **Computer Accounting Essentials with Microsoft Office Accounting 2007***, 007 352 7033

For Full Term Computer Accounting or AIS courses:

- *Yacht Crosson, Segovia **Computer Accounting with Microsoft Dynamics GP 10**, 2e*, 007 811 0793

- *Yacht **Computer Accounting with Peachtree Complete 2008**, 12e*, 007 337 9395

- *Yacht, Crosson **Computer Accounting with Microsoft Office Accounting***, 007 333 796X

- *Ulmer **Computer Accounting with QuickBooks Pro 2008** 10e* 0077262387

For more information, visit these websites:

www.mhhe.com/yacht

www.mhhe.com/ulmer2008

Software Installation

Software Installation includes the following:

1. System Requirements.
2. Installation of Microsoft Dynamics GP 10.0 (DGP).
3. Student Data DVD.
4. Windows Vista; Run as Administrator.
5. Start Dynamics GP and Opening Fabrikam, Inc.
6. Exit Dynamics GP.
7. Virtual Machine Installation.
8. File Organization of Dynamics GP 10.0-Education.
9. Uninstall Dynamics GP software.

 Read Me

Install the software Dynamics GP 10.0-Education or use a virtual instance of Dynamics GP 10.0 instead in the school's computer lab. Either option insures software compatibility between the school and student's off-site installation. If the school's computer lab has another version of Dynamics GP installed (for example, Dynamics GP 10.0 academic alliance version), two versions of Dynamics GP can be installed. If different Dynamics GP versions reside on the same machine, be sure to use a different directory for each version.
When you install Dynamics GP 10.0-Education, Microsoft SQL Server Express installs automatically.

Microsoft Dynamics GP 10.0-Education was used to write the textbook.

System Requirements

Operating System: Windows Vista Business, Ultimate, or Enterprise, (32-bit and 64-bit); or Microsoft Windows XP Professional with Service Pack 2 (32-bit and 64-bit); or Windows Server 2003 with Service Pack 2 (32-bit and 64-bit).

Processor: Pentium IV 2.4 GHz or higher

Hard Disk Space: 2 GB of available hard disk space

RAM Memory: 512 MB (1GB recommended)

Drive: DVD-ROM drive for installing Dynamics GP 10.0-Education software.

Video: SVGA (800 x 600) with 16-bit driver

External media: USB media, 2 GB recommended.

INSTALLATION OF MICROSOFT DYNAMICS GP 10.0[1] SOFTWARE

A DVD labeled Dynamics GP 10.0-Education is included with the textbook. There is also a Student Data DVD which contains the Empty Company Data and Sample Company Data folders that will be used with this textbook.

The steps that follow explain how to install the software and the sample company data. These steps assume you are installing Microsoft Dynamics GP10.0-Education *and* the Sample Company Data for the *first time*.

IMPORTANT INFORMATION; READ BEFORE INSTALLATION

Microsoft Dynamics GP 10.0-Education and the Windows Vista operating system were used to write the textbook. All the illustrations were done and steps completed using Windows Vista and Dynamics GP 10-Education. You may install the DVD that is packaged with the textbook on individual computers, on a virtual machine, or in a classroom computer lab.

Before installation check your computer system. System requirements are shown on pages iii-iv.

The installation is straightforward. Make sure you do the following:

1.   The folder that Dynamics GP is installed to *must* be empty. The ***default installation folder*** or ***program path*** is <Program Files>\Microsoft Dynamics\GP-Education. Make sure this folder is empty. The user may install to a different location.

---

[1]Dynamics GP 10.0 was formerly called Great Plains.

2.   The student must provide a password for the SQL Server administrator account. The installation *cannot* continue if a password is not provided.

3.   The student must select a country/region of either the United States or Canada.

4.   The student must be logged onto the machine as a user with administrative rights to the machine in order to install. The User ID is **sa**. (**sa** is an acronym for System Administrator. When you start DGP on page xi, you type **sa** in the User ID field.)

5.   The Student Data DVD includes a Sample Company Data folder. The Sample Company Data folder needs to be copied to your USB drive. When starting Dynamics GP, load data from your USB drive's Sample Company Data folder.

6.   Open the DYNAMICS.mdf file from your USB drive to start Fabrikam, Inc.

The Education Edition includes the option for students to use a computer in a lab or to be able to move data between computers. The authors suggest at least a 2 GB USB thumb drive for saving data.

Detailed steps for installing Dynamics GP 10.0 follow. *Check with your instructor before installing in the school's computer lab.* These instructions should be used if you are installing on an individual computer or laptop.

1.   Insert the Microsoft Dynamics GP 10.0 DVD that is included with the textbook in the DVD drive. An AutoPlay window appears. (*Hint:* These steps were written with Windows Vista. The author's DVD drive is identified with the letter F.)

AutoPlay

DVD Drive (F:) GPEDU10

☐ Always do this for software and games:

Install or run program

Run Setup.exe
Published by Microsoft Corporation

General options

Open folder to view files
using Windows Explorer

Set AutoPlay defaults in Control Panel

2.   Select Run Setup.exe. If a window appears that says A program needs your permission to continue, click Continue. The Component Installation window appears.

3. Click Install . Each component will show a checkmark next to it. Compare your Component Installation window to the one below.

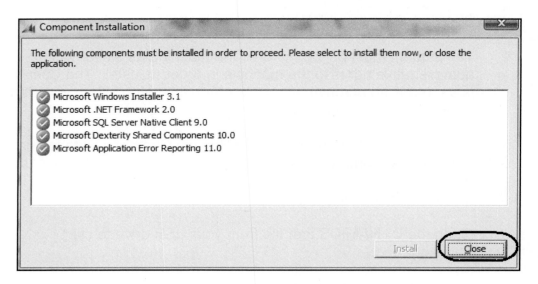

4. When all items are checked, click Close . Be very patient!!! Depending on your system's processing speed, the Welcome window may take several minutes to appear. The Welcome window finally appears.

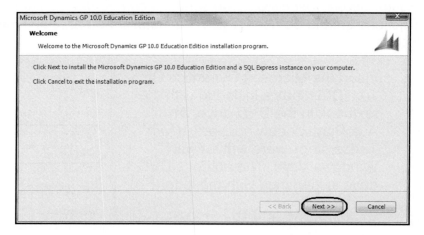

Troubleshooting

If a .NET Framework 2.0 is not installed; the installation cannot continue window appears, click OK. Refer to Appendix A, Troubleshooting.

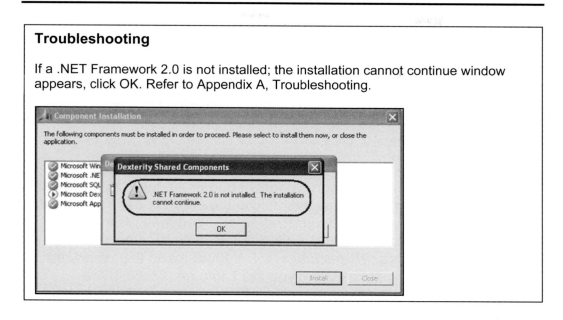

5.   Read the information on the Welcome window. Click Next >> to install.

6.   The Country/Region Selection window appears. Select either the United States or Canada. Click Next >>.

7.   The License Agreement window appears.

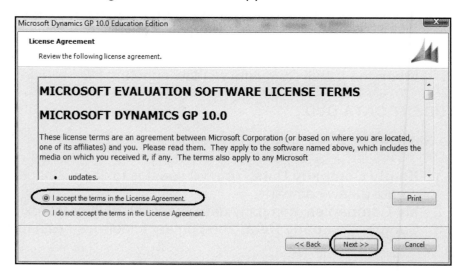

8.   Select I accept the terms in the License Agreement. Click
      [Next >>] .

9.   The Install Location window appears. The default location is
      C:\Program Files\Microsoft Dynamics\GP-Education. To accept
      the default location, click [Next >>] . *Or*, select Browse to go to
      another location.

10.   The SQL Server Password window appears. In the Password field,
      type a 6-12 character password. The password is ***case sensitive***.
      Do not *use a space between characters*. You may want to use
      lowercase letters only and a word that is easy to remember; for
      example **access**. *This is important*. You will need this password
      when using Dynamics GP. Type the *same* password in the
      Confirm Password field. The User ID is show below. *Write down
      your password.*

      User ID: **sa**

      Password: _____

11.   Click [Next >>] .

12.   The Ready to Install window appears. Click [Install] . The
      Installation Progress window appears. Installation will take a few
      minutes. Be patient!

13.   When the Install Complete window appears, click [Exit] .

STUDENT DATA DVD

The Student Data DVD includes three folders.

1. **Empty Company Data**. You will use this folder in Chapter 2 to
    create a new company.
2. **My Companies,** company data used with a different textbook.
3. **Sample Company Data**. The primary folder used with this text.

Complete the following steps to copy the Sample Company Data folder to your computer or USB drive. Then you will be ready to start Dynamics GP and open Fabrikam, Inc., the sample company.

Working on your own computer	**Computer Lab/Classroom and/or own Computer**
If you are working on your own computer, follow steps 1-7. In these steps, you copy the Sample Company Data folder from the Student Data DVD to your own individual PC. These steps describe how to copy the Sample Company Data folder to the installation path at C:\Program Files\Microsoft Dynamics\ GP-Education\ Student Data.	If you are working at school *and* at home, the authors recommend that you copy the Sample Company Data folder from the Student Data DVD to a USB drive (2GB minimum recommended).

1. Put the Student Data DVD into the drive.

2. If necessary, select the DVD Drive. (*Hint:* Right-click on the Start

    button [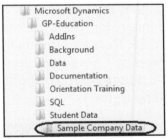 in Windows Vista]. Left-click
    Explore.)

3. Copy/paste or drag/drop the Sample Company Data folder to *either* your USB drive or your computer's Student Data folder. The computer default location of the Student Data folder is C:\Program Files\Microsoft Dynamics\GP-Education\Student Data.

4. Use Windows Explorer to make sure you copied the Sample Company Data folder to *either* your USB drive or the Student Data folder. (*Hint:* Right-click on the Start button; left-click Explore.)

5. Open the Sample Company Data folder. It includes 4 files.

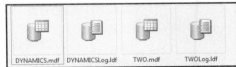

6. After checking that the Sample Company Data folder now resides *either* on your USB drive or in the program path at C:\Program Files\Microsoft Dynamics\GP-Education\Student Data\Sample Company Data, close the Explore window.
7. Remove the Student Data DVD.

WINDOWS VISTA: RUN AS ADMINISTRATOR

If you are using Windows Vista, the steps for Starting Dynamics GP and opening Fabrikam, Inc. on the next page assume you are using Dynamics GP for the first time. When using Windows Vista, you may need to select Run as administrator to start the program and open a company. (More information about Windows Vista and Permissions are in Appendix A, Troubleshooting.

When you start Dynamics GP, if a window appears that says *You don't have* **permission** *to open this file*, you should click 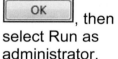, then select Run as administrator.

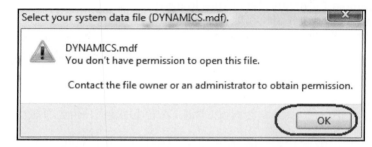

To select Run as administrator, right-click on the desktop shortcut for GP-Education. Then, left click Run as administrator. (If you do not have a desktop shortcut for Dynamics-GP, select the Start button, All Programs, Microsoft Dynamics, GP-Education 10.0. Right-click GP-Education, then left click Run as administrator.)

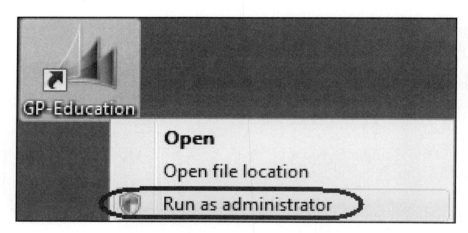

START DYNAMICS GP AND OPENING FABRIKAM, INC.

Follow these steps to start Dynamics GP 10.0-Education Edition.

1. Click 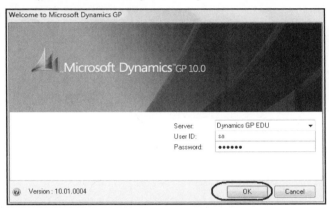 (Start); All Programs, Microsoft Dynamics.

2. Click GP-Education 10.0, GP-Education. (You may want to create a shortcut to have a GP-Education icon on the desktop.)

3. The Welcome to Microsoft Dynamics GP window appears. Type **sa** as the User ID. (sa is an acronym for system administrator.)

4. Type your password that you set up on p. viii step 10 (i.e., access).

5. Click OK. Be patient, the log in takes several minutes.

   NOTE—Script Error: If you receive an Internet Explorer Script Error, click Yes. This message appears because you do *not* have Microsoft Office 2003 Web Components installed on your computer. You do *not* need web components to use Dynamics GP.

6. The window prompts There isn't any data loaded. Do you want to load your data? (In Windows Vista, you may need to set permissions, see previous page.)

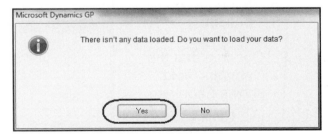

7. Click [Yes]. Follow the program path to where the Sample Company Data Folder and the DYNAMICS.mdf file is located. For example, if you installed it on your computer, go to the installation folder at C:\Program Files\Microsoft Dynamics\GP-Education\Student Data\Sample Company Data folder. If you copied the Sample Company Data folder to your USB drive, go there. Select the DYNAMICS.mdf file. Compare your select data file (DYNAMICS.mdf) window shown here.

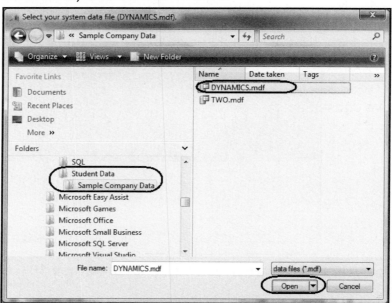

8. Click [Open]. After a few minutes, the Company Login window to appears. Be patient!

9. Observe that the Company field shows Fabrikam, Inc. Click [OK].

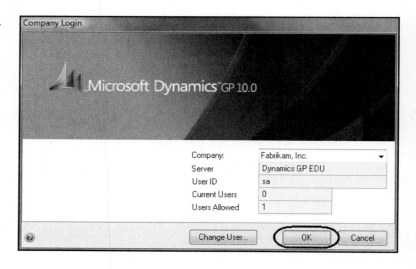

NOTE—VISTA users

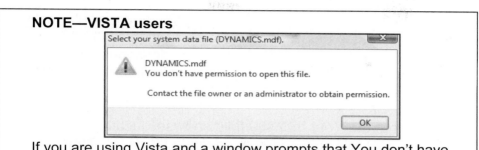

Select your system data file (DYNAMICS.mdf).   X

⚠ DYNAMICS.mdf
    You don't have permission to open this file.

    Contact the file owner or an administrator to obtain permission.

                                                    OK

If you are using Vista and a window prompts that You don't have permission to open this file, click OK to exit. Right-click on the GP-Education shortcut and select (left-click) Run as administrator. Restart Dynamics GP.

10. The Microsoft Dynamics GP window says You have chosen to use the sample company. Observe that the date is April 12, 2017.

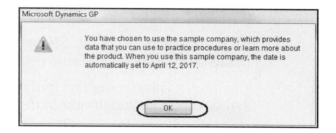

Microsoft Dynamics GP

⚠ You have chosen to use the sample company, which provides data that you can use to practice procedures or learn more about the product. When you use this sample company, the date is automatically set to April 12, 2017.

                              OK

11. Click [OK].

12. The Select Home Page, Welcome to Microsoft Dynamics GP, Choose your industry and role window appears.

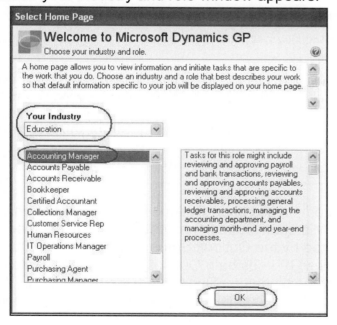

Select Home Page

Welcome to Microsoft Dynamics GP
Choose your industry and role.

A home page allows you to view information and initiate tasks that are specific to the work that you do. Choose an industry and a role that best describes your work so that default information specific to your job will be displayed on your home page.

Your Industry
Education

Accounting Manager
Accounts Payable
Accounts Receivable
Bookkeeper
Certified Accountant
Collections Manager
Customer Service Rep
Human Resources
IT Operations Manager
Payroll
Purchasing Agent
Purchasing Manager

Tasks for this role might include reviewing and approving payroll and bank transactions, reviewing and approving accounts payables, reviewing and approving accounts receivables, processing general ledger transactions, managing the accounting department, and managing month-end and year-end processes.

                              OK

A home page allows you to view information and indicate tasks that are specific to the work that you do. Dynamics GP allows you to choose an industry and a role that best describes your work so that default information specific to your job will be displayed on your home page.

Observe that the Your Industry field shows Education as the selection. The role selected is Accounting Manager. Tasks for this role include reviewing and approving payroll and bank transactions, reviewing and approving accounts payables, reviewing and approving accounts receivables, processing general ledger transactions, managing the accounting department, and managing month-end and year-end processes.

For purposes of using the Fabrikam, Inc. data, accept the default Industry (Education) and role (Accounting Manager) by clicking . Other roles and industries will be discussed later. Dynamics GP includes numerous industry and role selections.

13.   When the window appears that says you have 120 days to use the software before the evaluation period expires, click

OK

.

Read Me: 120-Day Evaluation Period

The 120-day evaluation period is associated with the data files *not* the software. The evaluation period starts the first time you load data. Once the data is loaded, you have 120 days to complete your work. **Write down the date when you started Dynamics GP for the first time.**

_____

---

14.   This step will omit if Microsoft Outlook is already setup on your computer. If Microsoft Outlook has not previously been setup, you will be prompted by the Outlook Setup wizard to setup Outlook now. Dynamics GP uses both Outlook and Internet Explorer to provide timely messages on Dynamics GP's home page. You will view Microsoft Office Outlook messages on your DGP's home

page in the next step. (*NOTE:* You do not need to install Outlook to use Dynamics GP. For more information about Microsoft Outlook, refer to Appendix A, Troubleshooting.

15.   After a while, the Home window appears. If necessary, enlarge it. The date (4/12/2017), company name (Fabrikam, Inc.), and User ID (sa) is shown at the bottom of the window. Compare your home page to the one shown here.

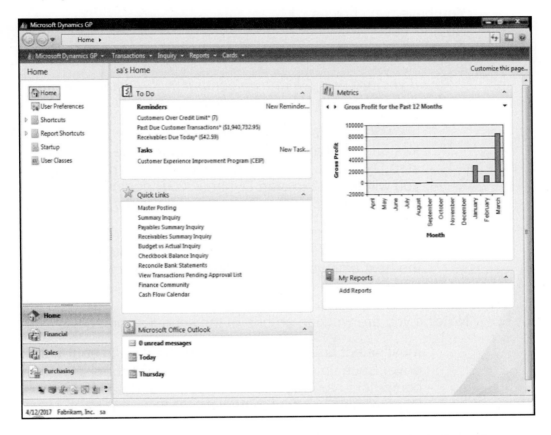

You will learn more about using Dynamics GP with Fabrikam, Inc. in Chapter 1. You may need to click on the arrows in the To Do, Quick Links, and Microsoft Office Outlook areas to expand the information.

EXIT DYNAMICS GP

1.   On the title bar, click on the down arrow next to Microsoft Dynamics GP. Click Exit. *Or,* click [X] on the title bar to exit.

2.   When the window prompts Do you want to unload your data? You have two choices, No and Yes.

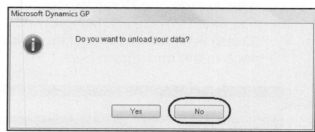

a.   *If you are using your own computer, the authors suggest that you select* No *when exiting Dynamics GP.* Click [No]. If you do *not* unload the data, you will be able to start Fabrikam, Inc. where you left off the next time you start Dynamics GP. To say it another way, by selecting No, you will be able to start Dynamics GP again without loading data from the Sample Company Data folder.

b.   If you select [Yes], then you will need to load data the next time you start Dynamics GP (refer to steps 1-8, pages xi-xii).

Note: If you are working on one of the school's computers, you must select [Yes] to unload the data to your USB drive. Each time you work on one of the school's computers, you will need to reload your data to start Dynamics GP and open the DYNAMICS.mdf file to use Fabrikam, Inc.

You should check with your instructor to ask his or her preference for loading and unloading data when you exit Dynamics GP.

Read Me: Computer Lab or Standalone Computer?

Computer Lab:

When using Dynamics GP, you will want to unload data before leaving the computer lab. Use external media (i.e., USB drive) for copying the Sample Company Data folder. When resuming work on Fabrikam, Inc. (or another company), start Dynamics GP, then open the DYNAMICS.mdf file from your USB drive. In Dynamics GP, files must be loaded and unloaded from the same location. Chapter 1 includes detailed steps for loading and unloading Dynamics GP data pages 22-23.

Standalone Computer:

For an individual computer (your own PC or laptop), unloading data may *not* be necessary. That means you select "No" to unloading data when exiting Dynamics GP.

BOTH Computer Lab and Standalone:

To use Dynamics GP in the computer lab and off-site on a standalone computer, unload data to external media (*or*, a network location where your work resides). This allows for convenient transfer and continuation of Dynamics GP work from school to home and vice versa via your USB drive.

VIRTUAL MACHINE INSTALLATION

Many computer labs are now using virtual machines to host software. The following steps provide lab instructions for students to load data into a virtual machine's Dynamics GP.

1. Turn on lab computer.
2. When Log on to Windows screen appears, click OK.
3. Agree to User terms.
4. Desktop appears. Select Start; All Programs, Business Accounting, Business Accounting. (Business Accounting is used as an example. Check with your instructor or lab personnel for course identification.)
5. Wait while VMware and Windows XP processes.

6.   When Log on to Windows screen appears, click OK.
7.   You are now on the virtual desktop. Notice the Business Accounting bar at the top of your screen.
8.   If you have an USB drive, plug it in now.
9.   Click Start; GP-Education.
10. When the Welcome to Microsoft Dynamics-GP window appears:

   Server: Dynamics GP EDU
   User ID: sa
   Password: 2008 [Check password with your instructor or lab personnel.]
11. Click OK
12. When Company Login Screen appears, Click CANCEL.
13. Then a screen prompts "Do you want to unload data? Click YES
14. Start GP-Education again.
15. When the Welcome to Microsoft Dynamics GP window appears:

   Server: Dynamics GP EDU
   User ID: sa
   Password: 2008 [Check password with your instructor or lab personnel.]
16. Click Yes
17. When There isn't any data loaded, Do you want to load your data? screen appears, Click Yes.
18. Browse to your student data location on your USB and select the Dynamics file.

Remember to unload data often and copy files to your USB flash drive!

FILE ORGANIZATION OF DYNAMICS GP 10.0-EDUCATION

Each Dynamics GP company is associated with a **_database ID_**. The company's database files end in .mdf and .ldf extensions, master data file and log data file, respectively. The table on the next page identifies the sample company included with Dynamics GP and the database ID associated with that company.

Company Name	Database ID
Fabrikam, Inc. is included on the DVD in the Sample Company Data folder)	*TWO.mdf* *TWOLog.ldf*

Dynamics GP also includes two DYNAMICS files: DYNAMICS.mdf and DYNAMICSLog.ldf. When you exit Dynamics GP, you can select an option to unload data. When you unload data, the DYNAMICS.mdf file is updated. This means that each company's data is accumulated in the DYNAMICS.mdf file.

For example, when you exited DGP, files associated with Fabrikam, Inc. were updated. Open your Sample Company data folder. Observe that the Date modified column shows today's date and the time that you exited the program. (*Hint:* If you do not have a Date modified column, click on a blank field on the Name row, select Date modified.) See below to see the files in the ….\Student Data\Sample Company Data folder.

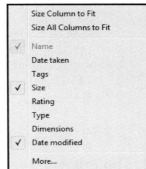

Name	Size	Date modified	Folder
DYNAMICS.mdf	73,728 KB	1/23/2008 1:53 PM	Sample Company Data (C:\Program Files\Microsoft Dynamics\GP-Education\S...
DYNAMICSLog.ldf	62,592 KB	1/23/2008 1:53 PM	Sample Company Data (C:\Program Files\Microsoft Dynamics\GP-Education\S...
TWO.mdf	380,928 KB	1/23/2008 1:53 PM	Sample Company Data (C:\Program Files\Microsoft Dynamics\GP-Education\S...
TWOLog.ldf	122,368 KB	1/23/2008 1:53 PM	Sample Company Data (C:\Program Files\Microsoft Dynamics\GP-Education\S...

Remember, if you unload data when exiting GP, the next time you start Dynamics GP a window prompts you to load data. You browse to the location of your Dynamics GP files, then open the DYNAMICS.mdf file. Because the DYNAMICS.mdf file contains the accumulated data for each company, this is the file that you select when you login to Dynamics GP. The authors suggest that you periodically unload data to external media, i.e., USB drive. If you need to use your data on another computer, the saved file can be accessed by the second computer using your USB drive. The textbook includes detailed steps for loading and unloading Dynamics GP data.

Fabrikam, Inc. files included on the Student Data DVD are shown on the next page. Work with the sample company, Fabrikam, Inc., is completed in Chapters 1.

Files on Student Data DVD \Sample Company Data	Chapter	Company Name
TWO.mdf* TWOLog.ldf	1	Fabrikam, Inc.

The files that are used for creating new companies are also included on the Student Data DVD in the Empty Company Data folder. The Empty Company Data folder files are used to create new companies. You will use these files in Chapter 2 to create a new company.

Files on Student Data DVD \Empty Company Data	Chapter	Company Name
DYNAMICS.mdf DYNAMICSLog.ldf GP.mdf GPLog.ldf	2	Student-designed service business

UNINSTALL DYNAMICS GP SOFTWARE

The following is provided for informational purposes only!

1. Click on the Start button [   ]; select Control Panel. In Windows Vista, use Control Panel's Classic View. Select Programs and Features. The Uninstall or change a program window appears.

   Uninstall or change a program

   To uninstall a program, select it from the list and then click "Uninstall", "Change", or "Repair".

   Or, If you are using *Windows XP*, go to Control Panel, Add Remove Programs.

2. Select Microsoft Dynamics GP-Education 10.0 from the list. Click Uninstall to remove it. (In Windows XP, select Change; Remove.)

3. Go to Windows Explorer (right-click the Start button; left-click Explore). Delete the C:\Progam Files\Microsoft Dynamcis folder.

4. Drag any Dynamics GP data folders into the Recycle bin.

5. Empty the Recycle Bin.

6. You are now ready to reinstall Dynamics GP from the DVD

Preface

Computer Accounting Essentials with Microsoft Dynamics GP 10.0, teaches you how to use Dynamics GP 10.0 software. For more than 20 years, Dynamics GP has been used by large and mid-sized businesses. Examples of businesses that use Dynamics GP 10.0 are retailers, sports franchises, manufacturers, service organizations, and accounting firms.

Dynamics GP 10.0 has the look and feel of Microsoft's popular Office Suite software. You will notice immediately that Dynamics GP 10.0 looks like Microsoft Outlook 2007. This familiar interface will help you navigate the software. This also means that Dynamics GP 10.0 and Microsoft Office products work well together.

The software, Dynamics GP 10.0-Education is included with the textbook. See pages v-xxii for software installation instructions.

Read Me
Microsoft Dynamics Partners are consulting firms that specialize in providing IT services to small and midsize businesses. To view a video to learn more about the advantages of pursuing a job or internship with a Dynamics Partner or to access all the other great resources Microsoft Dynamics provides to students, check out these sites:
Video: http://channel8.msdn.com/Posts/Jobs-with-Microsoft-Dynamics-Partners/
Student Resources and job listings: http://www.microsoft.com/studentstobusiness/

Computer Accounting Essentials with Microsoft Dynamics GP 10.0, shows you how a service business could implement and use the software. When you complete this textbook you have a basic working familiarity with Dynamics GP 10.0 software.

TEXTBOOK CONTENTS

The text includes 7 chapters with step-by-step instructions and screenshots. At the end of each chapter, you will answer Multiple Choice or True/Make True questions and demonstrate what you have learned in four Exercises.

CONVENTIONS USED IN THE TEXTBOOK

As you work through the chapters in this textbook, you are expected to read and follow the step-by-step instructions. Numerous screen illustrations help you check your work.

The following conventions are used.

1. Information that you type appears in **boldface**; for example, Type **2100** in the Find by Account Number field.

2. Keys on the keyboard that are pressed appear like this: <Tab>; <Enter>.

3. Unnamed buttons and icons are shown as they appear on the window; for example, , (Navigation Pane), Save, Post, etc.

4. Read Me boxes are shown in most chapters. The information in the Read Me box goes into more detail about the task you are completing. Whenever you see a Read Me box, review this information.

5. Read the **Troubleshooting** boxes.

6. Footnotes are used. Read each one for more information about the task you are completing.

Good luck in your study and use of Dynamics-GP 10.0 software.

Carol Yacht, Susan V. Crosson, and Joann Segovia, Authors
Computer Accounting Essentials with Microsoft Dynamics GP 10.0
www.mhhe.com/dynamicsgp10essentials

Table of Contents

Summary of Backups and their Size Made in this Text

Chapter 1	Sample Company Data	562MB
Chapter 2	Your Name Chapter 2 Begin	797MB
	Your Name Chapter 2 Exercises	797MB
Chapter 3	Student Name Chapter 3 October	797MB
	Student Name Exercise 3-4	797MB
Chapter 4	Unadjusted Trial Balance	797MB
	End of Year	797MB
Chapter 5	Chapter 5 End	797MB
Chapter 6	Chapter 6 End	797MB
Chapter 7	Your Name Chapter 7	797MB

Introduction

Computer Accounting Essentials with Microsoft Dynamics GP 10.0 introduces you how to use a popular mid-market accounting package for a service business. Microsoft Dynamics GP 10.0 (DGP) is known as a comprehensive business management solution for medium and large businesses that manage and integrate finances, e-commerce, supply chain, manufacturing, project accounting, field service, customer relationships, and human resources. Unlike small business accounting programs, DGP has many built-in internal controls and customizable features to protect a business and its users from errors and willful wrongdoing. You will notice as you set up your service business' accounts, vendors, and customers; the numerous options you must decide. In other words, you will customize your accounting system to specifically meet your needs.

Student users can install and use this education edition of the software at school either in a networked lab, on virtual machines, or on a stand-alone machine as well as at home on their personal computer. The education edition and the commercial software are identical with few exceptions, one of which is that the educational edition's data is only live for 120 days after installation. This 120 day education edition can be installed on a machine with another version of DGP as long as each is installed to a different directory. Thus it is possible to mix the 10.0 version with older versions on the same computer but each must have a different MSDE instance. For a more complete discussion of the system requirements of using DGP 10.0 Education Edition, consult the Software Installation section of this text.

As you learn this software take advantage of the help offered on all program screens, in software documentation and manuals, and on the DGP website www.microsoft.com/dynamics/gp Also, access DGP Student Resources and job listings: http://www.microsoft.com/studentstobusiness/

The McGraw-Hill Companies, Inc., *Computer Accounting Essentials with Microsoft Dynamics GP 10.0, 2e*

The text includes 7 chapters with step-by-step instructions and screenshots. Each chapter also contains a SmartList activity, a Sarbanes-Oxley compliance related activity, and an internal control activity. In Chapter 1 you will learn the basic features and navigation of DGP using Fabrikam, Inc., the sample company included with the software. In Chapter 2 you will setup a new corporation in DGP, enter beginning balances, and print its chart of accounts and opening balance sheet. In Chapters 3 and 4 you will record the fourth quarter cash receipts and payments for the business. At the end of each month, you will reconcile the bank statements and print the trial balance. In Chapter 4 you will record end-of-quarter adjusting entries, print an adjusted trial balance, prepare financial statements, close the fiscal year, and print a post-closing trial balance. In Chapter 5 you will begin the following year's first quarter accounting tasks and implement the payables management module to improve control over your business' acquisition and payment activities. In Chapter 6 you will implement the receivables management module to improve the management of customer sales and collection activities. In Chapter 7 you will complete first quarter's accounting tasks and will record end-of-quarter adjusting entries, print the adjusted trial balance, and prepare financial statements. At the end of each of these chapters, you will answer Multiple Choice or True/Make True questions and demonstrate what you have learned in several Exercises, including exercises that focus on internal controls and SmartLists.

Throughout the text you will be backing up your files to external media, especially if you are working on a computer other than your own. The size in megabytes of files you will copy to a hard drive, network, or external media are large (file size approximately 500 MB each). Specifically, you will create a folder on your USB drive or computer and unload your Dynamics GP files to that folder. (Refer to Software Installation or Chapter 1, for step-by step instructions.)

The authors suggest you use a USB drive (2 GB, minimum) for your external media but you can also use some other portable storage device (i.e., your iPod).

Chapter 1

Introduction to Fabrikam, Inc.

OBJECTIVES: In Chapter 1, you complete the following activities.

1. Start Dynamics GP 10.0 (DGP).[1]
2. Open the sample company, Fabrikam, Inc.
3. Select an industry and user role.
4. Set user preferences.
5. Operate Dynamics GP's drop-down lists, lookup fields, navigation pane, and menus.
6. Identify Dynamics GP's installation folder, student data folder, and sample data folder.
7. Save data.
8. Save using Backup and Restore.
9. Navigate the Help system.
10. Complete a search using SmartList.
11. Review Sarbanes-Oxley compliance.
12. Complete an internal control activity.
13. Identify security roles.
14. Exit Dynamics GP.

The textbook web site at <u>www.mhhe.com/dynamicsgp10essentials</u> has a link to Textbook Updates. Check this link for updates.

Dynamics GP 10.0 (DGP) is similar to other programs that use Windows. If you have used other Windows programs, specifically Microsoft Office, you will recognize the similarities.

MOUSE AND KEYBOARD BASICS

One of the first decisions you need to make is whether to use the mouse or keyboard. The instructions in this book assume that you are using a

---

[1]If Dynamics GP 10.0 is *not* installed see Software Installation, pages iv to viii. The Sample Company Data folder should be copied to either your USB drive or to the <Program Files>\Microsoft Dynamics\GP-Education\Student Data folder; refer to pages viii-x.

mouse. When the instructions refer to the word click this usually means to left-click with your mouse. (Sometimes the instructions mention right-click.) Note, you can also use the keyboard.

Using the Mouse

➢ To single click: position the mouse cursor over what you want to select and click the left mouse button once.

➢ To double-click: position the mouse cursor over your selection and click the left mouse button twice, quickly.

➢ Use the right mouse button the same way you use the left mouse button.

Using the Keyboard

➢ Hold down the **<Alt>**[2] key and the underlined letter to make the selection.

➢ If you have already held down the **<Alt>** key and the underlined letter and more selections appear with underlined letters, just type the underlined letter to select the item.

Using Shortcut Keys

Shortcut keys enable you to perform common operations by using two or more keys together.

<Ctrl>+<Letter> Shortcuts	
<Ctrl>+<X>	Cut
<Ctrl>+<C>	Copy
<Ctrl>+<V>	Paste
<Ctrl>+<P>	Print
<Ctrl>+<F>	Find
<Ctrl>+<A>	Search All
<Ctrl>+<Y>	Analysis
<Ctrl>+<L>	Lookup

[2]The greater and lesser signs are used around words to indicate individual keys on your keyboard; for example, **<Alt>** is for the Alternate key, **<Enter>** for the Enter/Return key, **<Ctrl>** is for the Control key, **<Esc>** is for the Escape key.

Function Key Shortcuts	
<F1>	Displays the online Help
<Ctrl>+<F4>	Closes the current window
<Alt>+<F4>	Closes the application
<Ctrl>+<F6>	Moves to the next window
<Shift>+<Ctrl>+<F6>	Moves to the previous window
Window Navigation Keyboard shortcuts	
Keyboard shortcut	**Navigation**
<Tab>	Move to next field
<Shift>+<Tab>	Move to previous field
<Ctrl>+<Tab>	Move from scrolling window to next field
<Shift>+<Ctrl>+<Tab>	Move from scrolling window to previous field
<Enter>	Default button on a window
<Ctrl>+W	Close the current window
<Atl>+<X>	Exit application

GETTING STARTED

Fabrikam, Inc. is the sample company included with DGP. The purpose of using the sample company in Chapters 1 is to help you become familiar with the software. In the remaining chapters, you use the software to work with service businesses.

To start Dynamics GP, do the following.[3]

1. Select [Start button]; All Programs, Microsoft Dynamics, GP-Education 10.0, GP Education. The Welcome to Microsoft Dynamics GP window appears. Type your password. (Refer to page viii, step 10.) **OR,** if you have a *desktop* icon for GP-Education, double-click on it.

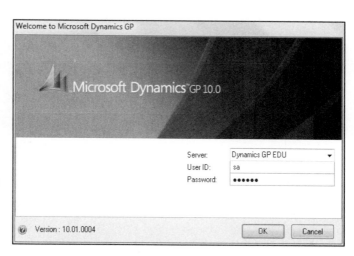

2. Click [OK]. Be

---

[3]These instructions assume that you have installed Dynamics GP 10.0 (pages iv-viii) and that you have copied the Sample Company Data folder to either your USB drive or to the installation path's Student Data folder (pages viii-x).

patient, it will take several minutes to log in.

 Read me

These instructions assume that **data was not unloaded** when you exited Fabrikam, Inc. For detailed steps see pages xvi-xvii, Exit Dynamics GP.

If you selected Yes (instead of No) when exiting the program, a screen message appears saying There isn't any data loaded. Do you want to load your data? Select Yes, then go to the Sample Company Data folder and open the DYNAMICS.mdf file. For detailed steps for loading data, refer to pages xi-xv, Starting Dynamics GP and Opening Fabrikam, Inc.

NOTE—Script Error: If you receive an Internet Explorer Script Error, click Yes. This message appears because you do *not* have Microsoft Office 2003 Web Components installed on your computer. You do *not* need web components to use Dynamics GP.

NOTE--VISTA users
If you are using Vista and a window prompts that You don't have permission to open this file, click OK to exit. Right-click on the GP-Education shortcut and select (left-click) Run as administrator. Restart Dynamics GP.

3.   The Company Login window appears. If necessary, in the Company field select Fabrikam, Inc.

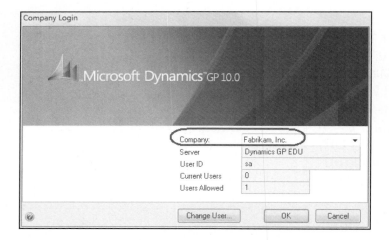

4.   Click OK.
5.   If necessary, wait a few minutes until the Microsoft Dynamics GP

windows appears saying that You have chosen to use the sample company. Read this information.

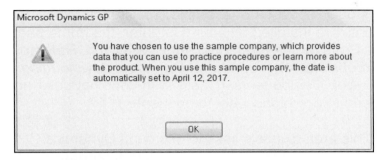

6.   Click OK . After a few moments, the *home page* appears.

The home page provides easy access to information that you need for your job. From the home page, you can see a summary of appointments, a list of tasks and reminders, and the number of unread e-mail messages that you have, as well as other information specific to your job.

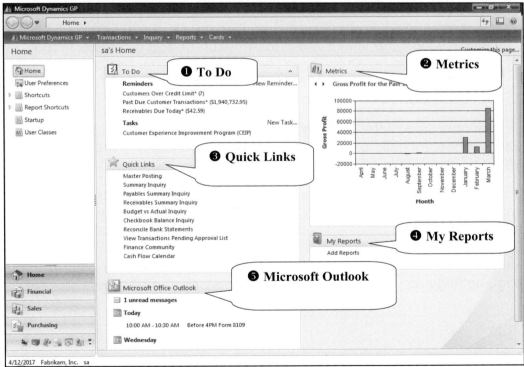

❶ **To Do**: This area displays the tasks assigned to you, predefined reminders, customized reminders, and the Workflow notifications that you have set up.

❷ **Metrics**: The metrics area of your home page displays graphic representations of DGP data. For example, if Microsoft Office 2003 Web Components are installed on your computer, the home page shows a Gross Profit for the Past 12 Months bar graph. *Refer to Appendix A, Troubleshooting for information about downloading Microsoft 2003 Web Components.* (Check with your instructor about whether you need to download web components.)

❸ **Quick Links**: This area displays links to Microsoft Dynamics GP windows, Web pages, navigation lists and external programs that you have set up as quick links.

❹ **My Reports**: When you click on the down arrow in the Reports area, the list expands showing frequently used reports or reports that you have added. You will work with this area later in Part 1 of the textbook.

❺ **Microsoft Office Outlook**: This area displays appointments and the number of unread e-mail message. Use the Microsoft Office Outlook Details window to select which information to display on the home page. (Click on up arrow, then the pencil to see the Microsoft Outlook Details window.) *Hint:* This area is available if you have MS Office Outlook installed on your computer.

On the right side of the home page, there is a link to Customize this page. When you link to Customize this page you can see the content areas that are selected for your home page.

Use the Customize Home Page window to display the home page's content areas and to modify the layout. You can also specify when your home page should be displayed and if it automatically should be updated. You can use the arrow buttons to indicate if specific content areas will be displayed on the right or left side of your home page. Home page settings are saved on a per-user basis and can be modified.

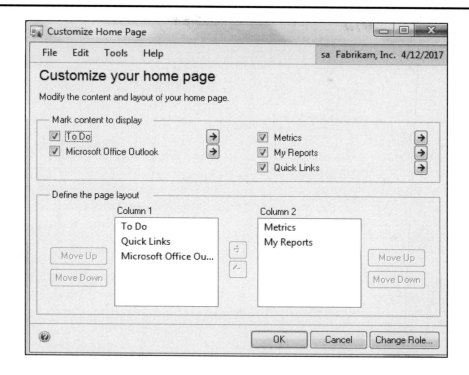

Observe the Change Role button on the Customize Home Page window. When you select Change Role..., a window appears reminding you if you change roles, the home page is also changed. If you select OK, the Welcome to Microsoft Dynamics GP Choose your industry and role window appears. This is the same window that was shown the first time you opened Fabrikam on page xiii. Cancel the window to return to the home page. No changes will be made at this time.

USER INTERFACE (UI)

One of the benefits of Windows is that it standardizes terms and operations used in software programs. Once you learn how to move around in DGP, you also know how to use other Windows applications.

The home page is used to show DGP's user interface. The numbered callouts are the terms used to identify these areas throughout the textbook.

❶ **Address bar**: The address bar displays the location of the current page within the navigation hierarchy of the application.

❷ **Menu:** The DGP menu provides access to administrative tasks, setup tasks, user and company information, the User Data window, and user preference.

❸ **Lists:** The lists are associated with a navigation pane selection. The home page list is shown because Home is selected on then navigation pane.

❹ **Navigation pane**: Use the navigation pane to select and display a list or page.

❺ **Status bar**: The status bar displays the user, date, and the company.

The top of the window includes the Microsoft Dynamics GP title bar. The title bar includes the Minimize 🔲 button, Double Window 🔲 button, and the Close 🔲 button.

TYPICAL DYNAMICS GP WINDOWS

Follow these steps to see the Transaction Entry window.

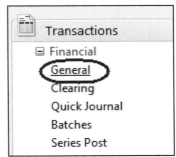

1. Click [Financial]. The address bar shows Home ▶ Financial ▶ Financial.

2. In the Transaction list, link to General. The Transaction Entry window appears.

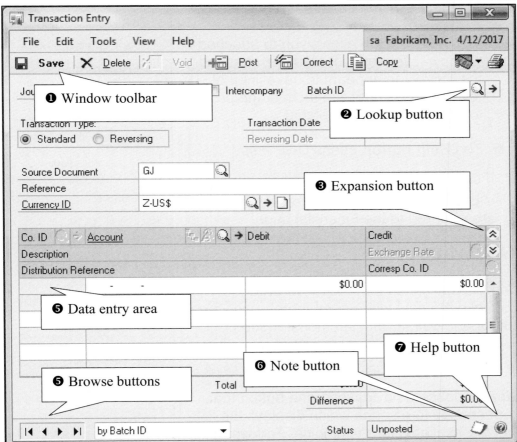

❶ The **Window toolbar** includes the Save, Delete, Post, Correct, Copy, and Print button.

❷ The **Lookup button** indicates that list of item is available for a particular field or window. You select an item from the list to enter in the window.

❸ The **Expansion button** opens a window where additional information for the field next to the button can be added, changed, or viewed.

❹ The **Data entry area** is where you enter information. Use the <Tab> key to move between fields.

❺ The **Browse buttons** allow you to scan information, such as accounts, transactions, and customer records.

❻ The **Note button** allows you to attached window-level notes. If a note is attached, the page icon appears to have lines of text in it. If no note is attached, the page icon will appear to be blank.

❼ The **Help button** opens DGP help.

3. If the Transaction Entry window is open, click  on its title bar to close it. You are returned to the Financial page.

NAVIGATION PANE

Use the navigation pane to move around DGP. To make the navigation pane larger, use your cursor and pull up with left mouse button.

Lists: Choose a navigation pane button that corresponds to a series which displays the lists that are available for that choice. For example, the financial list shows Financial, Accounts, Account Transactions, Checkbooks, General Ledger Batches, Report List, Assets.
Navigation pane: Choose a navigation pane

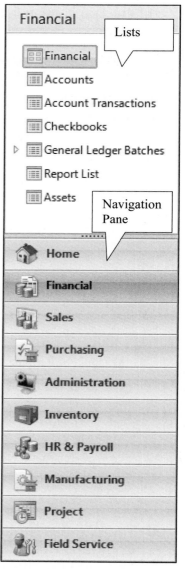

button that corresponds to a series that you want to display. The page that is associated with that selection will appear on the content pane on the right side.

The navigation pane selections identify DGP's **modules**. A module is an application that can be used to perform a specific set of tasks. Modules are combined to form a series. For example, the Financial series includes the general ledger and advanced financial analysis. The table that follows lists the series buttons or DGP modules that are available in the navigation pane and the lists associated with them.

Series buttons/ DGP Modules	Lists
Financial	Accounts, Account Transactions, Checkbooks, General Ledger Batches, Report list, and Assets.
Sales	Customers, Prospects, Salespeople, All Sales Transactions, Receivables Transactions, Sales Order Transactions, Invoicing Transactions, Receivables Batches, and the Report list.
Purchasing	Vendors, All Purchasing Transactions, Payables Transactions, Purchase Order Transactions, Payables Batches, and Report List.
Administration	All Report list, My Reports list, system Report list, Company Report list, Custom Report list, and SmartList Favorites.
HR & Payroll	Employees, Applicants, Attendance Transactions, and Report list.
Manufacturing	Bills of Materials, Picking Documents, Job Costing, Routings, and Manufacturing Orders.
Project	Projects, Timesheet Transactions, Billing Transactions, PA purchase order transactions, and Report list.
Field Service	Service Call Transactions, Contract Transactions, RMA Transactions, RTV Transactions, Depot Transactions, In-Transit Transfers, Equipment, and Report list.

USER PREFERENCES

Before you change user preferences, let's make sure that Show Required Fields is selected.

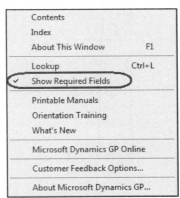

1.   To make sure Required Fields is selected, select 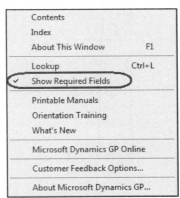 (Help).

2. Observe that one of the selections is Show Required Fields. There should be a checkmark next to it. If you do *not* see a checkmark, click Required Fields to place a checkmark next to it. *The instructions throughout the textbook assume Show Required Fields is selected.*

3. If necessary, select <Esc> to close the Help menu.

Follow these steps to change the User Preferences.

1. On the navigation pane, select 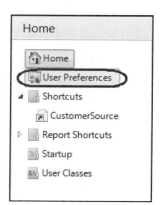.

2. From the Home list link to User Preferences.

3. User Preferences window appears. Make the following selections: Horizontal Scroll Arrows, Screen, Tab, Local. Compare your User Preferences window to the one below.

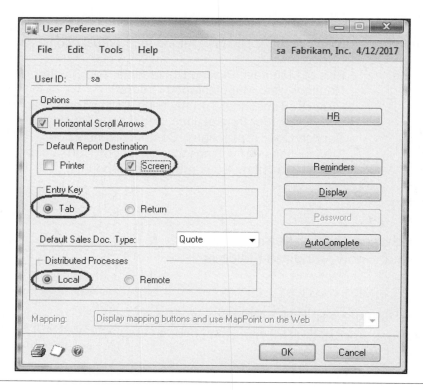

4. Click [Display] . The User Display Preferences window appears. In the Required Fields area, select Red as the Font Color. Once you select red as the font color, this will change all Dynamics GP companies. In other words, this is a global change.

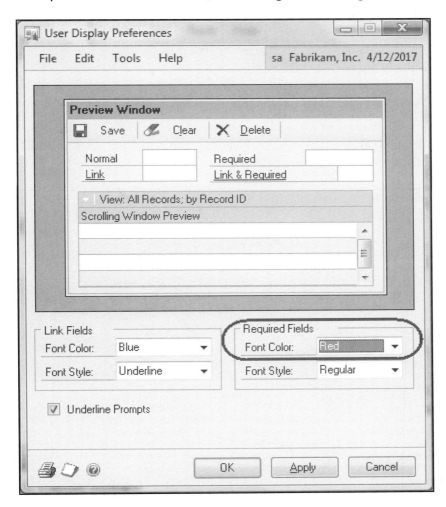

The User Display Preferences window includes selections to change how Dynamics GP looks on your computer. Various colors and styles are available for links and required fields.

5. Make sure that the Required Fields area shows that Font Color is Red is selected; then click [OK] to return to the User

Preferences window.

6. Click [OK] to return to the home page.

7. To see the red font color for required fields, do this. From the menu bar (click on the bar to see Transactions, Inquiry, etc.), select Transactions; Purchasing, Transaction Entry to open the Payables Transaction Entry window. Observe that the fields that need to be completed are shown in red. Close the Payables Transaction Entry window by clicking [X].

DISPLAYING PRODUCT INFORMATION

1. Click [?] (Help), then About Microsoft Dynamics GP. The About Dynamics GP window appears.

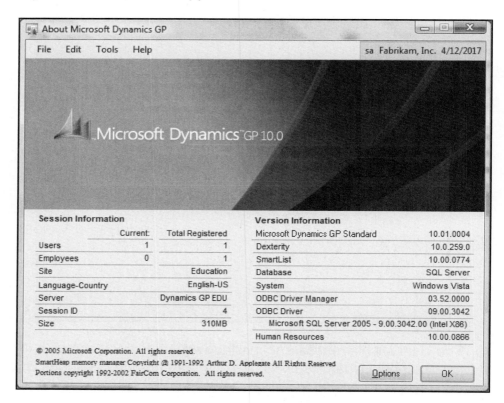

2. After reviewing the window, click [OK] to close it.

USING WINDOWS EXPLORER

The instructions that follow show you how to identify Dynamics GP's installation folder and data path on the hard drive of your computer. You also see the size of the Dynamics GP and sample company data.

Follow these steps to use Windows Explorer to identify DGP's location on your computer system.

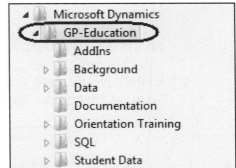

1.   Right-click 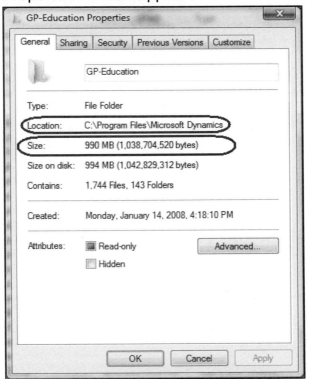 (Start button); left click Explore.

2.   Go to C:\Program Files\Microsoft Dynamics\GP-Education.

3.   Right-click on GP-Education; left click Properties. The GP-Education Properties window appears.

Observe the location (installation folder) of Dynamics GP is C:\Program Files\Microsoft Dynamics. The size of the file is 990 MB or 1,038.704,520 bytes and contains 1,744 files and 143 folders. Your file size, number of files, and folders may differ.

6. Close the GP-Education Properties window.

7. To see the size of the sample company data, follow these steps.

   a. If Sample Company Data folder is on your computer, double-click on the Student Data folder. Otherwise, go to your USB drive and select your Sample Company Data folder.
   b. Right-click Sample Company Data; left-click Properties. The Sample Company Data Properties window appears.

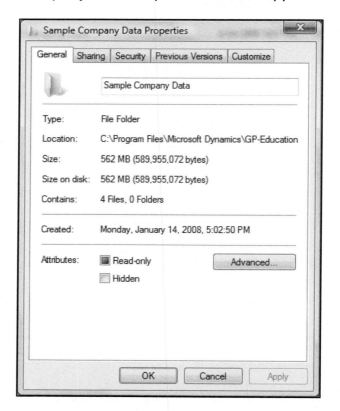

   c. Close the Sample Company Data Properties window.
8. Close the Explore window.

MENU BAR

Dynamics GP's menu bar has 5 selections: Microsoft Dynamics GP; Transactions; Inquiry, Reports, Cards. Click on the menu to change its color.

1.　From the menu bar, click on the down arrow (▾) next to Microsoft Dynamics GP to see its menu. The choices include User and Company, User Date, Edit, Tools, Maintenance, SmartList, Reminders, Tasks List, Process Monitor, User Preferences, Print Setup, Print, Exit.

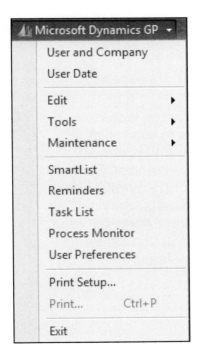

　　Menu choices followed by an ...*ellipsis* are associated with *dialog boxes* or windows that supply information about the open window. An arrow (▶) next to a menu item (for example, Edit) indicates that there is a submenu with additional selections. Also, observe that pressing **<Ctrl>+<P>** can be used to print.

The McGraw-Hill Companies, Inc., *Computer Accounting Essentials with Microsoft Dynamics GP 10.0, 2e*

2. From the menu bar, click on the down arrow (▾) next to Transactions to see its menu. The transactions menu allows you to view Financial, Sales, Purchases, Inventory, Payroll, Human Resources, Fixed Assets, Service Call Management, Contract Administration, Preventive Maintenance, Returns Management, and Depot Management features. Observe that when an arrow (▶) is next to an item, then mean that more choices are available.

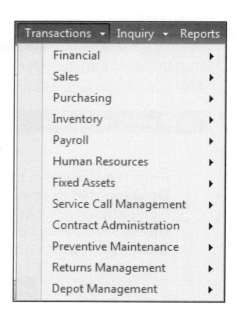

3. From the menu bar, click Inquiry. Inquires allow users to view information for open and historical years. The System, Financial, Sales, Purchasing, Inventory, Payroll, Human Resources, Fixed Assets, Service Call Management, Contract Administration, Returns Management, and Depot Management inquiry features are available.

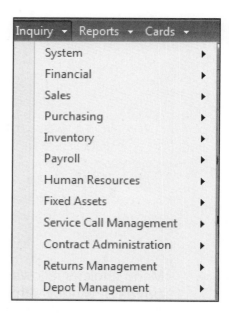

4. From the menu bar, select Reports. Reports provides access to windows where you can create System, Company, Financial, Sales, Purchasing, Inventory, Payroll, Customized, Combined Group, Human Resources and Fixed Assets, Service Call Management, Contract Administration, Preventive Maintenance, Returns Management, Depot Management and Workflow reports. You can also access the Letter Writing assistant.

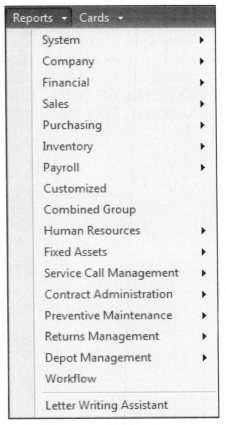

5. From the menu bar, select Cards. This selection provides access to cards used to enter master records for System, Financial, Sales, Purchasing, Inventory, Payroll, Human Resources, and Fixed Assets, etc.

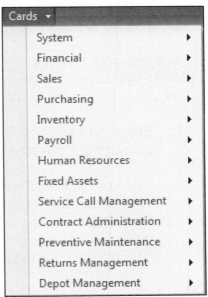

Above the menu bar is a selection for Help. A question mark identifies the Help icon ( ). Click to see its menu. The Help menu includes Contents, index, About this Window, Lookup, Show Required Fields is checked; Printable Manuals, Orientation Training, What's New, Microsoft Dynamics GP Online; Customer Feedback Options; About Microsoft Dynamics GP (refer to page16).

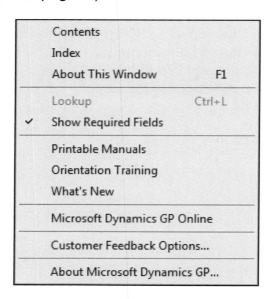

ADDING INFORMATION TO THE COMPANY NAME

Let's add your name to Fabrikam, Inc. Then, save (unload) and open (load) data to review newly added information. Follow these steps to do that.

1. From the Microsoft Dynamics GP menu, select Tools; Setup, Company, Company. The Company Setup window appears.

2. Add your first and last name to Fabrikam, Inc. in the Name field. The Company Setup window below shows Fabrikam, Inc.-Student Name in the Name field. Your instructor may prefer that you change other fields; for example, change the Contact field to your name; change the company's address, city and state to yours.

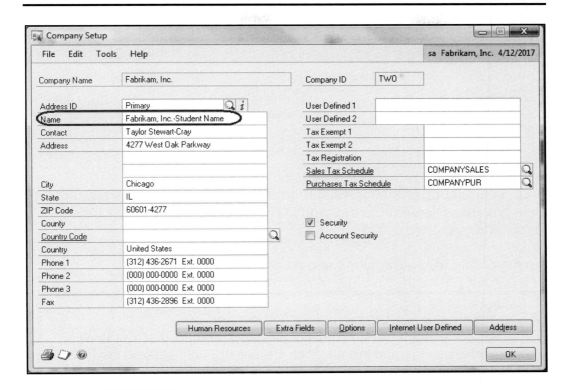

3. Click [OK] to return to the menu bar. Now that you have added some data, continue with the next section to learn about saving data.

SAVING DATA

Each time you add data to a company, the DYNAMICS.mdf file is updated. If you are working in both the computer lab and off-site with a standalone computer,[4] load and unload your data associated with Fabrikam, Inc. to your USB drive. When you want to return to the computer lab, reverse the process.

Four files are associated with Fabrikam, Inc:

1. DYNAMICS.mdf
2. DYNAMICSLog.ldf
3. TWO.mdf
4. TWOLog.ldf.

---

[4]A standalone computer refers to your own personal computer; for example, a laptop.

To see these files, go to your Sample Company Data folder.

Name	Date taken	Folder	Tags	Size
DYNAMICS.mdf		Sample Company ...		73,728 KB
DYNAMICSLog.ldf		Sample Company ...		62,592 KB
TWO.mdf		Sample Company ...		317,440 KB
TWOLog.ldf		Sample Company ...		122,368 KB

MDF is an abbreviation for master data file. LDF is an abbreviation or log data file. The DYANMICS.mdf and DYNAMICSLog.ldf file is updated *each* time you save data.

To save data follow the steps shown below.

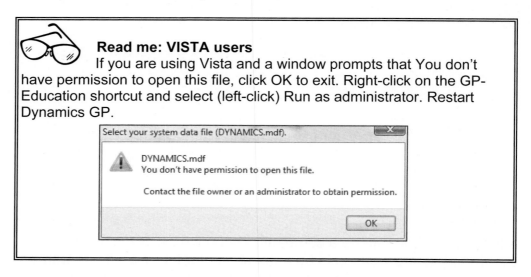

Read me: VISTA users
If you are using Vista and a window prompts that You don't have permission to open this file, click OK to exit. Right-click on the GP-Education shortcut and select (left-click) Run as administrator. Restart Dynamics GP.

1. If you loaded Sample Company Data from your USB drive, make sure it is plugged into your computer. Exit Dynamics GP. When the window prompts do you want to unload data, select Yes.

2. Confirm your Sample Company Data files have been updated by viewing the Sample Company Data folder on your USB. Look at the Date Modified column for the most current date and time.

3. To continue your work on another computer, plug your USB drive in and start Dynamics GP. When asked if you want to load data, select Yes and pick your DYNAMICS.mdf file in your Sample Company Data folder.

NOTE: If you are working off campus on a standalone computer and saving to your hard drive (Your own computer's <Program Files>\Microsoft Dynamics\GP-Education\Student Data\Sample Company Data), periodically save (unload) data to a USB drive to back it up. This will ensure that you have data to continue work.

STARTING DYNAMICS GP

When you exited Dynamics GP, you selected Yes to unload data. To restart Dynamics GP, follow these steps.

1. Double-click on the desktop shortcut, GP-Education. (Or click Start; All Programs, Microsoft Dynamics, GP-Education 10.0, GP-Education.) Type your password. Click | OK |.

2. The Microsoft Dynamics GP window appears. Click | Yes | to loading data. If necessary go to your Sample Company Data folder located either on your USB drive or your computer (<Program Files>\Microsoft Dynamics\GP-Education\Student Data\Sample Company Data). Open the DYNAMICS.mdf file. (*Hint:* If a window appears that says you do not have permission to open the file, close the window. DGP will also close. Right click on the GP-Education shortcut; left-click Run as Administrator.)

3. Check to see if you saved your changes.
   a.   From the Microsoft Dynamics GP menu, select Tools: Setup; Company, Company. Your Name should be at the end of the Name field.
   b.   From the Transactions menu, select Purchasing; Transaction Entry. The required fields should be shown in red.

You have now saved (unloaded) and opened (loaded) data. This is the procedure you use when you want to start where you left off the last time you used Dynamics GP.

BACKUP AND RESTORE

Another way you can save your work is to use the backup and restore feature of Dynamics GP. A **backup** is the process of saving to a hard drive location, external media such as DVDs, USB, or magnetic tape. **Restore** is starting data at the same place in the data as the last backup.

Backup – follow these steps.

1. From the Microsoft Dynamics GP menu, select Maintenance, Backup.

2. The Back Up Company window appears. In the Company Name field, notice you can select the appropriate company or system database to back up.

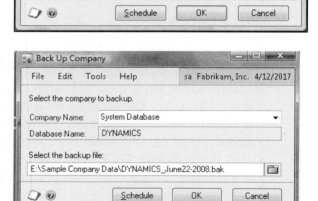

3. In the Select the backup file field, notice that a file path is automatically assigned: C:\Program Files\Microsoft Dynamics\GP-Education\backup\. If you are working from your USB drive instead of your computer, browse to your Sample Company Data folder on your USB drive. Dynamics GP automatically names backups by date. You can also schedule regular backups.

4. Click OK.

Restore – follow these steps to restore Dynamics GP data.

1. From the Microsoft Dynamics GP menu, select Maintenance, Restore. The Restore Company window appears.

2. Select the appropriate company name or system database.

3. In the Select the file to restore from field, browse to the location of your backup file.

4. When satisfied, click OK. The backed up data is restored and ready to use.

DYNAMICS GP HELP

Dynamics GP includes a couple levels of Help. In the instructions that follow, you look at Dynamics GP's Using Help file, and pressing <F1> for context-sensitive help.

1. On the right side of the Address bar, click (Help icon). Select Contents. The Microsoft Dynamics GP Help 10.0 window appears. Click on the Contents tab.

2. Click on the plus sign next to Microsoft Dynamics GP™ Help; then select Using Help.

3. Read the information on the right side of the window. On the left pane (under the tabs), make a few other selections to look at the Help windows. When through close the Help window.

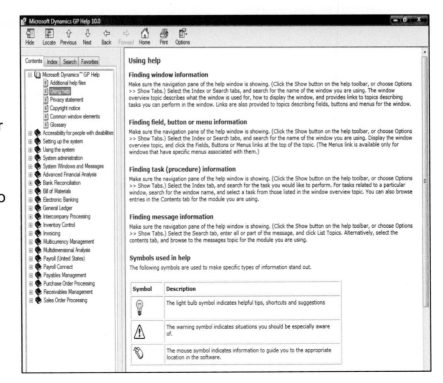

4. Another way to use the Dynamics GP's Help is to press the function key, **<F1>**, or ⊚ from most window. For example, select Transactions; Financial, General. The Transaction Entry window appears. Press the function key <F1>.

5. Observe that the Help window's left pane has Transaction Entry window selected. The right pane has numerous links.

6. Select <u>Fields</u>. The Transaction Entry window: Fields information appears. Each field on the Transaction Entry window is explained.

7. Link to a few other areas. Blue, underlined words identify links.

8. When you are through navigating the Help windows, exit the Help windows.

9. Close all windows.

SMARTLIST

The SmartList feature contains options for changing the information that is shown in the window. The options available in the menu vary among different windows or in some cases, the field that the user has selected.

You can use SmartList to create customized inquiries to provide easier, faster access to information stored in the Microsoft Dynamics GP system, including information about accounts, customers, employees, vendors, transactions, and items. You can print or export the search results, or display them on the screen.

SmartList uses sets of predefined search criteria, called favorites. The favorites are listed on the left side of the SmartList window. Some of the criteria within each SmartList favorite create a default search, or view, for each favorite. You can modify the view to create a variety of customized views. Access a list of SmartList Favorites that you can view, print, or modify when you select SmartList Favorites in the navigation pane.

In addition to the favorites that are included with Dynamics GP, a number of products integrate with SmartList. For example, SmartList results can be sent to Excel or Word. For example, you can search for information about your customers, export the results to Excel, and then use Excel and Word to create promotions targeted to specific groups of customers based on the volume of business transacted within your company, or how conscientious they are about paying their bills on time. By combining the capabilities of SmartList and Excel to organize and sort data with Word's mail merge capabilities, you can create mass mailings that tailor your message to individual customers.

Follow these steps to use the SmartList.

1.   From the Microsoft Dynamics GP menu, select SmartList. The SmartList window appears. Click on the plus sign next to Financial. Double-click Accounts. The Accounts list appears. A partial SmartList window is shown on the next page. The account list is also called the ***chart of accounts***. In accounting you learn that the chart of accounts is a list of all the accounts in the general ledger.

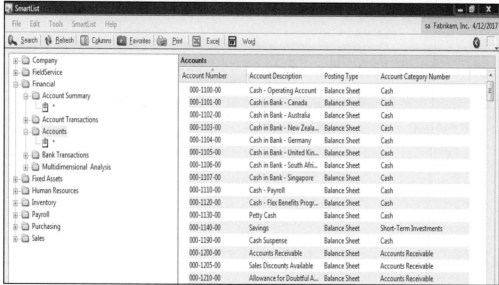

Observe that there are selections for Excel and Word. This means you can convert this list from Dynamics GP to Excel or Word formats.

2. Click [🔍 Search]. From the Search Accounts window, you can select Column Name, Filters, and Values. Complete the following search:

    Column Name: Select Account Category Number
    Filter: begins with
    Value: Type **Cash**

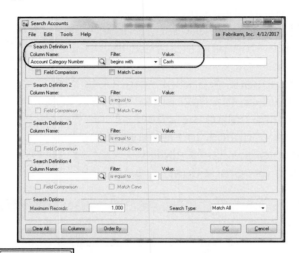

3. Select [OK]. The SmartList window appears with the Cash accounts listed.

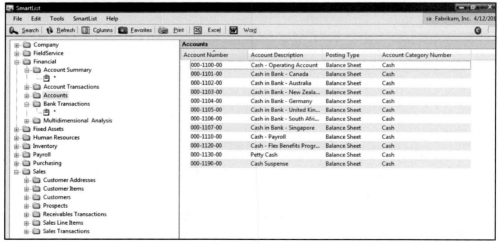

4. Close the SmartList.

SARBANES-OXLEY COMPLIANCE (SOX)

SOX Box
In response to a number of corporate and accounting scandals, the Sarbanes-Oxley Act of 2002 was enacted. This act is also called the Public Company Accounting Reform and Investor Protection Act of 2002. Two common ways of identifying this legislation are the abbreviations SOX or Sarbox. This law has had an effect on the way accounting data is collected and reported. The Sarbanes-Oxley Act of 2002 introduced major changes to the regulation of financial practice and corporate governance. For example, the law requires management and external auditors to assess risk and evaluate internal controls. One of the most important features of Dynamics GP is the internal controls built into every module. Dynamics GP's modules are identified by the selections on the navigation pane: Home, Financial, Sales, Purchasing, Administration, Inventory, HR & Payroll, Manufacturing, Project, and Field Service. Segregation of duties may be one of the most important internal controls. The Dynamics GP modules assist in assigning responsibility to specific tasks by applying a role. For example, on page xiii, when Fabrikam, Inc. was started for the first time, a role was selected. Roles identify what data a user can view or process. These roles are just one of many internal control features built into the software. Selecting a role assigns each employee responsibilities for specific tasks. In other words, not every employee, or everyone using Dynamics GP, has access to all parts of the system. This helps secure data from possible fraudulent use.

INTERNAL CONTROL[5]

Internal control is an integrated system of people, processes, activities, policies, and procedures that provide reasonable assurance that the organization achieves it objectives in efficiency and effectiveness of operations, reliability of financial reporting, and compliance of applicable

[5]For a more detailed definition, refer to Internal Control Definition and Importance, *Accounting Information Systems: Basic Concepts & Current Issues,* R. L. Hurt, McGraw-Hill/Irwin ©2008, pages 52-54.

regulations. In Dynamics GP, internal control is an important aspect of the system. In each chapter of this textbook, you will complete an Internal Control Activity to see how Dynamics GP protects company data. With the passage of the Sarbanes-Oxley Act of 2002, management and external auditors must annually assess a company's internal controls for companies traded on a stock exchange. This includes reporting to the Security and Exchange Commission (SEC) that management is responsible for the design and implementation of internal controls.

In Dynamics GP, numerous internal controls are built into the software. These controls minimize errors, reduce the time it takes to record entries, and secure data from fraud. Dynamics GP's internal controls include:

- **System controls**: Examples include User ID and password when logging into the software; passwords for restricting access to the software; and roles. Windows Vista permissions are another example of internal controls.

- **Transaction controls**: Examples include batch controls; edit checks; limit checks; preformatted data windows with defaults for automatic field completion for dates or other transaction terms, calculations, required fields; data prompts to edit, accept or reject transactions that are not complete or accurate; approvals; and comparisons of input data with master data.

When users make changes to company records, Dynamics GP's *audit trail* provides documentation. An audit trail allows internal management or external auditors to trace a transaction from any point in the Dynamics GP system back to its point of origination.

Dynamics GP has several methods to track information. For example, users can trace transactions and balances through a combination of the general ledger, journals, reports, and financial statements to determine when a user performed an action. Dynamics GP's audit trail provides this information. The audit trail provides accountability of users, deters users from fraudulent activity or mistakes, and tracks transaction history.

As you work through the Internal Control Activities in this textbook, examples of system security and transaction security are shown. In the example that follows, Fabrikam, Inc., is used to view examples of inquires and *audit trail codes*. Audit trail codes provide a precise record of each transaction, including how transactions are recorded and posted. Audit trail codes pinpoint the exact posting journal. Using audit trail codes, you can trace transactions to their origin quickly and accurately.

Two components comprise audit trails codes: the prefix and the journal number. The prefix indicates a particular type of posting journal; the journal number indicates which specific journal includes the recording of a transaction. The Internal Control Activity below shows you how to perform an audit trail inquiry.

	INTERNAL CONTROL ACTIVITY
	In this activity, use the Detail Inquiry window for tracing the audit trail codes for the financial module.
1.	To open a transaction inquiry window, from the Financial page's Inquiry area, select Financial, Detail. The Detail Inquiry window appears.
2.	In the Account field, select Account No. 000-1100-00, Cash – Operating Account. 
3.	If necessary select the 2017 as the year. 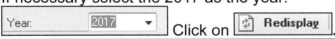 Click on
4.	Select the first item on the list (2/1/2017; Source Document 1,201; Reference, $3,263.24; Currency ID, $0.00). To see details, choose the Show Details button ( ). The Audit Trail codes for the line items are shown. 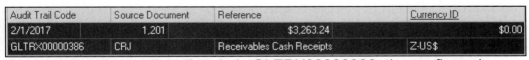 Observe that the audit trail code is GLTRX00000386, the prefix and journal number. The journal is identified as the CRJ for Cash Receipts Journal.
5.	When you are finished reviewing the information for the journal entry, choose Clear. The Detail Inquiry window is cleared. Close the Detail Inquiry window.

Security Roles

Security roles which contain the protective tasks that a user needs to do their job are another example of Dynamics GP's internal controls. System security controls access to system-wide setup information such as setting up new user records, assessing user security or printing reports. Some default security roles are created within the software. For example, the ACCOUNTING MANAGER* role contains security tasks that allow a user who is assigned to this role to view general ledger account information, enter journal entries, enter bank transactions, and perform other tasks assigned to an accounting manager might need to perform.

In Dynamics GP, individual security is role-based. Microsoft research has identified each user's typical, daily tasks. The system administrator assigns each user a security role before the user can access any forms, reports, or other data. To assign user security, a system administrator identifies the daily tasks that a user completes. Then the administrator assigns the user's role from either the default security roles or creates a new role.

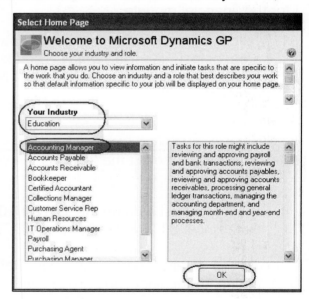

For example, user ABC is an accounting manager for Fabrikam, Inc., and needs access to set up general ledger, taxes, bank accounts, and credit cards as well as perform many other accounting tasks. Review the default security roles in Microsoft Dynamics GP to find one that grants access to the appropriate accounting functionality for user ABC. For our example, the ACCOUNTING MANAGER* security role is appropriate for user ABC. Use the User Security Setup Window to assign the ACCOUNTING MANAGER* security role to user ABC in the Fabrikam, Inc. company.

When Fabrikam, Inc. was started for the first time you were given the opportunity to choose an industry and role (page xiii). You were instructed to accept the defaults for Education as the Industry and

Accounting Manager as the role. The Select Home Page window includes industry and role selections.

The Accounting Manager role includes the following tasks: reviewing and approving payroll and bank transactions, reviewing and approving accounts payables, reviewing and approving accounts receivables, processing general ledger transactions, managing the accounting department, and managing month-end and year-end processes. Dynamics GP allows you to choose an industry and a role that best describes your work so that default information specific to your job is displayed on your home page.

From within the DGP, you can also review roles. Follow these steps to see the User Security Setup Window.

1. From the menu bar, click on the down arrow next to Microsoft Dynamics GP. Select Tools; Setup, System, Security Roles.

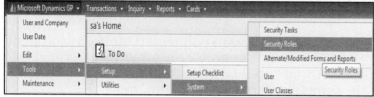

2. The Security Role Setup window appears. In the Role ID field, select the magnifying glass for the list of security roles. To see more roles, scroll down the list.

   The first time you started Fabrikam, Inc., a window appeared asking you to assign a role. On page xiii, you accepted the default role for Accounting Manager.

3. Click [Cancel] to return to the Security Role Setup window. Click

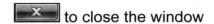 to close the window

Each time you start Dynamics GP, the User ID field shows **sa** (an acronym for system administrator). The User ID, sa, establishes you as the owner/administrator. This means you can create and delete company databases as well as perform maintenance. Along with using sa as the User ID, you also set up a password. (Refer to page viii, step 10.) The User ID and password set up during installation are part of Dynamics GP's internal control and security features.

EXITING DYNAMICS GP

When exiting Dynamics GP, the authors suggest you do *not* unload data if you are using your personal computer. If you are working at school and on your own laptop or PC, unload to your USB drive. Refer to page 22-23 for saving data to your USB drive.

SUMMARY AND REVIEW

OBJECTIVES: In Chapter 1, you completed the following activities.

1.   Start Dynamics GP 10.0 (DGP).
2.   Open the sample company, Fabrikam, Inc.
3.   Select an industry and user role.
4.   Set user preferences.
5.   Operate Dynamics GP's drop-down lists, lookup fields, toolbar, navigation pane, and menus.
6.   Identify Dynamics GP's installation folder, student data folder, and sample data folder.
7.   Save data.
8.   Save using Backup and Restore.
9.   Navigate the Help system.
10.   Complete a search using SmartList.
11.   Review Sarbanes-Oxley compliance.
12.   Complete an internal control activity.
13.   Identify security roles.
14.   Exit Dynamics GP.

Comment

The textbook web site at www.mhhe.com/dynamicsgp10essentials has a link to Textbook Updates. Check this link for updates.

True/Make True: Write the word True in the space provided if the statement is true. If the statement is not true, write the correct answer.

1. If there is an underlined letter in the menu or option you want to select, hold down the **<Alt>** key and the underlined letter to select it.

    _____

    _____

2. The menu items that have an arrow next to them indicate that there is another submenu with additional selections.

    _____

    _____

3. Shortcut keys enable you to use Dynamics GP's mouse.

    _____

    _____

4. The default location for copying the Sample Company Data is at <Program Files>\GP-Education\Students.

    _____

    _____

5. An integrated system of people, processes, and procedures that minimize or eliminate business risks are called internal controls.

    _____

    _____

6. Dynamics GP's internal controls include system access restrictions and transaction processing security.

    _____

    _____

7. Security roles include protective tasks that a user needs to do their job.

_____

_____

8. In Dynamics GP, individual security is based on the operating system being used.

_____

_____

9. The default user role is DP Manager.

_____

_____

10. Dynamics GP allows you to select industry and role preferences.

_____

_____

Exercise 1-1: Follow the instructions below to complete Exercise 1-1:

1. Start Windows, then Dynamics GP. Open Fabrikam, Inc. If data needs to be loaded go to step 2.

2. If necessary load data. (*Hint*: If necessary, browse to the Sample Company Data folder. Open the DYNAMICS.mdf file.)

3. Check the following information:

   a. User Preferences: Horizontal Scroll Arrows; Screen; Tab, and Local should be selected.
   b. Click <u>D</u>isplay: Required Fields shows the Font Color is red. Close windows.
   c. Microsoft Dynamics GP menu: Tools; Setup, Company,

Company. In the name filed, your name should appear after Fabrikam, Inc.

4.   Continue with Exercise 1-2.

Exercise 1-2

1.   Exit Dynamics GP.

2.   If you are working in the computer lab, unload data. Refer to unload data, steps 1-3, pages 22-23. *Remember, files unload to the same location where you loaded files from during login.* (*Hint:* If working on your own computer, select | No | when Dynamics GP asks if you want to unload data.)

Exercise 1-3: Internal Control

Follow these steps to print the audit trail codes.

1.   Start Dynamics GP. Open Fabrikam, Inc.

2.   Open the Audit Trail Codes Setup window. From the Microsoft Dynamics GP menu, select Tools; Setup, Posting, Audit Trail Codes. Posting setup is one of Dynamics GP's internal controls.

3.   If necessary, in the Series list select Financial. Choose File; Print.

4.   Answer the following questions.
   a. What is the Prefix, Next Sequence Number, and Source Document identification for Bank Deposit Entry?
   b. What are the audit trail codes for General Entry? Include the Prefix, Next Sequence Number, and Source Document identification.

Exercise 1-4: SmartList

1. Use SmartList to export the Accounts list to Excel.

2. The suggested file name is **Your** (Your first and last name) **Name Exercise 1-4_Account List.xls**.

3. Using the following account numbers, identify the Account Description, Posting Type, and Account Categories.

Account Number	Account Description	Posting Type	Account Categories
000-1100-00			
000-1200-00			
000-2400-00			
000-3010-00			
000-4110-00			
000-5100-00			
000-6170-04			

4. Exit Dynamics GP. (*Hint:* If working on your own computer, select | No | when Dynamics GP asks if you want to unload data. If working on a computer lab computer, select | Yes | and complete the steps on pages 22-23 to unload to your USB drive.)

Chapter 2

New Company Setup for a Service Business

OBJECTIVES: In Chapter 2, you will complete the following activities:

1. Copy Empty Company Data files from DVD.
2. Start Dynamics DGP 10.0-Education.
3. Create an additional company
4. Set up company information.
5. Enter the chart of accounts.
6. Set up fiscal periods.
7. Enter beginning balances.
8. Set up and print reports.
9. Use the SmartList.
10. Back up Chapter 2 data and exercises.
11. Review Sarbanes-Oxley compliance (SOX Box).
12. Complete an internal control activity.

In this text, you are the primary stockholder and accounting manager of a consulting and teaching services corporation that offers a variety of classes and private consultations. The business is called Student Name [Your first and last name] HELP, Inc. The business is growing and needs an information system that can grow with it. After doing research, you select Microsoft Dynamics GP 10.0. You will begin by using the software's accounting basics and will quickly move to use DGP's many features to expand the business. In this chapter you will set up the accounting records for Student Name HELP, Inc.

GETTING STARTED

In Chapter 1 you used the sample company Fabrikam, Inc. In this chapter you will copy files from the Empty Company Data folder on the Student Data DVD onto your desktop, rename the files, and copy them either into your computer's program path Student Data folder or on to your USB drive. From these files, you will create a new company, Student Name [Your first and last name] HELP, Inc.

Read Me: Windows Vista & Windows XP

Windows Vista: The data files must be located in the Student Data folder in the Microsoft Dynamics GP installation folder. The default location for this folder is C:\Program Files\ Microsoft Dynamics\GP-Education\Student Data.

Windows XP: Data files can be copied from hard drive, desktop, or USB drive locations. For optimal use with SQL, which runs alongside Dynamics GP, the authors suggest that data files be copied to the same place as your Sample Company Data folder. The steps that follow show that.

COPY EMPTY COMPANY DATA FILES

Follow these steps to copy the Empty Company Data files.

1.   Create a new folder for Empty Company Data files on your Desktop **using your first and last name** (i.e., Susan Crosson Data) (*HINT:* To add a folder on your Desktop, right click mouse anywhere on your desktop, scroll to New, and select Folder by clicking on it.)

2.   Insert the Student Data DVD into your DVD drive.

3.   Start Windows Explorer. (Start; All Programs, Accessories, Windows Explorer.)

4.   Click on your DVD Drive which shows Student Data DVD.

5.   Double-click on the Student Data folder to open it. Three subfolders are shown—Empty Company Data, My Companies, and Sample Company Data.

6.   Double-click on the Empty Company Data folder to open it. Four files are in the folder: DYNAMICS.mdf; DYNAMICSLog.ldf; GP.mdf; and GPLog.ldf .

7.   IMPORTANT. Copy just the GP.mdf and GPLog.ldf files from the DVD's Empty Company Data folder *on to your Desktop but NOT in the Your Name Data folder*.

8.   Rename only the GP.mdf and GPLog.ldf files *on your desktop* with **your three initials**, i.e., GP.mdf renamed to SNC.mdf and GPLog.ldf renamed to SNCLog.ldf . Remember that file names only have one extension, i.e., .mdf or .ldf.

9.   Drag these two renamed files from Desktop into the Sample Company Data folder which resides either on your USB drive or on your computer (C:\Program Files\Microsoft Dynamics\GP-Education\Student Data\Sample Company Data).

10.   When copied, the Sample Company Data folder has six files: DYNAMICS.mdf; DYNAMICSLog.ldf; SNC.mdf; SNCLog.ldf; TWO.mdf; TWOLog.ldf. (Remember, your files will show your 3 initials, *not* SNC.mdf and SNCLog.ldf)

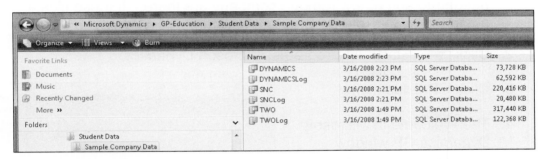

11.   After verifying that the Sample Company Data folder resides either on your USB drive or in your computer's program path C:\Program Files\Microsoft Dynamics\GP-Education\Student Data\Sample Company Data and contains the six files, close the Windows Explorer window.

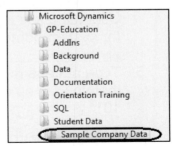

12.   Remove the Student Data DVD.

13.   Exit Windows Explorer.

Read Me

Why must six files reside in the Sample Company Data folder to use DGP?

- The DYNAMICS files contain the DGP operating database.
- The TWO files contain the database for Fabrikam Inc.
- The SNC or your 3 initials database (the renamed GP files) are ready for you to populate for the service business you will start in Chapter 2. (Each time you start another new business you will copy and rename the two GP files from the Student Data DVD.)

Each database, i.e., DYNAMICS, TWO, GP, and SNC require both .mdf files (master data files) and the .ldf files (log data files) to access and track their usage.

CREATE AN ADDITIONAL COMPANY

Follow these steps to create an additional company in Dynamics GP.

1. View your Sample Company Data folder to confirm the six files needed to add a new (empty) company are there. If these files are not in the folder, refer to Steps 2.-13. in the previous section.

2. Click ⊞ (Start); All Programs, Microsoft Dynamics.

3. Click GP-Education.

4. The Welcome to Microsoft Dynamics GP window appears. Type **sa** as the User ID. (sa is an acronym for system administrator.)

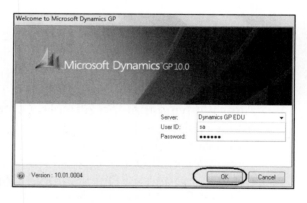

5. Type **access** (or password that you set up on p. viii step 10).

6. Click .

   NOTE—Script Error: If you receive an Internet Explorer Script Error, click Yes. This message appears because you do *not* have Microsoft Office 2003 Web Components installed on your computer. You do *not* need web components to use Dynamics GP.

7. The window prompts There isn't any data loaded. Do you want to load your data? Click

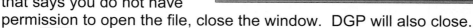

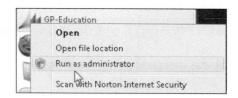

8. Go to your Sample Company Data folder either on your USB drive or your computer. Select the DYNAMICS.mdf file. Compare your select data file (DYNAMICS.mdf) window shown here.

   (Hint: If a window appears that says you do not have permission to open the file, close the window. DGP will also close.

   Click 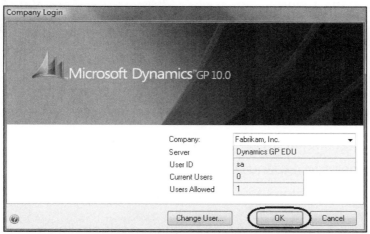 (Start); All Programs, Microsoft Dynamics. Right click on the GP-Education; then left click on Run as Administrator. Grant any Permissions, then go back to Step 2.)

9. Click Open ▾. After a few minutes, the Company Login window to appears.

10. Observe that the Company field shows Fabrikam, Inc., which is the

company used in Chapter 1. Click 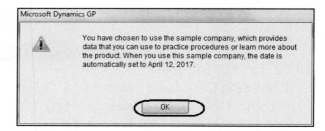.

11. The Microsoft Dynamics GP window says You have chosen to use the sample company. Observe that the date is April 12, 2017.

Microsoft Dynamics GP

You have chosen to use the sample company, which provides data that you can use to practice procedures or learn more about the product. When you use this sample company, the date is automatically set to April 12, 2017.

OK

12. Click OK .

13. If the Select Home Page, Welcome to Microsoft Dynamics GP, Choose your industry and role window appears, click OK to accept Education and Accounting Manager for your Industry and Role.

14. When the window appears that says you have 120 days to use the software before the evaluation period expires, click OK .

15. After a while, the Home window appears. If necessary, enlarge it. The date (4/12/2017), company name (Fabrikam, Inc.), and User ID (sa) is shown at the bottom of the window. Compare your home page to the one shown here.

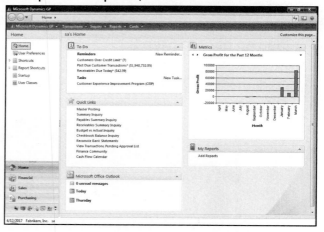

16. From the navigation pane, select Administration. (*Hint:* You may need to expand the Navigation pane and click on Show More buttons to see Administration.)

17. In the Utilities area of the Administration desktop, link to Create Company.

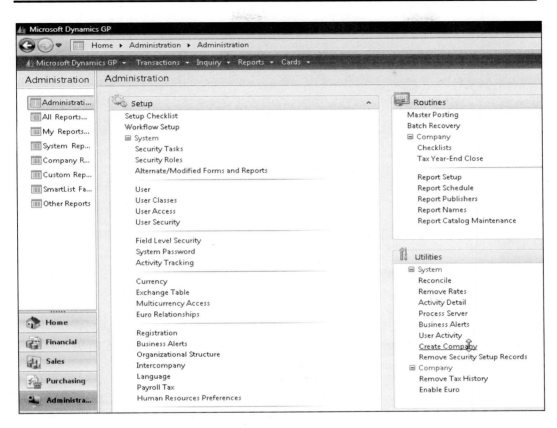

18. The Create Company window appears.

19. In the Company name field, type the company name, **Student Name [Your first and last name] HELP, Inc.**

20. Click on the folder [📁] in the Location of Database(.mdf) file field, go to the location of your program path files. The default location is C:\Program Files\Microsoft Dynamics\GP-Education\ Student Data\Sample Company Data.

21. Select the SNC.mdf file (*your 3 initials*). Confirm the File name shows SNC.mdf (your 3 initials). Click ⟦ Open ▼ ⟧.

22. When the Create Company window appears, observe that the Company Name field is completed; the Database Name field is completed; and the Location of Database (.mdf) file field is also completed.

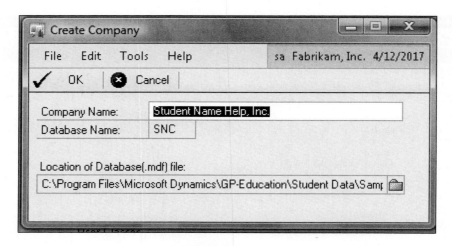

23. When satisfied, click [✓ OK]. The Creating Company….this may take a few minutes window appears.

24. Be patient while the company is be created. When the Create Company window appears (fields are blank), select File; Close Company.

25. From the dropdown Dynamics GP menu, click User and Company. The Company Login window appears.

26. In the Company field, select the company you just created, Student Name [Your first and last name] HELP, Inc. Click [OK].

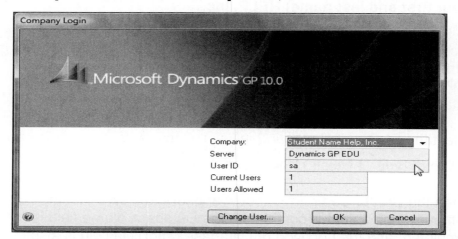

27. After a few minutes, the Microsoft Dynamics GP window appears

saying you have 120 days to use the software. Click OK . The
Home page appears. At the bottom left of your screen, the status bar
shows today's date, your HELP company name, and sa.

COMPANY ADDRESS

Follow these steps to add company address information.

1. From the navigation pane, select  ;
   on Administration desktop scroll down to Company;
   link to Company.

2. The Company Setup window appears.

   The Student Name [Your first and last name] HELP, Inc. is shown in
   the Company Name field.

   Complete the following fields:

   Address ID: PRIMARY
   Name: Your first and last name
   Contact: Your first and last name
   Address: Your address
   City: Your city
   State: Your state
   ZIP Code: Your zip code
   Phone 1:   Your phone
   Fax: Leave blank

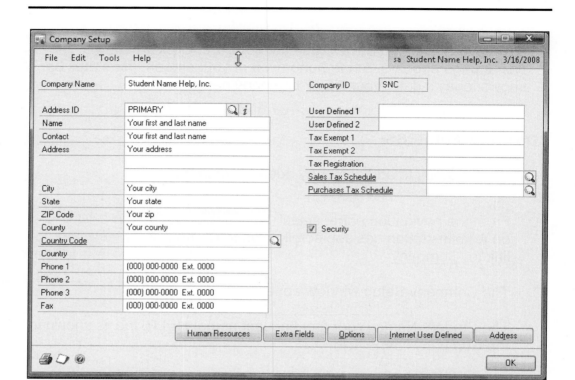

3. Proof your entries, when satisfied, click [OK]

INDUSTRY AND ROLES

In Chapter 1, pages 32-34, security roles are discussed. In Dynamics GP, security is role based. This means you can set up a company to protect records so that not everyone using the system can access data. In the following steps, you are going to select Accounting Manager as your role and Services as the Industry Type. The Accounting Manager role contains security tasks that allow the user to view general ledger accounting information, enter journal entries, enter bank transactions, and print reports, etc. This is an appropriate security role for the work you will do in this chapter.

Follow these steps to set up your role and industry type.

1. From the navigation pane, select [Home]. On the upper right side of the screen, link to <u>Customize this page</u>. The Customize Home Page window appears.

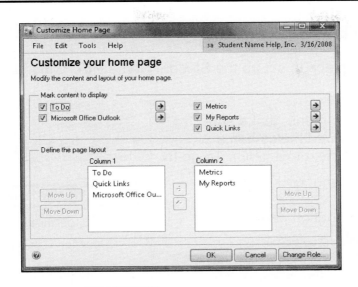

2. When you select Change Role..., a window appears saying that Any customizations that you have made. . .will be removed if you change roles. Click OK .

3. The Welcome to Microsoft Dynamics GP; Choose your industry and role window appears. In the Your Industry field, select **Services**. In the list, select **Accounting Manager**. Review the information about the Accounting Manager's tasks.

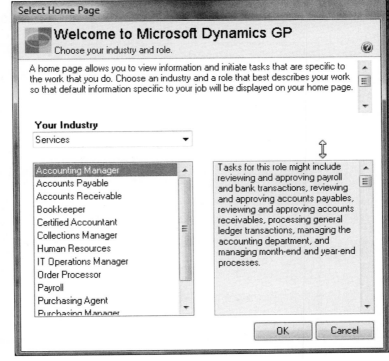

4. Click OK to return to the Home page.

USER PREFERENCES

Follow these steps to set up the Student Name HELP, Inc. user preferences.

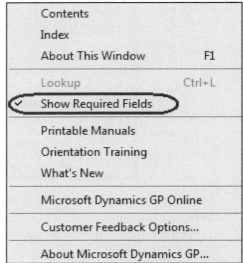

1. On the Help menu, make sure Show Required Fields has a checkmark next to it. (*Hint:* To go to the Help menu, click [⊙].)

2. On the navigation pane, select 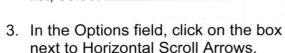. In the Home list, select [User Preferences].

3. In the Options field, click on the box next to Horizontal Scroll Arrows.

4. In the Default Report Destination field, select Screen. Compare your User Preferences window to the one shown below.

5. Click [Display]. In the Required Fields Font Color field, select Red. For Font Style, select Bold. Compare your User Display Preferences window to the one shown here.

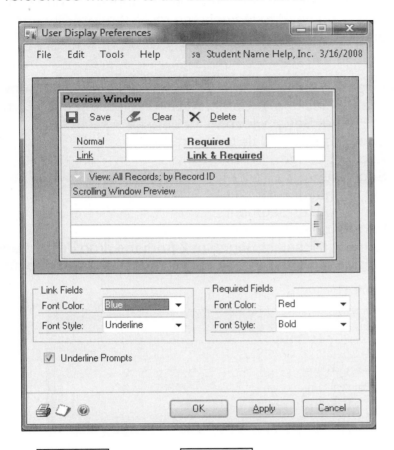

6. Click [OK] and then [OK] again to close both User Preferences windows.

CHART OF ACCOUNTS

The chart of accounts is a list of all the accounts in the general ledger. Chart of accounts commonly number accounts by type. For example, 1XXX are assets; 2XXX are liabilities, 3XXX are equities; 4XXX are revenues, 5XXX are expenses. Since no accounts exist for your Student Name HELP, Inc. in Dynamics GP, you must add all the accounts your company will use. Follow these steps to create your chart of accounts.

Account Framework

You currently use a four-digit account number to identify accounts in your business but realize you need to leave some room for flexibility and growth when you set up your account framework in DGP.

1. From the navigation pane, select **Administration**. Scroll down the Administration desktop to Company; and select <u>Account</u> Format.
2. The Account Format Setup window appears.(Notice the required fields are red.)
3. Type 9 for Account Length.
4. Type 3 for Segments.
5. Type 3 for the Length of Segment 1
6. Type 4 for the Length of Segment 2.
7. Type 2 for the Length of Segment 3.
8. For Main Segment ID, select Segment 2 from the drop down menu.
9. Compare your screen with the following screenshot and make any corrections.

☐ Company
   Company
   <u>Account Format</u>

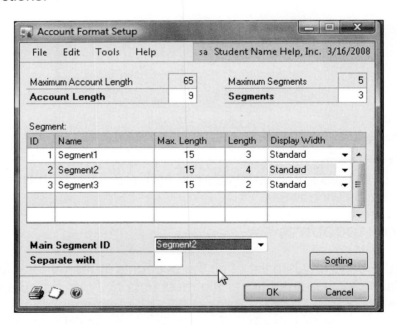

10. When satisfied, click OK to close the Account Format Setup window.

You are ready to enter your chart of accounts and beginning balances.

Add Accounts

1. From the navigation pane, select Financial. The Financials Lists shows Accounts, Account Transactions, Checkbooks, …Assets.

2. Link to Accounts. The Accounts window appears showing the default account list. Notice it is blank. Let's add your accounts. Click on 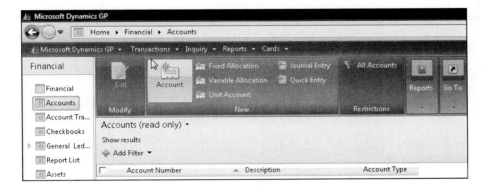 .

3. The Account Maintenance window appears.

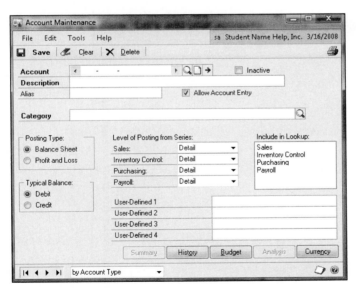

4. Type 000-1110-00 in the Account field. Press <Tab> to go to the Description field. If following screen appears, check the Do not

display this message again.   Click  .

5. Type Gainesville Checking for Description.

6. Type Cash for Alias.

7. Confirm Allow Account Entry is checked.

8. For Category, use the Lookup icon to select Cash as the Category.

9. Confirm Posting Type is Balance Sheet.

10. Confirm Typical Balance is Debit.

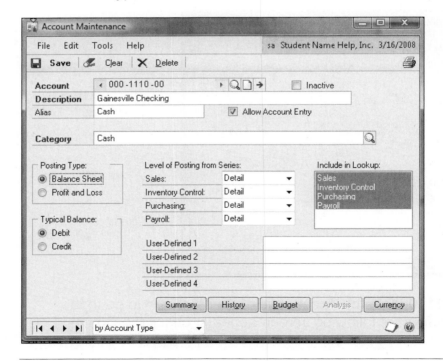

11. Proof your screen and click Save.

12. A new Account Maintenance screen appears. Click on 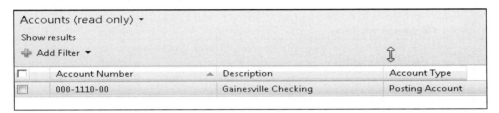 in the upper right hand corner of the screen to minimize it.

13. In the Accounts screen, click [🔄 Refresh]. The Accounts screen now contains the Gainesville Checking account.

Accounts (read only) ▾		
Show results		
➕ Add Filter ▾		
Account Number ▲	Description	Account Type
000-1110-00	Gainesville Checking	Posting Account

14. Click on [🖼 Accoun... 🗗 🗖] to maximize the Account Maintenance screen and add the following accounts.

Account Number	Account Description	Posting Type Typical Balance	Account Category
000-1110-00	Gainesville Checking	Balance Sheet Debit	Cash
000-1120-00	Sunshine Savings	Balance Sheet Debit	Cash
000-1130-00	FL State Savings	Balance Sheet Debit	Cash
000-1200-00	Prepaid Insurance	Balance Sheet Debit	Prepaid Expenses
000-1230-00	Prepaid Rent	Balance Sheet Debit	Prepaid Expenses
000-1430-00	Computer Equipment	Balance Sheet Debit	Property, Plant and Equipment
000-1435-00	Accum. Depr.-Computer Equipment	Balance Sheet Credit	Accumulated Depreciation
000-1440-00	Furniture and Fixtures	Balance Sheet Debit	Property, Plant and Equipment
000-1445-00	Accum. Depr.-Furniture and Fixtures	Balance Sheet Credit	Accumulated Depreciation
000-1450-00	Automobiles	Balance Sheet Debit	Property, Plant and Equipment
000-1455-00	Accum. Depr.-Automobiles	Balance Sheet Credit	Accumulated Depreciation
000-1720-00	Supplies	Balance Sheet Debit	Other Assets
000-2110-00	Accounts Payable	Balance Sheet Credit	Accounts Payable

000-2140-00	Notes Payable	Balance Sheet Credit	Other Current Liabilities
000-2310-00	Publisher Advances	Balance Sheet Credit	Other Current Liabilities
000-3000-00	Retained Earnings	Balance Sheet Credit	Retained Earnings
000-3100-00	Common Stock	Balance Sheet Credit	Common Stock
000-4100-00	Professional Fees	Profit and Loss Credit	Sales
000-4110-00	Teaching Income	Profit and Loss Credit	Sales
000-4120-00	Royalty Income	Profit and Loss Credit	Sales
000-5110-00	Advertising Expense	Profit and Loss Debit	Other Expenses
000-5120-00	Automobile Registration Expense	Profit and Loss Debit	Other Expenses
000-5130-00	Bank Charges	Profit and Loss Debit	Other Expenses
000-5135-00	Conference Expense	Profit and Loss Debit	Other Expenses
000-5145-00	Depr. Exp.-Automobiles	Profit and Loss Debit	Depreciation Expense
000-5147-00	Depr. Exp.-Computer Equipment	Profit and Loss Debit	Depreciation Expense
000-5149-00	Depr. Exp.-Furniture and Fixtures	Profit and Loss Debit	Depreciation Expense
000-5150-00	Dues and Subscriptions	Profit and Loss Debit	Other Expenses
000-5175-00	Insurance Expense	Profit and Loss Debit	Other Expenses
000-5180-00	Internet Service Provider	Profit and Loss Debit	Other Expenses
000-5185-00	Maintenance and Repairs Expense	Profit and Loss Debit	Other Expenses
000-5190-00	Postage and Delivery Expense	Profit and Loss Debit	Other Expenses
000-5195-00	Printing and Reproduction Expense	Profit and Loss Debit	Other Expenses
000-5235-00	Rent Expense	Profit and Loss Debit	Other Expenses
000-5245-00	Supplies Expense	Profit and Loss Debit	Other Expenses
000-5250-00	Telephone Expense	Profit and Loss Debit	Other Expenses
000-5255-00	Utilities Expense	Profit and Loss Debit	Other Expenses

15. Use the ▮◀ ▶ ▮ to review and correct your work, and Save changes.

16. When satisfied, close the Account Maintenance screen.

17. In the Accounts screen, click ⟳ Refresh to see all the accounts.

Change Accounts

1. If necessary, from the Financial list, link to <u>Accounts</u>. Select Account Number 2140, Notes Payable. Link to <u>2140: Notes Payable.</u>

2. The Account Maintenance window for the Notes Payable account appears. In the Description field, add your first and last name after Notes Payable. Also, notice the Category, Posting Type and Typical Balance selections. (Your Account Maintenance window should show your first and last name after Notes Payable.)

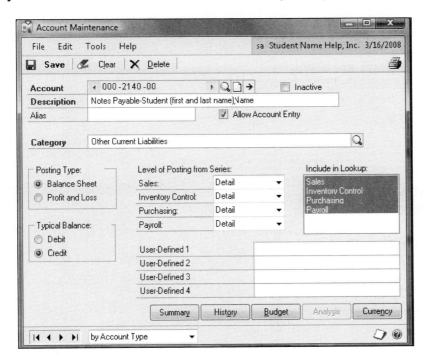

3. Click ⊟ Save , then click ✕ on the Account Maintenance window to return to the Accounts list.

---

4. Change the following accounts:

Acct. Number	Description
5130	Bank Charges **Expense**
5150	Dues and Subscriptions **Expense**

5. To make sure you have changed the accounts, go to the Financial page. Check that each account description is changed: Account No. 2140, Notes Payable-your first and last name; Account No. 5130, Bank Charges Expense; Account No. 5150, Dues and Subscriptions Expense.

6. Close the Account Maintenance window.

Printing the Chart of Accounts

1. From the Financial list, select [Financial]. The Financial page appears. In the Reports area, link to <u>Account</u>.

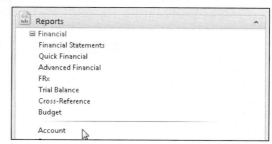

2. The Chart of Accounts Report window appears.

3. In the Reports field, select All Accounts.

4. Click [New].

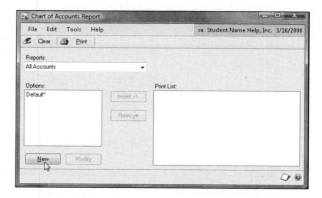

5. The Chart of Accounts Report Options window appears. Type **Chart of Accounts** in the Option field.

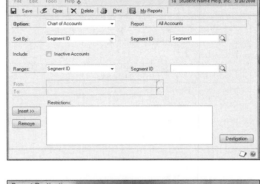

6. Click  .

7. Check Ask Each Time.

8. Select Screen and File.

9. Click ⬜ to browse to your computer desktop to save file in a new folder called Your [Your first and last name] Name Data folder. The suggested file name is **Chapter 2 Chart of Accounts.txt**.

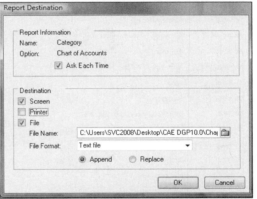

10. Click ⬜ Save ⬜.

11. When returned to the Report Destination window, Click ⬜ OK ⬜.

12. You are returned to the Chart of Accounts Report Options window. For Option, select Chart of Accounts.

13. Click ⬜ Print ⬜. The chart of accounts starts to print. A partial chart of accounts is shown here. Observe that the chart of accounts shows the category, whether the account is active, account type, posting type, and typical balance. Within the User-Defined 4 column, the chart of accounts classifies the accounts for the financial statements.

System:	3/16/2008	8:04:07 PM			ACCOUNTS LIST				Page: 1
User Date:	3/16/2008				Student Name Help, Inc.				User ID: sa
					General Ledger				

Ranges:	From:			To:			Sorted By: Segment1		
Account:	First			Last			Include:		
Account Description:	First			Last					

Account User-Defined 1	Description User-Defined 2		Alias	Category User-Defined 3	Active	Account Type User-Defined 4	Posting Type	Typical Balance
000-1110-00	Gainesville Checking		Cash	Cash	Yes	Posting Account	Balance Sheet	Debit
000-1120-00	Sunshine Savings			Cash	Yes	Posting Account	Balance Sheet	Debit
000-1130-00	FL State Retirement			Cash	Yes	Posting Account	Balance Sheet	Debit
000-1200-00	Prepaid Insurance			Prepaid Expenses	Yes	Posting Account	Balance Sheet	Debit
000-1230-00	Prepaid Rent			Prepaid Expenses	Yes	Posting Account	Balance Sheet	Debit
000-1430-00	Computer Equipment			Property, Plant and Equipment	Yes	Posting Account	Balance Sheet	Debit
000-1435-00	Accum. Depr.-Computer Equipment			Accumulated Depreciation	Yes	Posting Account	Balance Sheet	Credit
000-1440-00	Furniture and Fixtures			Property, Plant and Equipment	Yes	Posting Account	Balance Sheet	Debit
000-1445-00	Accum. Depr.-Furniture and Fixtures			Accumulated Depreciation	Yes	Posting Account	Balance Sheet	Credit
000-1450-00	Automobiles			Property, Plant and Equipment	Yes	Posting Account	Balance Sheet	Debit
000-1455-00	Accum. Depr.-Automobiles			Accumulated Depreciation	Yes	Posting Account	Balance Sheet	Credit
000-1720-00	Supplies			Other Assets	Yes	Posting Account	Balance Sheet	Debit
000-2110-00	Accounts Payable			Accounts Payable	Yes	Posting Account	Balance Sheet	Credit
000-2140-00	Notes Payable-Student (first and last name)Name			Other Current Liabilities	Yes	Posting Account	Balance Sheet	Credit
000-2310-00	Publisher Advances			Other Current Liabilities	Yes	Posting Account	Balance Sheet	Credit
000-3000-00	Retained Earnings			Retained Earnings	Yes	Posting Account	Balance Sheet	Credit
000-3100-00	Common Stock			Common Stock	Yes	Posting Account	Balance Sheet	Credit
000-4100-00	Professional Fees			Sales	Yes	Posting Account	Profit and Loss	Credit
000-4110-00	Teaching Income			Sales	Yes	Posting Account	Profit and Loss	Credit

14.   When you close the Chart of Accounts Report Options window, if a window prompts "Do you want to save changes to this report?", click [Discard].

15.   Close the Chart of Accounts Report window.

SETTING UP FISCAL PERIODS

Use the Fiscal periods Setup window to set up current fiscal periods for the Student Name HELP, Inc. You cannot post transaction until you create fiscal periods for that year.

Follow these steps to set up fiscal periods.

1.   From the Microsoft Dynamics GP menu, select Tools; Setup, Company, Fiscal Periods.

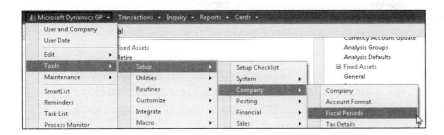

2. The Fiscal Periods Setup window appears.

3. Type **20XX (use your current year, i.e., 2008)** in the Year field.

4. Type **1/1/20XX (use your current year, i.e., 2008)** in the First Day field. The Last Day field shows 123120XX (your current year, i.e., 2008). Press <Tab>.

5. Click [Calculate]. Twelve periods are completed automatically.

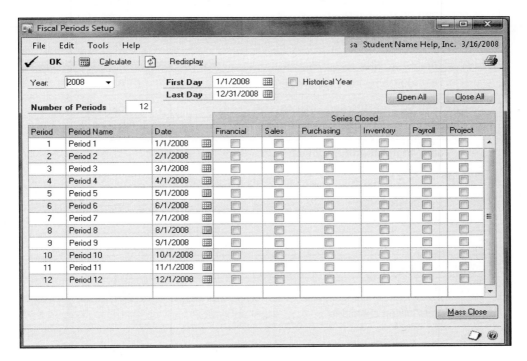

6. Click [OK].

ENTERING BEGINNING BALANCES

In order to begin accounting tasks, you start with a Balance Sheet that lists the types and amounts of assets, liabilities, and equity as of a specific date. A balance sheet is also called a *statement of financial position*. The October 1, 20XX balance sheet is shown here.

Student Name HELP, Inc. Balance Sheet **October 1, 20XX**		
ASSETS		
Current Assets		
000-1110-00 Gainesville Checking	$ 20,700.00	
000-1120-00 Sunshine Savings	4,500.50	
000-1130-00 FL State Savings	33,222.78	
000-1200-00 Prepaid Insurance	2,100.00	
000-1230-00 Prepaid Rent	600.00	
Total Current Assets		$61,123.28
Property and Equipment		
000-1430-00 Computer Equipment	$ 6,800.00	
000-1440-00 Furniture and Fixtures	5,000.00	
000-1450-00 Automobiles	19,000.00	
Total Property and Equipment		30,800.00
Other Assets		
000-1720-00 Supplies	1,771.83	
Total Assets		$ 93,695.11
LIABILITIES AND EQUITY		
Current Liabilities		
000-2110-00 Accounts Payable	$ 5,250.65	
Total Current Liabilities		$ 5,250.65
Equity		
000-3100-00 Common Stock		88,444.46
Total Liabilities and Equity		$ 93,695.11

The information in this Balance Sheet will be the basis for recording the

Student Name HELP Inc. beginning balances. Before you can enter beginning balances, you need to set up the Retained Earnings Account.

Follow these steps to set up the Retained Earnings account and record the Student Name HELP Inc. opening entry.

1. The steps to set up the Retained Earnings account are as follows:
    a. From the Financial page's Setup area, link to <u>General Ledger</u>.

    b. The General Ledger Setup window appears. In the <u>Account</u> field, select 000-3000-00, Retained Earnings.

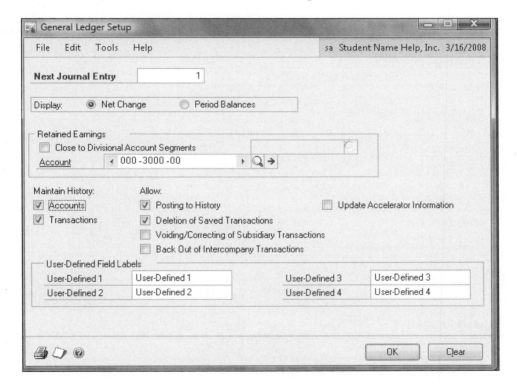

c. Click [OK].

2. From the Financial page's Transactions list, link <u>Batches</u>. The Batch Entry window opens.

3. Type **BBAL** (for Beginning Balances) in the Batch ID field.

---

4.   In the Origin field, select General Entry.

5.   Type **Beginning balance for October 1, 20XX (use your current year, i.e., 2008)** in the Comment field.

6.   If necessary, select Single Use as the frequency because you will post beginning balances and historical information only once. Compare your Batch Entry window to the one shown.

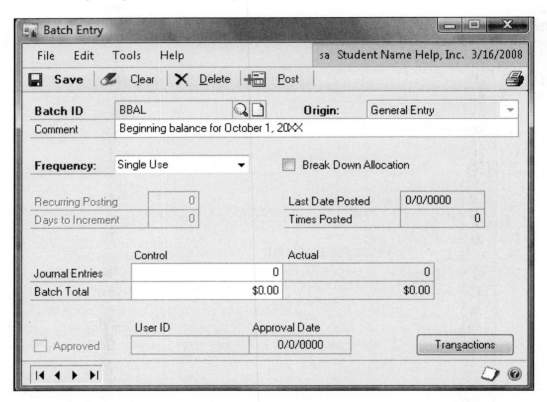

7.   Click [Transactions] to open the Transaction Entry window where you can enter beginning balance transactions. Observe that the Transaction Entry window shows Journal Entry 1; Batch ID, BBAL; Transaction Type, Standard; Source Document, GJ. Type **100120XX (use your current year, i.e., 2008)** in the Transaction date field, press <Tab>. The date appears as 10/1/2008. Compare your Transaction Entry window to the one shown here.

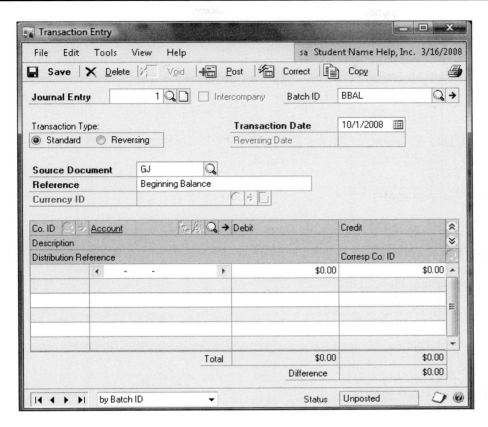

8.   Type **Beginning Balance** in the Reference field.

9.   Using the October 1, 20XX balance sheet on page 64, type the debit and credit entries. When the Difference field shows $0.00, debits and credits equal. Compare your Transaction Entry window with the one shown on the next page.

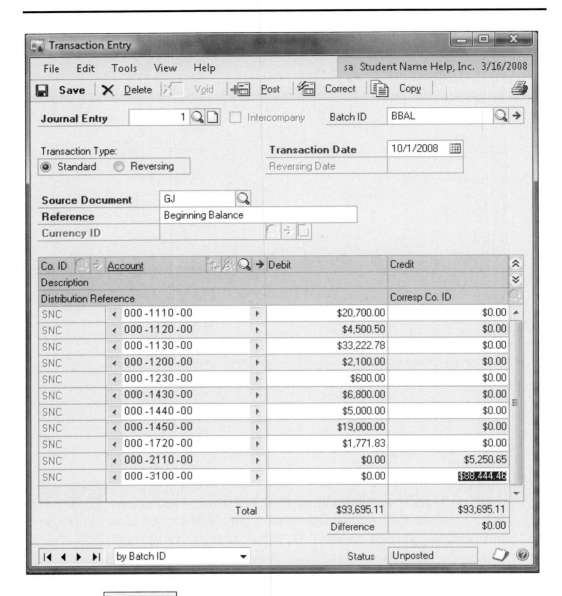

10.   Click [💾 Save]. A new Transaction Entry screen appears. *Before you post Journal Entry 1, let's make sure your entries are correct.*

11.   Use [◄ ◄ ► ►] to return to the Journal Entry 1 screen. Observe that there is a printer icon on the Transaction Entry window. Click [🖨]. Make sure the Screen and File Destination is checked. (If you do *not* want a print-out, uncheck Printer.) Click [📁] to browse to your

computer desktop to save file in the Your [Your first and last name] Name Data folder. The suggested file name is **Chapter 2 Beginning Balances.txt**. Your file path will differ.

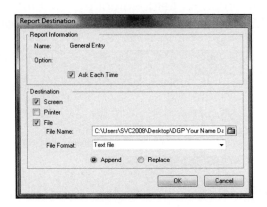

12.   Click [OK]. Make the selections to print. Compare your beginning balances for Oct. 1, 20XX with the balance sheet shown on page 64.

```
System:     6/23/2008  7:56:50 PM            Student Name HELP, Inc.                    Page:      1
User Date: 6/23/2008                      GENERAL TRANSACTION EDIT LIST                 User ID:  sa
                                                General Ledger


Batch ID:      BBAL
Batch Comment: Beginning balance for October 1, 2008.


Approved:      No            Batch Total Actual:        $187,390.22    Batch Total Control:      $0.00
Approved By:                 Trx Total Actual:                    1    Trx Total Control:           0
Approval Date:



    Journal      Transaction   Transaction   Reversing    Source    Transaction
    Entry          Type          Date          Date      Document   Reference
--------------------------------------------------------------------------------------------------------
        1      Standard     10/1/2008                     GJ       Beginning Balance


            Account            Description                              Debit           Credit
            ----------------   ----------------------------         -----------      -----------
            000-1110-00        Gainesville Checking                 $20,700.00
            000-1120-00        Sunshine Savings                      $4,500.50
            000-1130-00        FL State Savings                     $33,222.78
            000-1200-00        Prepaid Insurance                     $2,100.00
            000-1230-00        Prepaid Rent                            $600.00
            000-1430-00        Computer Equipment                    $6,800.00
            000-1440-00        Furniture and Fixtures                $5,000.00
            000-1450-00        Automobiles                          $19,000.00
            000-1720-00        Supplies                              $1,771.83
            000-2110-00        Accounts Payable                                       $5,250.65
            000-3100-00        Common Stock                                          $88,444.46
                                                                    -----------      -----------
        Total Distributions:        11                     Totals:  $93,695.11       $93,695.11
```

13.   Close the screen output. You are returned to the Transaction Entry window. Close the Transaction Entry window.

14.   From the Transactions list, link to <u>Batches</u>. The Batch Entry window appears. In the Batch ID field, select BBAL. Observe that the Comment field shows Beginning balance for October 1, 20XX.

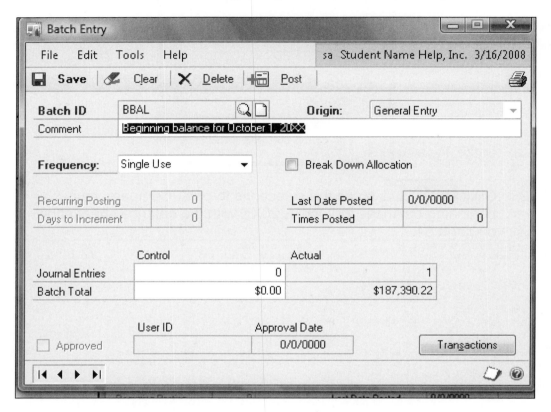

15.   Click [Post].

16.   Make the selections to print.

17.   Make the selections to print. The General Posting Journal prints showing the detail of the beginning balance entry. This posting journal shows the same account distribution as the General Transaction Edit List on the previous page.

18.   Close the Batch Entry window.

SETTING UP THE BALANCE SHEET

Before printing the balance sheet, you need to set up the financial reports. The steps below show how to set up the income statement, the balance sheet, and the statement of cash flows. Once the statements are set up, you complete balance sheet layout and print the balance sheet.

1. From the Financial page's Reports list, link to <u>Quick Financial</u>. The Quick Financial Setup window appears.

2. Type **Income Statement** in the Report field.

3. In the Type field, select **Profit and Loss**.

4. Click [💾 Save].

5. Type **Balance Sheet** in the Report field.

6. In the Type field, select **Balance Sheet**.

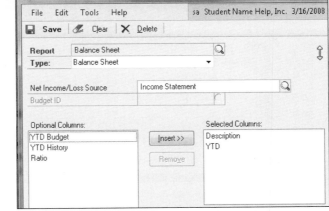

7. In the Net Income/Loss Source field, select Income Statement (Report Name); Profit and Loss (Report Type).

8. Click [💾 Save].

9. Type **Statement of Cash Flow** in the Reports field.

10. In the Type field, select **Statement of Cash Flows**.

11. In the Net Income/Loss Source field, select **Income Statement (Report Name); Profit and Loss (Report Type).**

12. Click [💾 Save]. Close the Quick Financial Setup window.

Balance Sheet Layout

Now that you have used the Quick Financial feature to identify financial statements, you need to set up the financial statements' accounting period. Follow these steps to set financial statements dates.

1. In the Reports list, link to <u>Advanced Financial</u>. The Advanced Financial Reports window appears. In the Reports list, select **Balance Sheet**.

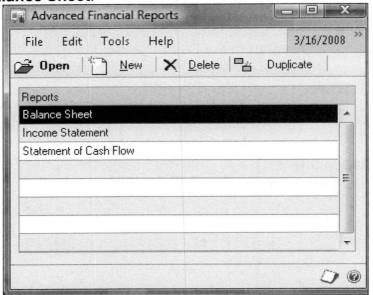

2. Click [Open]. The Advanced Financial Report Definition window appears. The Report and Type fields show Balance Sheet. The Net Income/Loss Source field shows Income Statement.

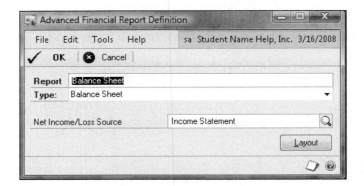

3. Click [Layout].

4. The Advanced Financial Report Layout window appears. Observe there are two gray columns below the icon bar that show C1 and C2

C1	C2

.

5. The account balance amounts appear in column C2 on the balance sheet. Double-click on column C2. This takes you to the Financial Column Definition window.

6. Observe that the Financial Column Definition window shows Year-To-Date in the Type field. In the Type field, select **Period Range**.

7. In the Period field, select **Other Period**.

8. For the Period, click [Q], then select **Period 10**; 10/1/20XX (your current year).

9. In the To field, select Other Period. For the Period, click [Q], the select **Period 12**. Compare your Financial Column definition window to the one shown here.

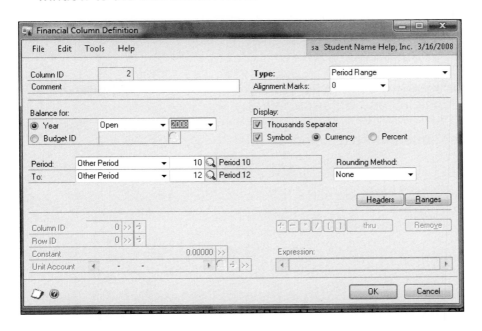

10.   Click [OK]. Close the Advanced Financial Report Layout
      window.

11.   When the window prompts Do you want to save changes to this
      report?, click [Save]. Close the Advanced Financial Report
      Definition window; close the Advanced Financial Reports window.

Printing the Balance Sheet

Follow these steps to print an October 1, 20XX Balance Sheet.

Read me: User Data

If a message appears that says the User Date falls within a fiscal year that hasn't been
set up, go to the Microsoft Dynamics GP menu; select User Date. On the User Date
window, type 10/01/20XX (Your current year) in the date field.

1.   In the Reports list, link to <u>Financial Statements</u>. The Financial
     Statement Report window appears.

2.   In the Report field, click 🔍, then double-click **Balance Sheet** to
     select it.

3.   Click [New].

4.   The Financial Statement Report Options window appears. In the
     Option field, type **Balance Sheet**.

5.   In the Amounts field, select **Detail.**

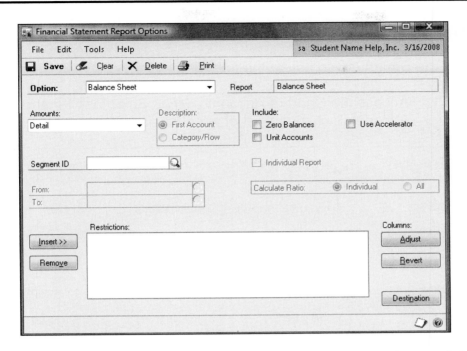

6. Make the selections to print to screen, save to file, or print to printer. (*Hint:* If you click [Destination], you can print to your screen and to file.) The suggested file name is **Chapter 2_Oct 1 20XX Balance Sheet.txt**. Click [printer icon], then compare the balance sheet to page 64.

7. Close all windows to return to Dynamics GP desktop. You should save these settings.

SMARTLIST

Using the SmartList, complete the following activity.

1.   Access the Chart of Accounts. (*Hint*: SmartList, Financial, Accounts). A partial list of accounts is shown.

Account Number	Account Description	Posting Type	Account Category Number
000-1110-00	Gainesville Checking	Balance Sheet	Cash
000-1120-00	Sunshine Savings	Balance Sheet	Cash
000-1130-00	FL State Retirement	Balance Sheet	Cash
000-1200-00	Prepaid Insurance	Balance Sheet	Prepaid Expenses
000-1230-00	Prepaid Rent	Balance Sheet	Prepaid Expenses
000-1430-00	Computer Equipment	Balance Sheet	Property, Plant and Equipment

2.   Export the file to Word and Save. The suggested file name is **Chapter 2_Account Number.doc**.

3.   What accounts are reported as current assets on a balance sheet? (*Hint*: The Account Category reflects the account classifications that a company uses on a classified balance sheet or a multi-step income statement.)

   ANSWER: Cash, short term investment, accounts receivable, inventory, prepaid expenses

4.   What types of account classifications exist for the income statement?

   ANSWER: Sales, Sales returns and discounts, cost of goods sold, other expenses, administrative expenses, depreciation expense, amortization of intangible assets, tax expense, selling expenses, salaries expenses, other income, other expenses.

EXITING DYNAMICS GP

You have completed a significant amount of work. You will want to save your data. At this point you should unload your data and make a back up of it to external media, i.e., USB flash drive. When using Dynamics GP, information is automatically saved to the location you loaded your data from—either your USB drive or your computer hard drive. Making a backup of your unloaded data simply means saving a copy of it to your USB drive. Unloading your data and making a backup of it means that it will be available if you want to work in Dynamics GP from this unloading point again, i.e., you make a mistake and want to redo your work.

In this textbook, detailed steps for unloading your data were shown in Chapter 1 pages 22-23. Since your data files will continue to grow in size with each chapter, before you backup to external media, such as a USB drive it is wise to check the file size. The authors recommend you make a backup periodically in case you make mistakes or want to transport your files between computers. The directions that follow are again the step-by-step guide to unloading and then backing up to external media your chapter data.

When you unload now, you are saving the company information, the revised chart of accounts, and the beginning balances that you recorded.

Steps to Unload Data

1. From Dynamics GP's menu bar, select File; Exit.

2. Window appears which asks Do you want to unload data? Select Yes. (Data will detach and the DYNAMICS.mdf file is updated.)

3. Data can now be copied for backup or be transported to another computer.

4. On your USB drive or in your computer's Program folders, double click on the Sample Company Data folder to verify that it contains your six data files:
    SNC.mdf (your 3 initials)
    SNCLog.ldf (your 3 initials)
    DYNAMICS.mdf
    DYNAMICSLog.ldf

TWO.mdf
TWOLog.ldf

5.   Leave the window open for step 7.

6.   Open the Your Name Data folder which is located on your Desktop. Create a New Folder named Your Name [Your first and last name] Chapter 2 Begin. (i.e., Susan Crosson Chapter 2 Begin) *Hint:* Each time you back up a chapter or exercise use a different folder and folder name.

7.   Copy the six data files from the Sample Company Data folder into the newly created Your Name Chapter 2 Begin folder.

8.   Copy the Your Name [Your first and last name] Chapter 2 Begin folder from your Desktop to your USB drive.

9.   Your files are now backed up and can be transported to continue work on a different computer. You can also reload them if you want to start over from this point.

Comment

When you back up, you are saving your work to its current point in Dynamics GP. Each time you make a backup, you should type a different backup name (folder name) to distinguish between them, i.e., Your First and Last Name Chapter 2. In this way, if you need to go to an earlier backup, you have the data for that purpose. Remember, you can go back to an earlier point in the company's data by loading that data file. Without these backup files, you cannot go back to an earlier point in the data. Since all the chapters work together, your backup files are important. In the business world, backups are unique to each business: daily, weekly, monthly. *Remember to back up before you leave the computer lab or your computer! IMPORTANT!*

Backup Folder Size

Follow these steps to see the size of the backup file on your external media.

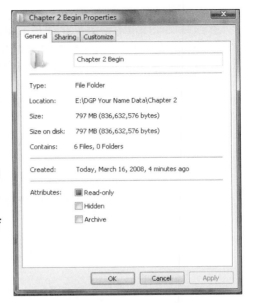

1. Go to Windows Explorer.

2. From Windows Explorer, go to the location of your external media. Right click on the Chapter 2 Begin folder, select Properties. Compare your window to the one shown here. The Name of the file is Your Name Chapter 2 Begin; the Size of the file is 797 MB. (The size of your backup file may differ; this is okay.)

3. Close Windows Explorer.

4. Close all open windows.

SARBANES-OXLEY COMPLIANCE

SOX Box
The Sarbanes-Oxley legislation established new standards for all U.S. public company boards and their management. It does not apply to privately held companies. The legislation also covers public accounting firms. SOX contains 11 sections ranging from additional Corporate Board responsibilities to criminal penalties. The act requires the Securities and Exchange Commission (SEC) to implement rulings or requirements to comply with the new law. An aspect of SOX is the strengthening of corporate accounting controls.   For example, SOX establishes a new oversight board called the Public Company Accounting Oversight Board (PCAOB). The PCAOB oversees, regulates, inspects, and disciplines accounting firms in their roles as auditors of public companies. SOX also covers auditor independence, corporate governance, internal control assessment, and improved financial disclosure. As you can see, internal control is a key element of the Sarbanes-Oxley Act of 2002.

SYSTEM INTERNAL CONTROLS

Managers implement various unique internal control systems within their organizations but some internal controls are common to most businesses. The following list introduces the internal controls that you would likely encounter within an accounting information system. The list is in alphabetical order for easy reference.[1]

- Adequate documentation via flowcharts or data flow diagrams
- Background checks of employees
- Backup of computer files
- Backup of power supplies and disaster recovery systems
- Bank reconciliation and reconciliation of other accounts
- Batch control totals
- Data encryption
- Document matching of paper or electronic based document
- Edit checks
- Firewalls
- Insurance or bonding of key employees to prevent financial losses
- Internal audits to reveal fraud, waste, inefficiency
- Limit checks
- Lockbox systems
- Physical security of computers and related equipment
- Preformatted data entry screens
- Pre-numbered documents
- Restrictive endorsement and daily deposits of checks received
- Segregation of duties
- User training

Internal controls are comprised of three types: (1) preventive controls help prevent errors and irregularities from occurring, (2) detective controls determine when an error or irregularity has occurred, and (3) corrective controls focus on fixing a problem, error, or irregularity after it has occurred. The Dynamics GP software offers several system internal controls. Some of these are described below.

Digital approvals: Authorization within the system is required to approve the processing of an event.

Preformatted screens: To facilitate the data entry process, the cursor

---

[11]For a detailed explanation, review Internal Control Examples, pages 61-63, *Accounting Information Systems: Basic Concepts & Current Issues* by R. L. Hurt, McGraw-Hill/Irwin ©2008 or another AIS textbook.

moves automatically to the next field. Certain data fields such as current date are automatically populated. Fields are restricted to the input of either text or numeric data or a specific number of characters.

Online prompting: The user must answer requests for user input or questions about the data. These questions include accept, edit, or reject a completed screen.

Master data populates input screens: When a user enters a specific identification code such as a vendor number, the system accesses master tables and automatically completes detail information about the vendor such as name or address.

Limit checks: The system tests whether the contents or values of a field fall within predetermined limits. For example, vendor numbers may need to fall within a specific range.

Calculated fields: The system accesses information and automatically calculates values for fields. For example, based on the number of items ordered and the price per item, the total costs are calculated.

Drop down lists or look up tables: The user uses these features to find acceptable data within the master tables to enter for these fields such as vendor number.

Sign check: Determines that a data field has an appropriate sign; for example, the number of items ordered is a positive value.

Completeness check: The user has entered all required fields within the screen.

Validity check: The system compares data entered within a screen with data in a master table to determine that the item exists. For example, a vendor number must exist within the master table for vendors for confirm the vendor is a valid vendor.

Prompting: The system requests the user to enter specific data and processing will not continue until the data is entered within the field.

SUMMARY AND REVIEW

OBJECTIVES: In Chapter 2, you completed the following activities:

1.   Copy Empty Company Data files from DVD.
2.   Start Dynamics DGP 10.0-Education.
3.   Create an additional company
4.   Set up company information.
5.   Enter the chart of accounts.
6.   Set up fiscal periods.
7.   Enter beginning balances.
8.   Set up and print reports.
9.   Use the SmartList.
10. Back up Chapter 2 data and exercises.
11. Review Sarbanes-Oxley compliance (SOX Box).
12. Complete an internal control activity.

The textbook web site at www.mhhe.com/dynamicsgp10essentials has a link to Textbook Updates. Check this link for updates.

Multiple Choice Questions: In the space provided, write the letter that best answers each question.

_____1.   In Chapter 2 you set up the additional company, Student Name HELP Inc. What other company is included in Dynamics GP?

   a. Fabrikam, Inc.
   b. Your Name Data.
   c. Student Name, Inc.
   d. World Online, Inc.
   e. None of the above.

_____2.   Student Name HELP Inc. is what type of business?

   a. Nonprofit business.
   b. Merchandising business.
   c. Manufacturing business.
   d. Service business.
   e. None of the above.

_____3. Student Name HELP Inc.'s type of business is a:

    a. Corporation.
    b. Partnership.
    c. Sole proprietorship.
    d. Non-profit.
    e. None of the above.

_____4. What is the maximum account length in DGP's account framework?

    a. 5.
    b. 9.
    c. 65.
    d. Unlimited length.
    e. None of the above.

_____5. The list of all the accounts in the general ledger is called a/an?

    a. Income statement.
    b. Balance Sheet.
    c. Posting report.
    d. Chart of accounts.
    e. None of the above.

_____6. Student Name HELP Inc. account structure is segmented?

    a. 3-4-2.
    b. 2-3-4.
    c. 4-3-2.
    d. 1-5-3.
    e. None of the above.

_____7. How many accounts were added to Student Name HELP Inc. in the chapter?

    a. 11.
    b. 13.
    c. 37.
    d. 63.
    e. None of the above.

_____8.   Another term for the Balance Sheet is:

a. Income statement.
b. Assets and liabilities.
c. Statement of financial position.
d. Statement of cash flow.
e. None of the above.

_____9.   Student Name HELP Inc.'s Balance Sheet at the beginning of
           October 20XX shows the following current assets:

a. $93,695.11
b. $61,123.28
c. $30,800.00
d. $ 00.00
e. None of the above.

_____10.   Student Name HELP Inc.'s Balance Sheet at the beginning of
           October 2005 shows total equity of:

a. $ 00.00
b. $ 5,250.65
c. $88,444.46
d. $93,695.11
e. None of the above.

Exercise 2-1: In order to complete Exercise 2-1, you must complete the activities in Chapter 2. The work started with Student Name HELP Inc. is continued in Exercises 2-1 and 2-2. Follow the instructions below to complete Exercise 2-1:

1. Start Dynamics GP. Browse and load (attach) the DYNAMICS.mdf file from your Sample Company Data folder. For Company, select Student Name HELP Inc. and you are ready to do the following:

    a. From Navigation pane, select Financial and link to Accounts.
    b. Change account 000-5110-00 Advertising Expense Description field to Advertising and Marketing Expense. Save.
    c. Change account 000-5180-00 Internet Service Provider Description field to Internet Service Provider Expense.
    d. Verify the changes by clicking Refresh in the Accounts window.
    e. Close all open windows.
    f. Print to printer and file a Chart of Accounts. (*HINT:* Financial; Financial, Reports, Account or see step-by-step directions on pages 60-62.) The suggested text file name, **Your** (Your first and last name) **Name Ex 2-1 Chart of Accounts**.
    g. Close all open windows.

2. Continue with Exercise 2-2.

Exercise 2-2: You must complete Exercise 2-1 before you can complete Exercise 2-2.

1. Print the beginning balance entry you made in the chapter. (*Hint:* From menu bar: Inquiries; Financial, Journal Entry Inquiry. Use Lookup icon to select entry. Click on Printer icon. In Report Destination window, check Printer and File then OK. Click OK to print.) The suggested text file name, **Your** (Your first and last name) **Name Ex 2-2 Journal Entry 1.**

Exercise 2-3: Internal Control

Follow these steps to print the audit trail codes.

1.   Open the Audit Trail Codes Setup window. From the Microsoft Dynamics GP menu, select Tools; Setup, Posting, Audit Trail Codes. Posting setup is one of DGP's internal controls.

2.   If necessary, in the Series list select Financial. Choose File; Print. Print to printer and file. The suggested file name is **Your** (Your first and last name) **Name Ex 2-3 Audit Trail Codes**.

3.   Answer the following questions:

     a.   What are the Prefix, Next Sequence Number, and Source Document for the Origin identified as Bank Deposit Entry?

     b.   Why is the next sequence number 2 for the GLTRX prefix?

Exercise 2-4: SmartList

1.   Use SmartList to export Journal Entry 1 to Excel. (*HINT:* Smartlist; Account Transaction)

2.   Set up worksheet to print landscape on one page. Print to printer and save to file. The suggested file name is **Your** (Your first and last name) **Name Ex 2-4.xls**.

3.   Exit Dynamics DGP and unload your data. When you unload, you are saving the company information after completing Chapter 2 exercises. (*HINT:* DGP will unload to the same location where it was loaded from, i.e., Sample Company Data folder.)

4. Copy/paste or drag/drop the 6 files from Sample Company Data folder to a new folder named Your Name Chapter 2 exercises on your Desktop. Copy this folder to external media. (*HINT:* Refer to the unload and back up steps listed on pages 77-78.

Chapter 3

Processing Cash Receipts and Payments

OBJECTIVES: In Chapter 3, you complete the following activities.

1. Start DGP and open the Student Name HELP, Inc. company.
2. Record and post deposits and checks.
3. Complete bank reconciliation.
4. Complete an inquiry for the checkbook register.
5. Print the trial balance.
6. Print financial statements.
7. Use the SmartList.
8. Review Sarbanes-Oxley compliance (SOX Box).
9. Complete an internal control activity.

The textbook web site at www.mhhe.com/dynamicsgp10essentials has a link to Textbook Updates. Check this link for updates.

In Chapter 2, you set up the accounts and entered the beginning balances for Student Name HELP, Inc. using the October 1, 20XX balance sheet as the source document. In Chapter 3, you will complete basic businesses processes involving cash receipts and payments for the corporation as it offers a variety of classes and private consultations. You will use the Student Name HELP, Inc.'s checkbook register and bank statement as source documents. In accounting, you learn that source documents show written evidence of a business transaction. Chapter 3 also includes Dynamics GP's SmartList, a SOX Box, and an internal control activity.

GETTING STARTED

Student Name HELP, Inc. is a consulting and teaching services corporation that offers a variety of classes and private consultations. The Student Name HELP, Inc.'s sources of income are from professional fees, book royalties, and part-time teaching income.

Follow these steps to open the Student Name HELP, Inc.

1. Start Dynamics GP. Type your password.
2. On the Company Login window, in the Company field, select Student Name HELP, Inc.

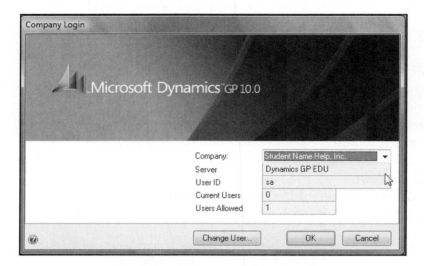

Click [OK]. The Student Name HELP, Inc. appears on the status bar, along with today's date and sa. (sa is an acronym for System Administrator) *(Hint:* If a window appears that says you do not have permission to open the file, close the window. DGP will also close.

Click (Start); All Programs, Microsoft Dynamics. Right click on the GP-Education; then left click on Run as Administrator. Grant any Permissions, then go back to Step 1.)

3. You are ready to begin.

Printing the Balance Sheet

To confirm that you are starting with the proper October 1, 20XX (your current year), follow these steps to print an October 1 Balance Sheet.

Read me: User Data

If a message appears that says the User Date falls within a fiscal year that hasn't been set up, go to the Microsoft Dynamics GP menu; select User Date. On the User Date window, type 10/01/20XX (your current year) in the date field.

---

1. In the Reports list, link to Financials; <u>Financial Statements</u>. The Financial Statement Report window appears.

2. In the Report field, click 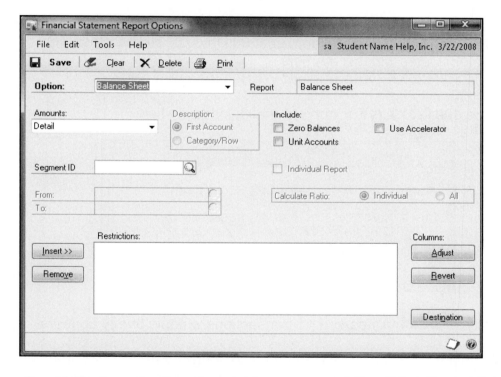, then double-click Balance Sheet to select it.

3. Click New .

4. The Financial Statement Report Options window appears. In the Option field, type Balance Sheet.

5. In the Amounts field, select Detail.

6. Make the selections to print to screen and file. (*Hint:* If you click Destination , you can print to your screen and to file.) The suggested file name is **Your Name Chapter 3_Oct 1 20XX Balance Sheet.txt**. Click , then compare the balance sheet to the one on page 64.

7. Close all windows. You should save these settings.

OCTOBER 1 ACCOUNT TRANSACTIONS

In Chapter 2 you learned how to use information from a Balance Sheet to record an opening entry. Now you are going to see how the check register provides information for bank reconciliation.

Before you continue, let's check that the beginning balances have been recorded. Follow these steps to see account transactions.

1.   From the navigation pane, select [Financial]. In the Financial list, double-click [Account Transactions].

2.   Select the Restrictions ribbon, Last 90 Days, Custom Dates. The Custom Dates window appears.
3.   Type **100120XX (your current year)** in the From field.

4.   Type **100120XX (your current year)** in the To field.

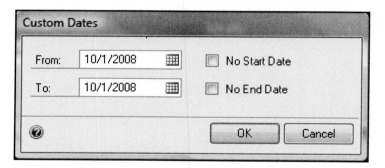

5.   Click [OK]. A Loading 11 transactions window briefly appears.

6.   Highlight the first transaction. Link to <u>Journal Entry 1</u>. The Journal Entry Inquiry window appears. Observe that the Transaction Date is 10/1/20XX; the Batch ID is BBAL; the Audit Trail Code is specified. The Journal Entry Inquiry window shows the account distribution for the beginning balances.

	Date ▼	Entry Number	Account Description	Debit Amo...	Credit Am...
☐	10/1/2008	1	Gainesville Checking	$20,700.00	$0.00
☐	10/1/2008	1	Sunshine Savings	$4,500.50	$0.00
☐	10/1/2008	1	FL State Savings	$33,222.78	$0.00
☐	10/1/2008	1	Prepaid Insurance	$2,100.00	$0.00
☐	10/1/2008	1	Prepaid Rent	$600.00	$0.00
☐	10/1/2008	1	Computer Equipment	$6,800.00	$0.00
☐	10/1/2008	1	Furniture and Fixtures	$5,000.00	$0.00
☐	10/1/2008	1	Automobiles	$19,000.00	$0.00
☐	10/1/2008	1	Supplies	$1,771.83	$0.00
☐	10/1/2008	1	Accounts Payable	$0.00	$5,250.65
☐	10/1/2008	1	Common Stock	$0.00	$88,444.46

Journal Entry 1

7. Expand. Now the account description displays below the account number. Scroll down to see all the transactions. After checking the 11 transactions, close the window and return [Home].

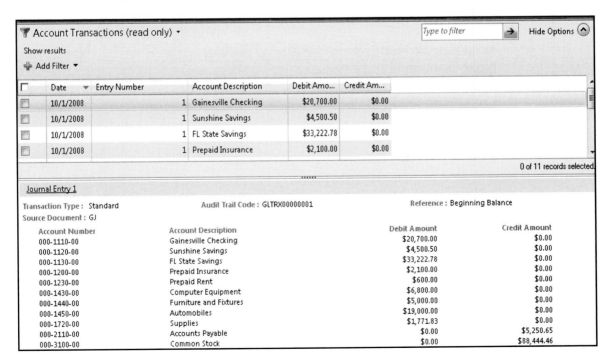

The McGraw-Hill Companies, Inc., *Computer Accounting Essentials with Dynamics GP 10.0, 2e*

BANK RECONCILIATION

In Dynamics GP, you use Bank Reconciliation to set up, enter, and maintain cash receipts and cash disbursements. You will learn how to enter transactions that affect checkbook balances and the reconciliation process.

Checkbooks

You need to set up a Checkbook ID to use the bank reconciliation module. Follow these steps to set up a new checkbook.

1. In the Financial list, double-click [Financial]. In the Cards area, link to Financial; <u>Checkbook</u>. The Checkbook Maintenance window appears.

2. Type **CHECKBOOK** in the Checkbook ID field.

3. Type **Checkbook** in the Description field.

4. In the Cash Account field, select or type Account Number 000-1110-00, Gainesville Checking. Complete these fields.

Next Check Number:	**4001**
Next Deposit Number:	**01**
Last Reconciled Balance:	**20700.00**
Last Reconciled Date:	**93020XX (your current year)**

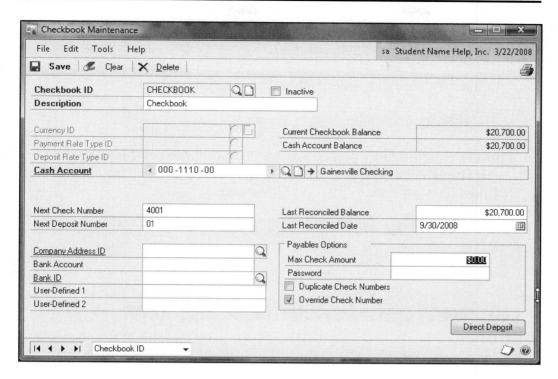

5. Observe that the Current Checkbook Balance and Cash Account Balance field shows $20,700.00. This is the beginning balance that you entered for Account Number 000-1110-00, Gainesville Checking. Refer to the October 1, 20XX balance sheet on page 64 to verify this amount.

    The Last Reconciled Balance also shows $20,700.00. The Last Reconciled Date filed shows 9/30/20XX.

8. Click ☐ Save .

9. Close the Checkbook Maintenance window.

Setup

You need to complete setup procedures before you can enter or post transactions, or reconcile your checkbook. Once you set up the bank reconciliation, you can enter or void transactions and deposits.

1. From the Financial page's Routines list, link to <u>Checklists</u> to open the Financial Checklists window.

2. In the Module field, select Bank Reconciliation.

3. In the Frequency field, select Month End.

4. In the Routine field, select Reconcile. Compare your Financial In the Routine list, click Reconcile to select it. Compare your Financial Checklists window to the one shown here.

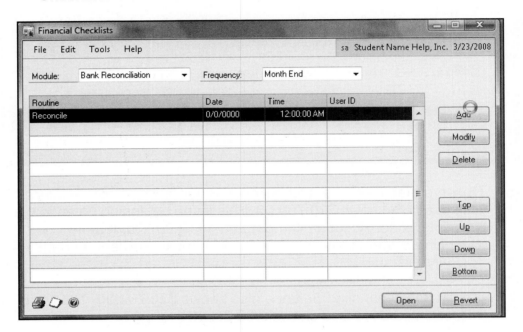

5. Click [Open].

6. In the <u>Checkbook ID</u> field, select CHECKBOOK.

7. Type **20700.00** in the Bank Statement Ending balance field.

8. Type **93020XX** (your current year) in the Bank Statement Ending Date.

9. Type **93020XX** (your current year) in the Cutoff Date.

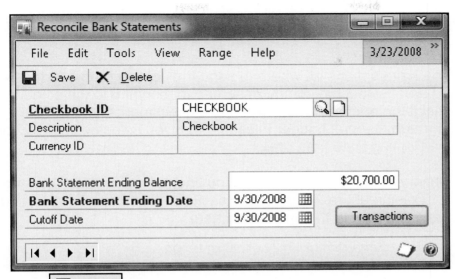

10.   Click [💾 Save]. Close the Reconcile Bank Statements window.

11.   Observe that the Financial Checklists window shows the Date and Time that you set up the bank reconciliation. Close the Financial Checklists window.

Posting Setup

Posting moves transactions to a permanent record known as the general ledger. In order for these transactions to update the general ledger, you need to go to Dynamics GP's posting setup.

To specify posting settings, follow these steps.

1.   From the Microsoft Dynamics GP menu, select Tools; Setup, Posting, Posting. The Posting Setup window appears.

2.   In the Series field, select Financial.

3.   In the Origin field, select Bank Transaction Entry.

4.   **Steps 4 and 5 *are very important*.** Click on the box next to **Post Through General Ledger Files**. When you make this selection to post bank transaction entries, you update the cash account (Account Number 000-1110-00, Gainesville Checking).

5. In the Posting Date From area, click on the radio button next to **Transaction**.

6. You have options on where to send the posting report. In the Send To area, select the computer screen for sending to the screen or check the printer. Confirm you have checkmarks next to Post Through General Ledger Files and that you selected Transaction in the Posting Date from area.

7. Observe that the Bank Trx Posting Journal has a checkmark next to it. Trx is an abbreviation for transactions. Compare your Posting Setup window to the one shown here.

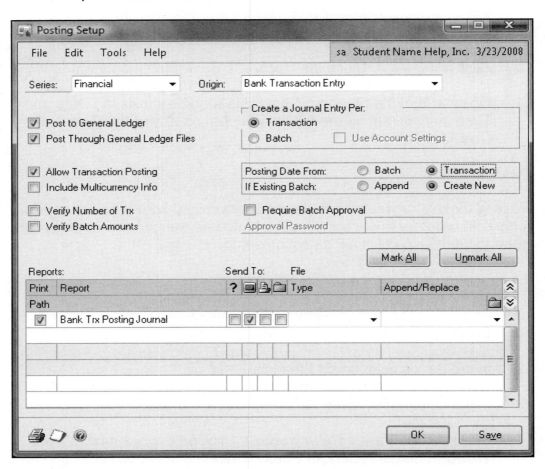

8. Click [Save].

9. Make the same selections for Series, Financial; Origin, Reconcile Bank Statement (scroll down the list); Post Through General Ledger Files; Posting Date From, Transaction. In the Send to area, select the screen; uncheck printer. Compare your Posting Setup window to the one shown below. *This is a very important step.*

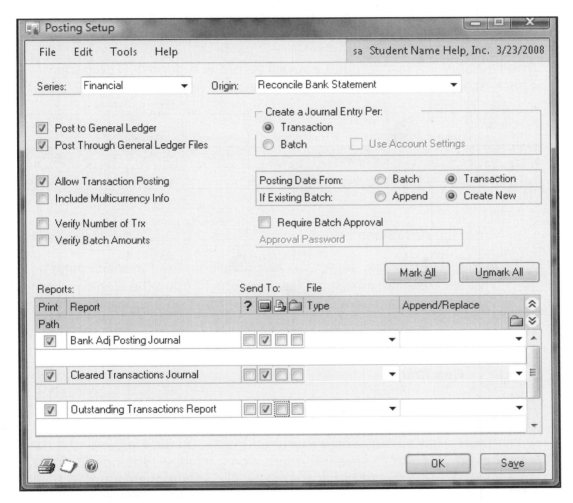

10. Observe the reports that have checkmarks next to them and the location to send the reports. You have selected to automatically print to screen after completing bank reconciliation.

11. Click [Save], then [OK].

RECORDING TRANSACTIONS

In Dynamics GP, you use the Bank Transaction Entry window to record deposits and checks. In the previous section, you updated the bank reconciliation posting records. When you post a deposit or check, Dynamics GP automatically updates the general ledger.

Entering Receipts

The first bank transaction that you will record is a deposit. The partial check register shown below identifies the 10/1 deposit.

Check Number	Date	Description of Transaction	Payment	Deposit	Balance
	10/1	Beginning Balance			20,700.00
	10/1	Publisher's advance (deposit)		6,000.00	26,700.00

1. From the navigation bar, select Financial . If necessary in the Financial list, select ⊞ Financial . From the Financial page's Transactions list, link <u>Bank Transactions</u> to open the Bank Transaction Entry window. Remember that you are required to complete all fields shown in red font.

👓 **Read me**

Does your Bank Transaction Entry window show the required fields in red? If *not*, refer to step 5 on pages 53. This is a system internal control within DGP. Remember, Show Required Fields, on the Help menu must be checked. In order to save information on a window, you need to enter data into the ***required fields***. If a warning appears that says not all fields have been completed, you have skipped one or more of the required fields. Another way to check that required fields are active is to click on Help to make sure that Show Required Fields has a checkmark next to it.

---

2. In the Option field, select Enter Receipt. Press <Tab> to move between fields.

3. If necessary, select Check in the Type field.

4.   Type **100120XX** in the Transaction Date field.

5.   Select CHECKBOOK in the <u>Checkbook ID</u> field.

6.   Accept the default for the receipt number shown in the Number field.

7.   Type **Publisher** in the Recvd From field.

8.   Type **Advance** in the Description field.

9.   Type **6000.00** in the Amount field. Press <Tab>.

10.   Observe that the Distribution Reference table shows that the Originating Debit is $6,000.00. This is correct. When you enter a receipt (deposit to checking account), Account No. 000-1110-00, Gainesville Checking, is debited. Now you need to enter the correct account to credit. (*Hint:* Expand the distribution table. Gainesville Checking is shown below Account No. 000-1110-00.)

11.   Your cursor should be in the Distribution Reference line for the credit; click on the line below Gainesville Checking (Account No. 000-1110-00). Type **000-2310-00** on the row that has a left arrow at the beginning of the field, and a right arrow at the end of the field. On the Bank Transaction Entry window, observe that the Distribution Reference field shows 000-2310-00. (Account 000-2310-00 is unearned revenue since the publisher paid before the work has been done. You may recall that unearned revenue is classified as a liability account.)

12.   Press <Tab> or click on the Originating Credit column. Type **6000.00** in the credit column. Press <Tab>. Observe that the Difference shows 0.00. This means that the debits and credits equal. Compare your Bank Transaction Entry window with the one shown on the next page.

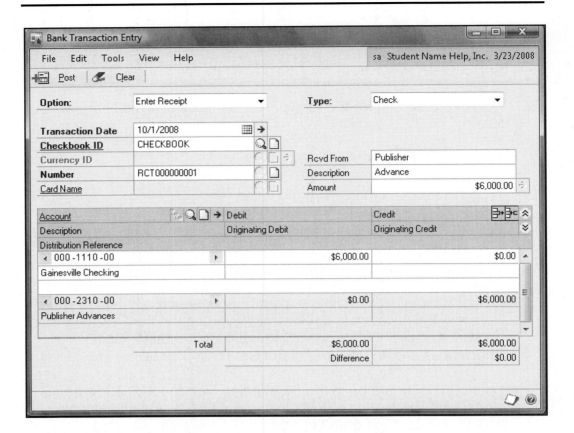

13. Click . The Bank Transaction Entry window is ready for the next transaction.

👓 **Read me**

The Bank Reconciliation module uses *transaction-level posting*. Transaction-level posting is a method in which you enter and post transactions without having to create a batch. Transaction-level posting is also known as real-time posting. Refer to the Posting Setup information in this chapter for more information.

Entering Checks

A partial check register on the next page shows the Student Name HELP, Inc.'s next transaction, Check No. 4001; a check issued to Office Staples for computer equipment in the amount of $1,005.35. You will now enter this transaction.

Check Number	Date	Description of Transaction	Payment	Deposit	Balance
	10/1	Beginning Balance			20,700.00
	10/1	Publisher's advance (deposit)		6,000.00	26,700.00
4001	10/2	Office Staples (computer equipment)	1,005.35		25,694.65

1.   Access the Bank Transaction Entry window if you do not have it on your screen.

2.   If necessary, select Enter Transaction in the Option field. Press <Tab> and then <Tab> again to accept Check as Type.

3.   Type **100220XX** (your current year) as the Transaction Date. CHECKBOOK should appear in the Checkbook ID field. (If not, select it.) Press <Tab>.

4.   Observe that the Number field shows 4001.

5.   Type **Office Staples** in the Paid To field.

6.   Type **Computer equipment** in the Description field.

7.   Type **1005.35** in the Amount field. Observe that Account No. 000-1110-00, Gainesville Checking, is credited for $1,005.35. (*Hint:* Expand the distribution table.)

8.   Your cursor should be in the Distribution Reference line for the debit; click on the line below Gainesville Checking (Account No. 000-1110-00). Type **000-1430-00** on the row that has a left arrow at the beginning of the field, and a right arrow at the end of the field. On the Bank Transaction Entry window, observe that the Distribution Reference field shows 000-1430-00 and Computer Equipment. Press <Tab>.

9.   Type 1005.35 in the Originating Debit field. Press <Tab>.

10.   Compare your Bank Transaction Entry window with the one on the next page. Observe that the Difference shows 0.00. This means that the debits and credits equal.

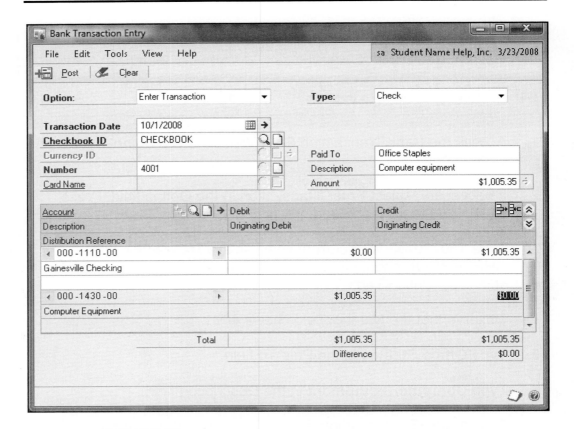

9.   Click . The Bank Transaction Entry window is ready for the next transaction.

In accounting, you learn that source documents show written evidence of a business transaction. Examples of source documents are sales invoices, purchase invoices, and in this case, the Student Name HELP, Inc.'s check register for their checking account (Account No. 000-1110-00, Gainesville Checking).

Continue with the October 4 deposit of $3,750.15 to record the bank transaction entries (Transaction Nos. 4-14) shown on the check register which follows. Record and post each check and deposit. Each deposit (receipt) is a debit to Account No. 000-1110-00, Gainesville Checking; each check issued (payment) is a credit to the Gainesville Checking account. *Remember to click* Post *after entering each bank transaction entry.*

Trans No.	Ck. No.	Date	Account No. and Description	Payment	Deposit	Balance
1		10/1	000-1110-00 - Beginning Balance			20,700.00
2		10/1	000-2310-00 - Publisher's advance (deposit)		6,000.00	26,700.00
3	4001	10/2	000-1430-00 - Office Staples (computer equipment)	1,005.35		25,694.65
4		**10/4**	**000-4120-00 - Book royalty from publisher (deposit)**		**3,750.15**	**29,444.80**
5	4002	10/9	000-5190-00 - U.S. Post Office (postage)	37.00		29,407.80
6	4003	10/9	000-5150-00 - The Courier (subscription)	145.00		29,262.80
7	4004	10/9	000-5255-00 - Midwest Gas Co. (utilities)	132.61		29,130.19
8	4005	10/10	000-5250-00 - MCA Bell (telephone)	96.58		29,033.61
9		10/14	000-4110-00 - Gainesville College (teaching income)		2,655.00	31,688.61
10	4006	10/14	000-5120-00 - MDOT (automobile registration)	201.00		31,487.61
11	4007	10/14	000-5195-00 - AD King (printing)	110.00		31,377.61
12	4008	10/29	000-5185-00 - Victor Albert (repairs)	210.00		31,167.61
13	4009	10/29	000-5235-00 - Greene Rentals (rent)	1,250.00		29,917.61
14	4010	10/30	000-5180-00 - Internet Service Provider (internet)	29.90		29,887.71

10.   When you close the Bank Transaction Entry window, the Bank Transaction Posting Journal appears with each transaction's debit and credit. Review this report. Then close the Screen Output.

11.   Make sure you have recorded each transaction by displaying the Account Transactions window (From the Financial list, select

▤ Account Transactions .)

12.   Select Restrictions; Custom Date, Custom Dates From 100120XX (your current year) to 103020XX (your current year). To see the transactions in numeric order, click on the Entry Number field to resort the entries from 1-14. Review entries 2 through 14. Observe that when you select a transaction, the Audit Trail Code for that entry number and the Accounts debited and credited are shown. A partial Account Transactions window is shown on the next page.

The McGraw-Hill Companies, Inc., *Computer Accounting Essentials with Dynamics GP 10.0, 2e*

	Date	Entry Number	▲	Account Description	Debit Amo...	Credit Am...	
☐	10/1/2008		2	Publisher Advances	$0.00	$6,000.00	
☐	10/1/2008		3	Gainesville Checking	$0.00	$1,005.35	
☐	10/1/2008		3	Computer Equipment	$1,005.35	$0.00	
☐	10/4/2008		4	Gainesville Checking	$3,750.15	$0.00	
☐	10/4/2008		4	Royalty Income	$0.00	$3,750.15	
☐	10/9/2008		5	Gainesville Checking	$0.00	$37.00	
☐	10/9/2008		5	Postage and Delivery Exp...	$37.00	$0.00	
☐	10/9/2008		6	Gainesville Checking	$0.00	$145.00	
☐	10/9/2008		6	Dues and Subscriptions E...	$145.00	$0.00	
☐	10/9/2008		7	Gainesville Checking	$0.00	$132.61	
☐	10/9/2008		7	Utilities Expense	$132.61	$0.00	
☐	10/10/2008		8	Gainesville Checking	$0.00	$96.58	

0 of 37 records selected.

Journal Entry 2

Transaction Type : Standard   Audit Trail Code : GLTRX00000002   Reference : Advance
Source Document : CMTRX

Account Number	Account Description	Debit Amount	Credit Amount
000-1110-00	Gainesville Checking	$6,000.00	$0.00
000-2310-00	Publisher Advances	$0.00	$6,000.00

13. Scroll down the Account Transactions window to see all 14 transactions. Select individual transactions to see the accounts debited and credited.

 Read me: What if you make a mistake? The following steps assume a Journal entry was incorrect.

If you have not posted, click on [✐ Clear] to remove what you have written in the Bank Transaction Entry window.
If you discover your mistake after you have posted, Open a Bank Transaction Entry window. In Option field, select either Void Transaction or Void Receipt.
Make selections based on incorrect entry data. Click Void.
Now record and post the correct debits and credits. Observe that the Journal Entry field shows a new Journal Entry number.
If you reprint the General Posting Journal report, notice that an extra transaction number prints with the correct accounts debited and credited. For auditing purposes, Dynamics GP shows an additional journal entry number so that the accounting records show that an entry was deleted.

What if you make too many mistakes?
If you want to start over from the last time you unloaded and copied your data to external media, exit DGP. Unload your faulty data and drag the files to Trash.

Identify and use your most recently unloaded good files and copy them into your program path. Restart Dynamics GP and load DYNAMICS.mdf from these restored files.

Bank Deposit Entry

You use the Bank Deposit Entry window to choose the receipts to deposit and post. You do this every time you physically make a deposit at the bank. All the selected checkbook receipts that are available for deposit appear in the Bank Deposit Entry window. When you post, the checkbook balance will update by the deposit amount. The General Ledger account will *not* update until you post each receipt (deposit to checking account).

Follow these steps to post deposits.

1. If necessary, start DGP, load data, and open the Student Name HELP, Inc.

2. From the navigation pane, select [Financial]. In the Financial list, select [Financial] to go to the Financial page. In the Transactions list, link <u>Bank Deposits</u> to open the Bank Deposit Entry window.

3. If necessary, in the Option field, select the Enter/Edit option. Press <Tab> to move between fields.

4. The Type field shows Deposits with Receipts. If not, select it.

5. Type **103120XX** (your current year) as the Deposit Date.

6. Select CHECKBOOK as the <u>Checkbook ID</u>.

7. Accept the default Deposit Number 01.

8. Type **October deposits** in the Description field.

9. The three deposits appear in the table: 10/1/20XX for $6,000.00; 10/4/20XX for $3,750.15; 10/14/20XX for $2,655.00.

10. Click [Mark All]. Enter checkmarks next to each deposit. Compare your Bank Deposit Entry window with the one shown here.

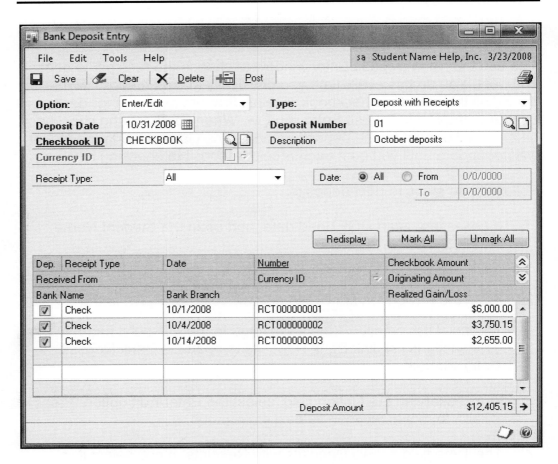

11. Click 🔲 Post .

12. When you close the Bank Deposit Entry window a Print window appears. The Bank Deposit Posting Journal prints showing the individual deposits and total deposits of $12,405.15.

RECONCILE THE BANK STATEMENT

The Student Name HELP, Inc. receives a bank statement every month from Gainesville Checking for their account (Account No. 000-1110-00, Gainesville Checking). The bank statement lists the checks and deposits that have cleared the bank. In DGP, *bank reconciliation* is the process of making the bank statement cash balance and the checkbook cash balance match as of a certain date. The Student Name HELP, Inc.'s bank statement is shown on the next page.

Statement of Account			Student Name HELP, Inc.	
Gainesville Checking			1235 W. 75th Street	
October 1 to October 31, 20XX Account # 0908-33-5689			Gainesville, FL 32192	
REGULAR CHECKING				
Previous Balance		$20,700.00		
3 Deposits (+)		12,405.15		
7 checks (-)		1,736.54		
Service Charges (-)	10/31/XX	15.00		
Ending Balance	10/31/XX	**$31,353.61**		
DEPOSITS				
	10/04/XX	6,000.00		
	10/07/XX	3,750.15		
	10/17/XX	2,655.00		
CHECKS (Asterisk * indicates break in check number sequence)				
	10/07/XX	4001	1,005.35	
	10/15/XX	4002	37.00	
	10/17/XX	4003	145.00	
	10/17/XX	4004	132.61	
	10/18/XX	4005	96.58	
	10/31/XX	4007*	110.00	
	10/31/XX	4008	210.00	

Follow these steps to reconcile the bank statement balance to Account No. 000-1110-00, Gainesville.

1. In the Transaction list, link to <u>Reconcile Bank Statement</u>. The Reconcile Bank Statement window appears.

2. Select CHECKBOOK as the <u>Checkbook ID</u>.

3. Type **31353.61** in the Bank Statement Ending Balance field.

4. Type **103120XX** in the Bank Statement Ending Balance and Cutoff Date fields.

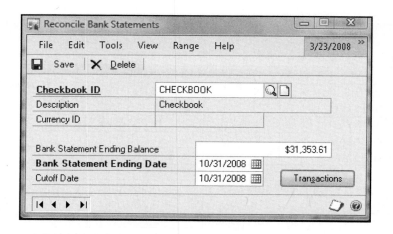

5. Click Transactions .

6. Click on column C to put a checkmark next to each transaction that has cleared the bank. The arrows on the sides of the scrolling window indicate what line your cursor is located. Observe that the Difference field shows ($15.00). This is the amount of the service charge. Compare your Select Bank Transactions window to the one shown here.

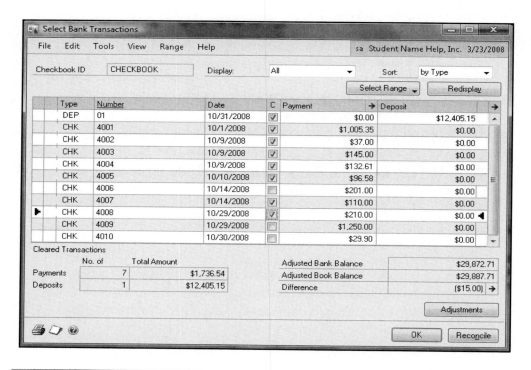

8. Click [Adjustments] to record the bank service charge. When the Reconcile Bank Adjustments window appears, select Service Charge in the Distribution Reference column. Then Account Number 000-5130-00, Bank Charges Expense, for the Account. Type **15.00** as the amount of the service charge. (*Hint:* Expand the account distribution.) Observe the Difference field shows $0.00. Compare your Reconcile Bank Adjustments window to the one shown here.

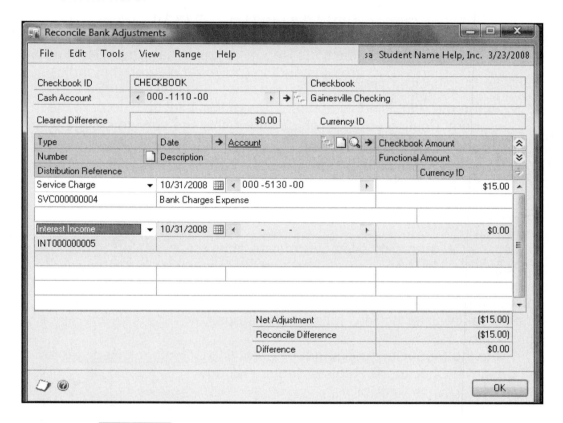

9. Click [OK]. You are returned to the Select Bank Transactions window. Observe that the Adjusted Bank and Book Balance fields show $29,872.71. This is the correct amount (check register balance $29,887.71 – 15.00 = $29,872.71). Click [Reconcile].

10. When the Print window appears, make the selections to print. Four reports display:

1) Reconciliation Posting Journal—the difference shows $0.00. Close the report.

2) Bank Adjustments Posting Journal—this shows the service charge entry. Close the report.

3) Marked Transaction Report—this shows the deposits and checks that have cleared the bank. There are seven payments and one deposit. Close the report.

4) Outstanding Transactions Report—shows that Check Nos. 4006, 4009, and 4010 are outstanding (have *not* cleared the bank.)

11. When the print window appears, make the selections to print the General Posting Journal, which shows that the service charge was posted to the general ledger.

12. Close all windows.

INQUIRIES

Dynamics GP stores detailed information about cash-related transactions. You can use inquiries and reports to view and analyze information about transactions. To use inquiry window to access information about transactions posted to your checkbook and view checkbook register activity, follow these steps.

1. From the Financial page's Inquiry area, link Checkbook Register to open the Checkbook Register Inquiry window.

2. In the Checkbook ID field, select Checkbook. The Checkbook Register Inquiry window appears. Observe that this window displays total deposits of $12,405.15, and each check. The Current Balance field shows $29,872.71. This is the Student Name HELP, Inc.'s checkbook register balance minus the bank service charge. Compare your Checkbook Register Inquiry window to the one shown on the next page.

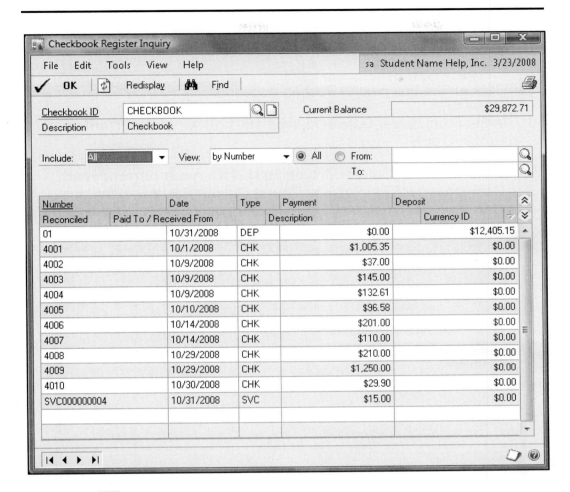

3. Click 🖨️ to print to screen and file. The suggested file name is **Your Name Chapter 3_October Checkbook Register.txt**.

4. Close all windows.

PRINTING THE TRIAL BALANCE

Follow these steps to print the trial balance.

1. In the Reports area, link to <u>Trial Balance</u>.

2. In the Reports field, select Summary.

3. Click New.

4. The Trial Balance Options window appears. Type **Trial Balance** in the Option field.

5. Click on the box next to Posting Accounts.

6. In the From, Enter Date field, type **100120XX (your current year)**. Press <Tab>.

7. In the To, Enter Date field, type **103120XX (your current year)**. Compare your Trial Balance Report Options window to the one shown below. (*Hint:* Make sure Posting Accounts is checked.)

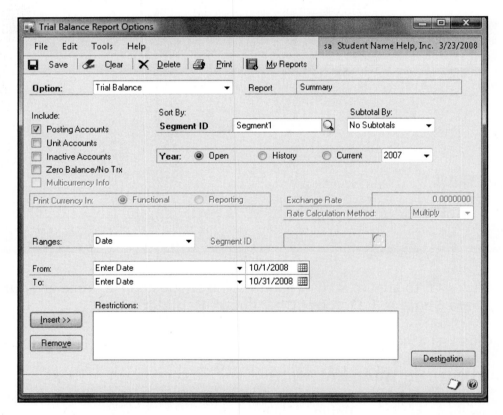

8. Click [Destination]. Print the Screen and File. (If necessary, uncheck Printer.) The suggested file name is **Your Name Chapter 3_October Trial Balance.txt**. Click Save, then click [OK].

9. In the Trial Balance Report Options window, click [Print]. Compare your Trial Balance Summary for 20XX report to the one

shown below. Depending on the percentage you have set, you may need to scroll across to see all the columns. (Error Hint: If Grand Totals for Accounts do *not* show 24 accounts, confirm Posting Setup earlier in the chapter.)

Range c:	From:		To:			Sorted By:	Segment1			
Date:	1/1/2008		12/31/2008			Include:	Posting			
Account	First		Last							

Inactive	Account	Description	Beginning Balance	Debit	Credit	Net Change	Ending Balance
	000-1110-00	Gainesville Checking	$0.00	$33,105.15	$3,232.44	$29,872.71	$29,872.71
	000-1120-00	Sunshine Savings	$0.00	$4,500.50	$0.00	$4,500.50	$4,500.50
	000-1130-00	FL State Retirement	$0.00	$33,222.78	$0.00	$33,222.78	$33,222.78
	000-1200-00	Prepaid Insurance	$0.00	$2,100.00	$0.00	$2,100.00	$2,100.00
	000-1230-00	Prepaid Rent	$0.00	$600.00	$0.00	$600.00	$600.00
	000-1430-00	Computer Equipment	$0.00	$7,305.35	$0.00	$7,305.35	$7,305.35
	000-1440-00	Furniture and Fixtures	$0.00	$5,000.00	$0.00	$5,000.00	$5,000.00
	000-1450-00	Automobiles	$0.00	$19,000.00	$0.00	$19,000.00	$19,000.00
	000-1720-00	Supplies	$0.00	$1,771.83	$0.00	$1,771.83	$1,771.83
	000-2110-00	Accounts Payable	$0.00	$0.00	$5,250.65	($5,250.65)	($5,250.65)
	000-2310-00	Publisher Advances	$0.00	$0.00	$6,000.00	($6,000.00)	($6,000.00)
	000-3100-00	Common Stock	$0.00	$0.00	$83,444.46	($83,444.46)	($83,444.46)
	000-4110-00	Teaching Income	$0.00	$0.00	$2,655.00	($2,655.00)	($2,655.00)
	000-4120-00	Royalty Income	$0.00	$0.00	$3,750.15	($3,750.15)	($3,750.15)
	000-5120-00	Automobile Registration Expense	$0.00	$201.00	$0.00	$201.00	$201.00
	000-5130-00	Bank Charges Expense	$0.00	$15.00	$0.00	$15.00	$15.00
	000-5150-00	Dues and Subscriptions Expense	$0.00	$145.00	$0.00	$145.00	$145.00
	000-5180-00	Internet Service Provider Expense	$0.00	$29.90	$0.00	$29.90	$29.90
	000-5185-00	Maintenance and Repairs Expense	$0.00	$210.00	$0.00	$210.00	$210.00
	000-5190-00	Postage and Delivery Expense	$0.00	$37.00	$0.00	$37.00	$37.00
	000-5195-00	Printing and Reproduction Expense	$0.00	$110.00	$0.00	$110.00	$110.00
	000-5235-00	Rent Expense	$0.00	$1,250.00	$0.00	$1,250.00	$1,250.00
	000-5250-00	Telephone Expense	$0.00	$96.58	$0.00	$96.58	$96.58
	000-5295-00	Utilities Expense	$0.00	$132.61	$0.00	$132.61	$132.61

	Accounts	Beginning Balance	Debit	Credit	Net Change	Ending Balance
Grand Totals:	24	$0.00	$105,332.70	$105,332.70	$0.00	$0.00

10.   If a print window appears, make the selections to print. Close all Windows. When the window appears asking if you want to save changes to this report, click [Save] .

PRINTING THE FINANCIAL STATEMENTS

Since this company records quarterly adjusting entries on December 31, 20XX instead of making monthly adjustments, you will not record any adjusting entries at the end of October. Instead, you print the Student Name HELP, Inc.'s financial statements—income statement, balance sheet, statement of cash flow. In Chapter 2 the balance sheet was set up, and then printed. When you completed the balance sheet layout on page 72-75, one column was set up to show the month's activity (Period 10) and the other column for the end-of-quarter results (Period 12). In the next section, you complete a similar layout for the Income Statement and Statement of Cash Flow.

Income Statement Layout

Before you can print the income statement, you need to define its layout. Follow these steps to set up the income statement for Chapter 3.

1. From the Financial page's Reports area, link to <u>Advanced Financial</u>. The Advanced Financial Reports window appears.

2. Double-click on Income Statement. Click Layout.

3. Observe the three gray columns on the Advanced Financial Report Layout window: C1, C2, and C3. The account balances for the Current Period appear in C2; the Current YTD (year-to-date) balances will appear in C3.

4. Double-click on C2. You will set the Financial Column Definitions for the second column. Observe that the Column ID field shows 2.

5. In the Period field, select Other Period. Then click to select Period 10 for October.

6. In the To field, select Other Period. Then click to select Period 10 for October.

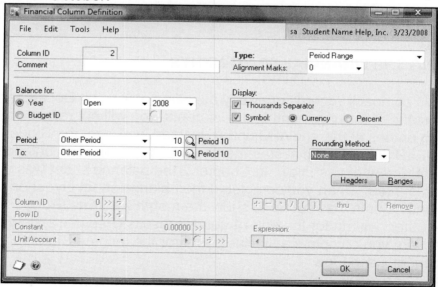

7.   Click [OK]. You are returned to the Advanced Financial
     Report Layout window.

8.   Double-click on C3. In the Type field, select Period Range. In the
     Period field, select Other Period, Period 10; set the To field to Other
     Period, Period 12.

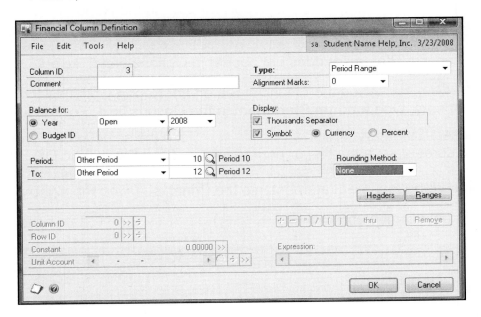

9.   Click [OK].

10. Close the Advanced Financial Report Layout window. Click
     [Save].

11. Close the Advanced Financial Report Definition window.

12. Close the Advanced Financial Reports window.

Income Statement and Balance Sheet

Follow these steps to print the income statement and balance sheet.

1.   From the Financial page's Reports area, link to <u>Financial
     Statements</u> to print, save, or view financial statements.

2. On the Financial Statement Report window, in the Report field, select Balance Sheet. Insert the Balance Sheet into the Print list. (*Hint:* Highlight Balance Sheet; click | Insert >> |. If Balance Sheet does not appear in the Options list, pick New and make selections to print (see page 88).)

3. On the Financial Statement Report window, in the Report field, select Income Statement.

4. If Income Statement does not appear in Options panel, select | New |. When the Financial Statement Report Options window appears, type **Income Statement** in the Options field. For Amounts, select Summary. Click | Destination |. Make the selections to print to screen, save the file, or print to printer. Click Save; then OK.

5. Insert the Income Statement into the Print List. (*Hint:* Highlight Income Statement; click | Insert >> |.)

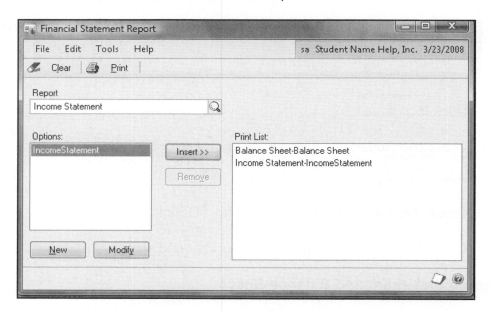

6. To print the balance sheet and the income statement, click | Print |. Compare your screen output with the following check figures:

Balance Sheet Check Figures:
Total Assets: $103,873.17
Note, the Balance Sheet's Net Profit amount, agrees with the
Income Statement's Net Income amount of $4,178.06.

Income Statement Check Figures:
Scroll down the Income Statement report. Current Period and
Current YTD Net Income is $4,178.06

7.   Close all windows.

Statement of Cash Flow Layout

Before you can print the statement of cash flow, you need to define its
layout. Follow these steps to set up the statement of cash flow.

1.   In the Reports area, link to <u>Advanced Financial</u>. The Advanced
     Financial Reports window appears.

2.   Double-click on Statement of Cash Flow. Click [Layout].

3.   Observe the three gray columns on the Advanced Financial Report
     Layout window: C1, C2, and C3. The account balances for the
     Current Period will appear in C2; the Current YTD (year-to-date)
     balances will appear in C3.

4.   Double-click on C2. You are going to set the Financial Column
     Definitions for the second column. Observe that the Column ID field
     shows 2.

5.   In the Period field, select Other Period. Then click [ ] to select
     Period 10 for October.

6.   In the To field, select Other Period. Then click [ ] to select Period
     10 for October.

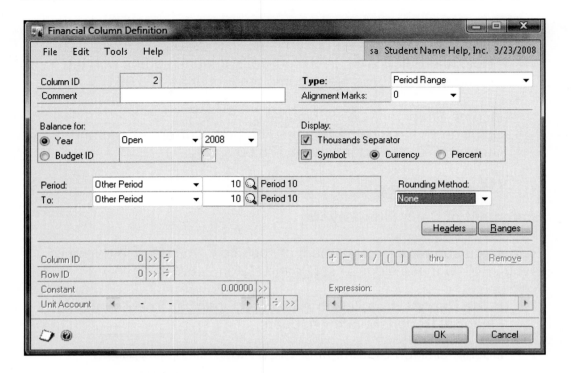

7. Click [OK]. You are returned to the Advanced Financial Report Layout window.

8. Double-click on C3. In the Type field, select Period Range. In the Period field, select Other Period, Period 10; set the To field to Other Period, Period 12.

9. Click [OK].

10. Close the Advanced Financial Report Layout window. Click [Save].

11. Close the Advanced Financial Report Definition window.

12. Close the Advanced Financial Reports window.

Printing the Statement of Cash Flow

1. In the Reports area, link to <u>Financial Statements</u>. In the Report field, select Statement of Cash flow; click New .

2. Type **Cash Flow Statement** in the Type field. For Amounts, select Summary. Click Destination . Make the selection to print to screen, save to file, or print to printer. Click Save; then OK.

3. On Financial Statement Report window, insert the Cash Flow Statement into the Print List. (*Hint:* Highlight Cash Flow Statement; click Insert >> .)

4. Make the selections to print to screen. Compare your screen with the following check figures.

    Statement of Cash Flow Check Figures:

    Current Period, Ending Cash balance: $67,595.99
    YTD, Ending Cash Balance: $67,595.99
    Observe that the ending cash balance on the statement of cash flow is the same as the Total Cash balance on the Balance Sheet. Review the information in the Read Me box on the next page.

Read Me: My financial statements show zero balances. Why?

You need to set up the financial column definitions and specify the period in order for the financial statements to show amounts. For example, if the Statement of Cash Flow does not show amounts, do the following.

1. From the Financial page, go to the Reports area; link to Advanced Financial.

2. Open the Statement of Cash Flow; click Layout .
3. Double-click column heading C2 (in the gray area).
4. In the Type field, select Period Range.
5. In the Period field, select Other Period. Select Period 10.
6. In the To field, select Other Period. Select Period 10. You have just set the Current Period column on the Statement of Cash Flow to

    Period 10 for October. Click OK .
7. Double-click C3 (Current YTD) column heading.
8. In the type field, select Period Range.
9. In the Period field, select Period 10.
10. In the To field, select Other Period. Select Period 12. You have just

    set the Current YTD field for December. Click OK .
11. Close the Advanced Financial Report Layout window; save your settings.

Now when you print the Statement of Cash Flow, the report will have account balances in both the Current Period and Current YTD columns.

5. Save your changes to the report.

6. Close all windows.

SMARTLIST

Using SmartList's [Search] capabilities (*HINT:* Microsoft Dynamics GP; SmartList), complete the following activities.

1. We will verify that the entries from the bank reconciliation posted to the appropriate account. Using the SmartList [Search], do a search that lists entries prepared during a Bank Reconciliation for CHECKBOOK. (*Hint:* SmartList; Financial; Bank Transactions.)

Column Name:	Checkbook ID
Filter:	is equal to
Value:	CHECKBOOK

Column Name:	Source Document
Filter:	is equal to
Value:	CMADJ

Your printout will include any entries made during the bank reconciliation process. Each month required recording a $15 service charge.

SOX BOX

One of the tools accountants use to analyze and assess the effectiveness of a company's internal controls for Sox section 404 compliance is a risk/control matrix.[1] The formats and details of the matrix can vary but the key objective is to assist in the identifying risks and establishing effective internal controls.

SOX Box
A risk/control matrix identifies, documents, and evaluates the internal controls. The key components of a control matrix include the following: **Identify the internal control objectives or control goals**. These goals include both operational and information processing controls for the business process. Operational goals address the effectiveness of the operations, efficient employment of resources, and the security of

---

[1] For a more detailed discussion of an example of a risk/control matrix, refer to Accounting *Information Systems: Basic Concepts and Current Issues*, pages 83-85 or another AIS text.

resources. Information process goals address the input validity, input completeness, and input accuracy of the data as well as the update completeness and update accuracy of the input data.

Identify and evaluate the internal controls. Accountants frequently use flowcharts or data diagrams of business processes to identify the steps and procedures of a specific business process. As an accountant reviews the graphical representation of the business process, internal controls are identified that appear to accomplish internal control objectives or goals. This analysis will document the internal controls that are present as well as potential internal controls that are missing. This process relates the internal controls to the internal objectives. If an internal control is missing, then the accountant needs to determine whether additional controls are needed to eliminate potential weaknesses within the process or strengthen present controls.

Evaluate the risk level. In assessing the internal controls, the accountant identifies the potential risk level to the organization. Controls that do not operate as designed or missing internal controls with high risks are reported as significant material weaknesses within SOX Section 404 report. The identification of these risks are assisted through the use of an internal control framework such as the COSO enterprise risk management framework.

Identify the type of internal controls. As internal controls are evaluated, the controls are identified as preventive, detective, or corrective as well as manual or automated. Preventive controls are designed to stop problems, errors, deviations, or risks from occurring. Detective controls are designed to discover problems have occurred soon after they arise. Corrective controls will remedy discovered problems by identifying the cause of the problems, correcting the errors, and modifying the system to minimize or eliminate future problems. The analysis of internal controls also includes the further classification as general controls and application controls. General controls address the control environment such as information systems management controls, security management controls, IT infrastructure controls, and software acquisition, development, and maintenance controls. Application controls address the prevention, detection, and correction of transaction errors and emphasize accuracy, completeness, validity, and authorization of the input, processing, storage, and transmission of data. Both manual and automated controls are evaluated for Section 404 report.

	INTERNAL CONTROL ACTIVITY
	To assure appropriate segregation of duties, an independent accountant or someone not responsible for handling cash receipts has the separate task of reconciling a bank statement. If specific error messages occur, Dynamics GP's Help explains them. Perform the following steps to explore some of these messages, a description of the potential situation, and an explanation of how to solve the problem.
1.	From the Microsoft, Dynamics GP menu, access the Help by either clicking [icon] or using shortcut <Alt>+<H>
2.	Under module help, select Bank Reconciliation. On the next screen select Bank Reconciliation messages.
3.	Click on the first error message: A cash account must be assigned to this checkbook. Notice the description of the situation and suggested solution. One of DGP's system controls requires that a cash account be assigned to a checkbook. If this was not done, then the checkbook maintenance screen needs accessing to set up this internal control.
4.	Close this screen.
5.	Scroll down the messages and select the message: Adjustments are out of balance. Notice the description of the situation and suggested solution. One of Dynamics GP's system controls requires adjusting entries balance; if debit and credit does not equal, the user must access the adjusting entry and verify that an account was set up as the debit or credit account.
6.	Close this screen.
7.	Scroll down the messages and select the message: A fiscal period for this date has not been set up. Notice the description of the situation and suggested solution. One of Dynamics GP's system controls requires that the date of a transaction fall within the fiscal period.
8.	Close this screen.
9.	Scroll down the messages and select the message: The difference must be zero before you can reconcile this checkbook. Notice the description of the situation and suggestion solution. The system automatically calculates the difference between the adjusted bank balance and the adjusted book balance. One of Dynamics GP's system controls requires that the calculated amount must be zero. The user must review the cleared items and required adjustments; the cleared transactions and appropriate adjustments must be entered within the bank reconciliation screens that result in a zero balance.
10.	Close this screen.
11.	Notice many other messages exist. Remember that the Help will provide the user with information to resolve problems for recording, processing, and printing information. This resource is readily available and explains many of Dynamics GP's internal control features.

The McGraw-Hill Companies, Inc., *Computer Accounting Essentials with Dynamics GP 10.0, 2e*

SAVING CHAPTER 3: STUDENT NAME CHAPTER 3 OCTOBER FOLDER

 Read me: Create a Your Name Chapter 3 October folder

It is a good business practice to periodically unload data files to your external media. For instance, create a Your Name Chapter 3 October folder on your external media. Then, exit Dynamics GP and unload data into that folder.

To resume work, start Dynamics GP. Click "Yes" to loading data, browse your external media to the Student Name Chapter 3 October folder and pick the DYNAMICS.mdf file. Finally, select the company, Student Name HELP, Inc. when asked.

---

1. *Before* exiting DGP, review the information in the Read me box.

2. If you are copying files, select "Yes" to unloading data. If you are working on your own computer, select "No" to unloading data.

SUMMARY AND REVIEW

OBJECTIVES: In Chapter 3, you completed the following activities.

1. Start DGP and open the Student Name HELP, Inc. company.
2. Record and post deposits and checks.
3. Complete bank reconciliation.
4. Complete an inquiry for the checkbook register.
5. Print the trial balance.
6. Print financial statements.
7. Use the SmartList.
8. Review Sarbanes-Oxley compliance (SOX Box).
9. Complete an internal control activity.

The textbook web site at www.mhhe.com/dynamicsgp10essentials has a link to Textbook Updates. Check this link for updates.

Multiple Choice Questions: In the space provided, write the letter that best answers each question.

_____1. In Chapter 3 you use the Student Name HELP, Inc.. What other companies are included in Dynamics GP?

   a. Fabrikam, Inc.
   b. Jessica Richards, MD.
   c. Aurum Jewelers.
   d. World Online, Inc.
   e. None of the above.

_____2. In Chapter 3 of the book, you complete monthly accounting for which type of business?

   a. Nonprofit.
   b. Merchandising.
   c. Manufacturing.
   d. Service.
   e. None of the above.

_____3. The Student Name HELP, Inc.'s revenues include:

   a. Teaching income.
   b. Book royalties.
   c. Consulting services.
   d. All of the above.
   e. None of the above.

_____4. The account category for Gainesville Checking is:

   a. Other assets.
   b. Equity.
   c. Cash.
   d. Retained earnings.
   e. None of the above.

_____5. The list of all the account balances in the general ledger is called a/an?

   a. Income statement.
   b. Balance Sheet.
   c. Posting report.
   d. Trial Balance.
   e. None of the above.

_____6. The financial statements include these reports.

   a. Income statement, balance sheet, general ledger.
   b. Chart of accounts, general ledger.
   c. Trial balance, balance sheet, income statement, statement of cash flow.
   d. Income statement, balance sheet, statement of cash flow.
   e. None of the above.

_____7. The October 1, 20XX account balance in Account No. 000-3100-00, Common Stock, is:

   a. $83,695.11.
   b. $88,444,46.
   c. $99,332.70.
   d. $51,123.28.
   e. None of the above.

_____8. Another term for Balance Sheet is:

   a. Income statement.
   b. Assets and liabilities.
   c. Statement of financial position.
   d. Statement of cash flow.
   e. None of the above.

_____9. The Student Name HELP, Inc.'s Balance Sheet at the end of October 20XX shows the following total assets:

    a. $57,595.99.
    b. $103,873.17.
    c. $120,232.84.
    d. $104,482.19.
    e. None of the above.

_____10. The Student Name HELP, Inc.'s net income for the month of October is:

    a. $2,700.00.
    b. $5.600.00.
    c. $3,955.15.
    d. $4,178.06.
    e. None of the above.

Exercise 3-1: In order to complete Exercise 3-1, you must complete all the activities in Chapter 3. The work started with the Student Name HELP, Inc. is continued in Exercises 3-1 and 3-2. Follow the instructions below to complete Exercise 3-1:

1. Start Dynamics GP. Open the Student Name HELP, Inc. If necessary, load data.

2. Use the check register to journalize and post transactions. (*HINT: Financial; Financial, Bank Transaction*)

Trans. No.	Ck. No.	Date	Account No. and Description	Payment/ Dr (-)	Deposit/ Cr. (+)	Balance
15		*10/31/08*	*Balance Forward*			*29,872.71*
16	4011	11/3/08	000-2110-00 - VISA (Accounts payable)	5,250.65		24,622.06
17		11/8/08	000-2310-00 - Publisher (Advance payment)		2,250.00	26,872.06
18	4012	11/9/08	000-5255-00 - Midwest Gas Co. (utilities)	140.98		26,731.08
19	4013	11/10/08	000-5110-00- Richards Advertising, Inc. (advertising)	115.00		26,616.08
20	4014	11/13/08	000-5190-00 - U.S. Post Office (postage)	37.00		26,579.08
21	4015	11/13/08	000-5150-00 - AAA (dues)	195.00		26,384.08
22	4016	11/15/08	000-5250-00 - MCA Bell (telephone)	90.40		26,293.68
23		11/15/08	000-4110-00 - Gainesville College (teaching income)		2,655.00	28,948.68
24	4017	11/16/08	000-5180-00 - Internet Service Provider (internet)	29.90		28,918.78
25	4018	11/28/08	000-1720-00 - Office Staples (supplies)	137.80		28,780.98
26	4019	11/29/08	000-5235-00 - Greene Rentals (rent)	1,250.00		27,530.98

3. Display/Print the General Posting Journal; General Ledger report.

4. Post the bank deposit entry on 11/30/20XX (your current year). (*Hint:* Refer to pages 105-106 Bank Deposit Entry. Enter 11/30/20XX (your current year), Deposit Number 2, November deposits, All, Mark All, Post.)

5. Display/Print the Bank Deposit Posting Journal.

6. Exit Dynamics GP or continue with Exercise 3-2.

Exercise 3-2: You must complete Exercise 3-1 before you can complete Exercise 3-2.

1. If necessary start Dynamics GP; open the Student Name HELP, Inc.

2. Use the Bank Statement below to complete bank reconciliation. (*HINT:* See pages 107-110. Remember to adjust for Bank Service Charge (Account Number 000-5130-00) of $15.00.)

Statement of Account Gainesville Checking November1 to November 30, 20XX Account # 0908-33-5689			Student Name HELP, Inc. 1235 W. 75th Street Gainesville, FL 32192	
REGULAR CHECKING				
Previous Balance	10/31/08	31,353.61		
2 Deposits(+)		4,905.00		
9 Checks (-)		7,249.43		
Service Charges (-)	11/30/08	15.00		
Ending Balance	11/30/08	**$28,994.18**		
DEPOSITS				
	11/9/08	2,250.00		
	11/16/08	2,655.00		
CHECKS (Asterisk * indicates break in check number sequence)				
	11/3/08	4006	201.00	
	11/5/08	4009	1,250.00	
	11/5/08	4010	29.90	
	11/10/08	4011	5,250.65	
	11/10/08	4012	140.98	
	11/24/08	4013	115.00	
	11/27/08	4014	37.00	
	11/27/08	4015*	195.00	
	11/30/08	4017	29.90	

4. Display/Print the Reconciliation Posting Journal, Bank Adjustments Posting Journal, Cleared Transactions Journal, and the Outstanding Transactions Report. Your Adjusted Book balance is $27,515.98. (The ending Check Register balance minus the service charge.)

5.   Use inquiry to view, then print the Checkbook Balance Inquiry. The checkbook register shows October and November transactions and the Current Checkbook and Cash Balances are $27,515.98. Print to screen and file. The suggest file name is **Your Name Exercise 3-2_Oct and Nov Check Register.txt**.

6.   Print a Trial Balance Summary report from 100120XX to 113020XX (your current year). Click New or Modify to get to the Trial Balance Report Options window to complete the From and To fields.

| From: | Enter Date | ▼ 10/1/2008 ▦ |
| To: | Enter Date | ▼ 11/30/2008 ▦ |

Print to screen and file. The suggested file name is **Your Name Exercise 3-2_Trial Balance.txt**.
Check Figure: Account 000-1110-00, Gainesville Checking has a balance of $27,515.98.

7.   Before printing the income statement, update the report definition for Column 2. (*Hint:* Refer to pages 114-115. In the Reports area, link to <u>Advanced Financials</u>, Income Statement, Layout, C2; Period 11, Period 11.) This insures that the Current Month Column will show November, Period 11, revenues and expenses. Confirm that column C3 settings are Period 10 to Period 12 since this is the Current YTD column that shows the accumulated amounts for Periods 10 through 12, October, November and December.

8.   Print the income statement to screen and file. The suggested file name is **Your Name Exercise 3-2_Income Statement.txt**.
Check Figure: The Current Period income is $781.72; the Current YTD net income is $4,959.78.

9.   Print a balance sheet to screen and file. The suggested file name is **Your Name Exercise 3-2_Balance Sheet.txt**.
Check Figure: The total assets equal the total liabilities and equity of $101,654.24. Compare the net income amount to the YTD column on the income statement.

10. After updating the report definitions for column C2, print a statement of cash flow to screen and file. (*Hint:* See step 7 or pages 117-118.)

The suggested file name is **Your Name Exercise 3-2_Statement of Cash Flow.txt**.
Check Figure: The Current YTD ending cash balance is the same as the balance sheet's total cash balance, $65,239.26.

11.   Exit Dynamics GP or continue with Exercise 3-3 or 3-4.

Exercise 3-3: Internal Control

Access the Public Company Accounting Oversight Board Standard No. 5 at http://www.pcaobus.org/Rules/Rules_of_the_Board/Auditing_Standard_5.pdf

Answer the following questions:

1. What is a material weakness in internal control over financial reporting?

2. What is meant by management's assessment of the effectiveness of internal control over financial reporting?

3. What are preventive controls? Name two controls within DGP.

4. What are detective controls? Name two controls within DGP.

5. Paragraph 24 addresses centralized processing and controls. Provide three examples of processing controls within DGP.

Exercise 3-4: SmartList

Using SmartList's (*HINT:* Microsoft Dynamics GP; Smartlist), complete the following activities.

1. What was the total amount of cash receipts recorded on October 4, 20XX?

2. Save. The suggested file name is **Your Name Exercise 3-4_Cash Receipts.xls**. (*Hint:* Excel 2007 files end in the extension, .xlsx. Excel 2003 files end in the extension, .xls.)

3. What was the total amount of cash payments recorded on October 9, 20XX?

4. Save. The suggested file name is **Your Name Exercise 3-4_Cash Payments.xls**.

5. *Before* exiting Dynamics GP, review the information in the Read me box.

> **Read me: Create a Student Name Exercise 3-4 folder**
>
> Periodically unload data to external media. For instance, create a Student Name Exercise 3-4 folder on your external drive. Then, exit Dynamics GP and unload data in to the Student Name Exercise 3-4 folder on your external drive.

Chapter 4

Completing Quarterly Activities and Closing the Fiscal Year

OBJECTIVES: In Chapter 4, you will complete the following activities.

1. If necessary, load Exercise 3-4 data.
2. Record and post deposits and checks for December.
3. Complete bank reconciliation.
4. Complete an inquiry for the checkbook register.
5. Print the trial balance (unadjusted).
6. Journalize and post quarterly adjusting entries in the general journal.
7. Print financial statements.
8. Close the fiscal year.
9. Print a Post-Closing Trial Balance.
10. Use the SmartList.
11. Review Sarbanes-Oxley compliance (SOX Box).
12. Complete an internal control activity.

Chapters 2-4 work together. In Chapter 4, you continue recording financial information for the Student Name HELP, Inc. The December checkbook register and bank statement are used as source documents. At the end of December, which is also the end of the fourth quarter, you complete adjusting entries for the Student Name HELP, Inc, print financial statements, and close the fiscal year.

The steps of the accounting cycle completed in Chapter 4 are:

Dynamics GP's Accounting Cycle	
1.	Record and post bank transactions
2.	Bank reconciliation
3.	Print the unadjusted trial balance.
4.	Record and post adjusting entries.
5.	Print the adjusted trial balance.
6.	Print the financial statements: Income Statement, Balance Sheet, and Statement of Cash Flow.
7.	Close the fiscal year.
8.	Print the post-closing trial balance.

GETTING STARTED

Follow these steps to open the Student Name HELP, Inc.

1. Start Dynamics GP. Type your password.

2. Open the Student Name HELP, Inc.

3. To make sure you are at the correct starting point, view the Summary Trial Balance. The account balance in Gainesville Checking is $27,515.98. Make sure your Summary Trial Balance report agrees with the one in step 6, Exercise 3-2.

CHECKBOOK REGISTER AND BANK STATEMENT: DECEMBER 20XX (your current year)

Use the Student Name HELP, Inc's checkbook register to record and post transactions for the month of December. The December check register is shown below.

Trans. No.	Check No.	Date	Account No. and Description	Payment	Deposit	Balance
27		11/30	*Bank Service Charge*	*15.00*		*27,515.98*
28		12/6	000-4110-00 - Gainesville College (teaching income)		2,655.00	30,170.98
29	4020	12/10	000-5255-00 - Midwest Gas Co. (utilities)	165.95		30,005.03
30	4021	12/12	000-5250 -00- MCA Bell (telephone)	91.96		29,913.07
31	4022	12/15	000-5180-00 - Internet Service Provider (internet)	29.90		29,883.17
32	4023	12/16	000-1720-00 - Business Gallery (business cards; debit, Supplies)	115.25		29,767.92
33	4024	12/16	000-5195-00 - AD King (Printing)	60.39		29,707.53
34	4025	12/16	000-5135-00 - Conference (Conference Expense)	203.60		29,503.93
35	4026	12/30	000-5235-00 - Greene Rentals (rent)	1,250.00		28,253.93

1. Record and post bank transaction entries using the check register shown above.

2. Print the General Posting Journal. You have recorded eight transactions (numbered 28-35 on the check register). Check each debit and credit entry to make sure they are correct. When through checking each entry, close the report.

3. Post the 12/31/20XX bank deposit entry. (*Hint:* From the Financial page's Transaction's area, link to Bank Deposits. For detailed steps, refer to pages 105-106.)

4. Print the Bank Deposit Posting Journal.

5. Use the Gainesville Checking bank statement to reconcile. Remember to record the bank service charge (Account No. 000-5130-00). (*Hint:* From the Financial page's Transactions section, link to Reconcile Bank Statement.)

    The bank statement is shown on the next page.

Statement of Account Gainesville Checking December 1 to December 31, 20XX Account # 0908-33-5689			Student Name HELP, Inc 1235 W. 75th Street Gainesville, FL 32192	
REGULAR CHECKING				
Previous Balance	11/30/08	$28,994.18		
1 Deposits(+)		2,655.00		
8 checks (-)		1,941.65		
Service Charges (-)	12/31/08	15.00		
Ending Balance	12/31/08	**$29,692.53**		
DEPOSITS				
	12/8/08	2,655.00		
CHECKS (Asterisk * indicates break in check number sequence)				
	12/3/08	4016*	90.40	
	12/3/08	4018	137.80	
	12/3/08	4019	1,250.00	
	12/15/08	4020	165.95	
	12/17/08	4021	91.96	
	12/27/08	4022	29.90	
	12/27/08	4023	115.25	
	12/31/08	4024	60.39	

6. Print the Reconciliation Posting Journal, Bank Adjustments Posting Journal, Cleared Transactions Journal, and the Outstanding Transactions Report. Your Adjusted Book balance is $28,238.93. (This represents the ending check register balance minus the service charge.)

7. Print the following bank reconciliation reports: Reconciliation Posting Journal, Bank Adjustments Posting Journal, and Cleared Transactions Journal.

8. Print to screen a Trial Balance Summary report from 100120XX to 123120XX (your current year). The suggested file name is **Chapter 4_Trial Balance Summary.txt**. This is the unadjusted trial balance. The financial statements will be printed after completing the adjusting entries.

| | | To:
12/31/2008
Last | | Sorted By:
Include: | Segment 1
Posting | | |

Description	Beginning Balance	Debit	Credit	Net Change	Ending Balance
Gainesville Checking	$0.00	$40,665.15	$12,426.22	$28,238.93	$28,238.93
Sunshine Savings	$0.00	$4,500.50	$0.00	$4,500.50	$4,500.50
FL State Retirement	$0.00	$33,222.78	$0.00	$33,222.78	$33,222.78
Prepaid Insurance	$0.00	$2,100.00	$0.00	$2,100.00	$2,100.00
Prepaid Rent	$0.00	$600.00	$0.00	$600.00	$600.00
Computer Equipment	$0.00	$7,805.35	$0.00	$7,805.35	$7,805.35
Furniture and Fixtures	$0.00	$5,000.00	$0.00	$5,000.00	$5,000.00
Automobiles	$0.00	$19,000.00	$0.00	$19,000.00	$19,000.00
Supplies	$0.00	$2,024.88	$0.00	$2,024.88	$2,024.88
Accounts Payable	$0.00	$5,250.65	$5,250.65	$0.00	$0.00
Publisher Advances	$0.00	$0.00	$8,250.00	($8,250.00)	($8,250.00)
Common Stock	$0.00	$0.00	$88,444.46	($88,444.46)	($88,444.46)
Teaching Income	$0.00	$0.00	$7,965.00	($7,965.00)	($7,965.00)
Royalty Income	$0.00	$0.00	$3,750.15	($3,750.15)	($3,750.15)
Advertising and Marketing Expense	$0.00	$115.00	$0.00	$115.00	$115.00
Automobile Registration Expense	$0.00	$201.00	$0.00	$201.00	$201.00
Bank Charges Expense	$0.00	$45.00	$0.00	$45.00	$45.00
Conference Expense	$0.00	$203.60	$0.00	$203.60	$203.60
Dues and Subscriptions Expense	$0.00	$340.00	$0.00	$340.00	$340.00
Internet Service Provider Expense	$0.00	$89.70	$0.00	$89.70	$89.70
Maintenance and Repairs Expense	$0.00	$210.00	$0.00	$210.00	$210.00
Postage and Delivery Expense	$0.00	$74.00	$0.00	$74.00	$74.00
Printing and Reproduction Expense	$0.00	$170.39	$0.00	$170.39	$170.39
Rent Expense	$0.00	$3,750.00	$0.00	$3,750.00	$3,750.00
Telephone Expense	$0.00	$278.94	$0.00	$278.94	$278.94
Utilities Expense	$0.00	$439.54	$0.00	$439.54	$439.54

	Accounts	Beginning Balance	Debit	Credit	Net Change	Ending Balance
Grand Totals:	26	$0.00	$126,086.48	$126,086.48	$0.00	$0.00

NOTE: Account numbers are not shown because the Trial Balance Summary is displayed at 125%.

Check Figure: Gainesville Checking shows a balance of $28,238.93

TROUBLESHOOTING: What if my summary trial balance does not agree with the one shown?

1. First check the company name. Does it show Student Name HELP, Inc. Now check the account balances. You may have logged in to the wrong company; *or*, incorrectly entered, then posted transactions. Exit DGP, unload data.

2. Start DGP; load data. Open the DYNAMICS.mdf file from the Exercise 3-4 folder. Login in to Student Name HELP, Inc.

3. Redo.

INQUIRY

Follow these steps to display or print the checkbook register.

1. From the Financial page's Inquiry area, link to <u>Checkbook Register</u>. The Checkbook Register Inquiry window appears.

---

2. In the <u>Checkbook ID</u> field, select checkbook. The Checkbook Register Inquiry window appears. Observe that the deposits for October, November and December are shown. Checks 4001 through 4026 are listed and the three $15.00 service charges for October, November and December. The Current Balance field shows $28,238.93, which is The Student Name HELP, Inc's checkbook register balance minus the bank service charge.
   A partial Check Register Inquiry window is shown here. The December checks (4020 – 4026) are shown. Scroll down the window to see the December entries and the three bank service charges.

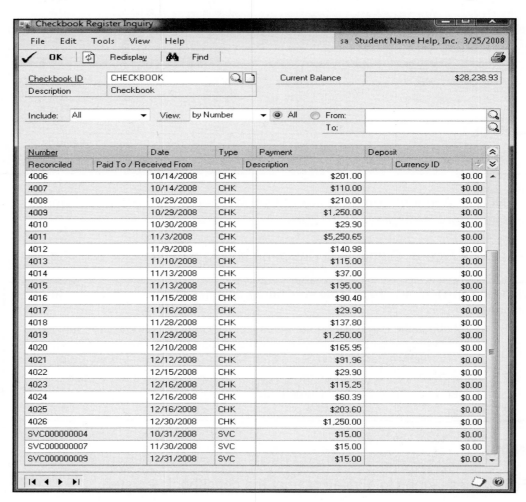

3. Close the Checkbook Register Inquiry window.

EXIT Dynamics GP: CHAPTER 4 UNADJUSTED TRIAL BALANCE

Before exiting Dynamics GP, review the information in the Read me box.   Select "Yes" to unload data to your external media. If you are working on your own computer, select "No."

 Read me: Create a Chapter 4 Unadjusted Trial Balance folder

Periodically unload data to external media. For instance, create a Chapter 4 Unadjusted Trial Balance folder. Then, exit Dynamics GP and unload data to it.

END-OF-QUARTER ADJUSTING ENTRIES

The Student Name HELP, Inc's policy is to record adjusting entries at the end of the quarter. You have recorded all of the accounting transactions through December 31, 20XX. You will now record the following adjusting entries in the general journal.

Follow these steps to record and post the adjusting entries shown.

1.   Start Dynamics GP and open Student Name HELP, Inc. if it is not already open.

2.   From the Financial page's Transactions area, link to <u>General</u> to open the Transaction Entry window. Observe that the Journal Entry number is 37. In October, November and December, you recorded and posted 36 entries. These entries include the bank service charge entries.

3.   Type **12/31/20XX (your current year)** in the Transaction Date field. The Source Document field defaults to GJ (General Journal).

4.   Type **Adjusting entry** in the Reference field.

5.   In the Distribution Reference table, select the accounts to debit and credit. See the adjusting entries listed on the following pages for account distribution information.

6.   Click ⊞ Post .

Record and post the December 31, 20XX adjusting entries listed below.

1. Office supplies on hand are $1,850.00. This is Journal Entry number 37. The Transaction Entry window for this entry is shown below. (*Hint:* Expand account distribution.)

Acct. #	Account Name	Debit	Credit
000-5245-00	Supplies Expense	174.88	
000-1720-00	Supplies		174.88

Computation:　Supplies　　　　　　　　$2,024.88
　　　　　　　　Office supplies on hand　 - 1,850.00
　　　　　　　　Adjustment　　　　　　　$　174.88

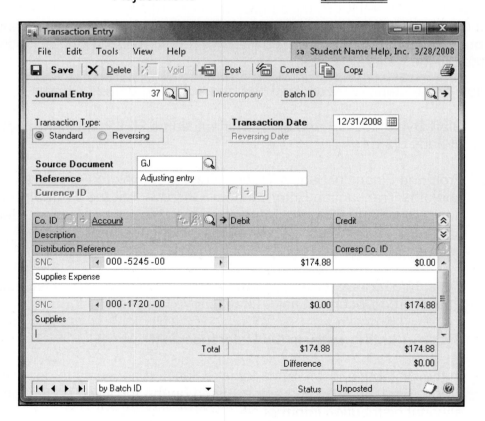

Hint: Click [Post] *after each transaction entry.*

2. Adjust three months of prepaid insurance ($2,100 X 3/12 = $525). The Student Name HELP, Inc paid a one year insurance premium on 10/1/XX. This is Journal Entry number 38.

Acct. #	Account Name	Debit	Credit
000-5175-00	Insurance Expense	525.00	
000-1200-00	Prepaid Insurance		525.00

1. Adjust prepaid rent: $600. This is Journal Entry number 39.

Acct. #	Account Name	Debit	Credit
000-5235-00	Rent Expense	600.00	
000-1230-00	Prepaid Rent		600.00

2. Use straight-line depreciation for the Student Name HELP, Inc's computer equipment. The computer equipment has a three-year service life and a $1,000 salvage value. This is Journal Entry number 40.

    To depreciate computer equipment for the fourth quarter, use this calculation:

    $7,805.35 - $1,000 ÷ 3 years X 3/12 = $567.11

Computer Equipment, 10/1/XX	$6,800.00
Hardware Upgrade, 10/4/XX	1,005.35
Total computer equipment, 12/31/XX	$7,805.35

Acct. #	Account Name	Debit	Credit
000-5147-00	Depr. Exp.- Computer Equipment	567.11	
000-1435-00	Accum. Depr. - Computer Equipment		567.11

5. Use straight-line depreciation to depreciate the Student Name HELP, Inc's furniture. The furniture and fixtures have a 5-year service life and a $500 salvage value. This is Journal Entry number 41.

    To depreciate furniture for the fourth quarter, use this calculation:

    $5,000 - $500 ÷ 5 X 3/12 = $225.00.

    Add Account No. 000-5149-00, Depr. Exp.-Furniture and Fixtures; Category, Other Expenses; Posting Type, Profit and Loss; Typical Balance, Debit.

Acct. #	Account Name	Debit	Credit
000-5149-00	Depr. Exp.- Furniture and Fixtures	225.00	
000-1445-00	Accum. Depr.-Furniture and Fixtures		225.00

6. The Student Name HELP, Inc purchased their automobile on October 1, 20XX. Use the following adjusting entry. This is Journal Entry number 42. The computation is:

    $19,000 X 20% X 3/12 = $950.00

Acct. #	Account Name	Debit	Credit
000-5145-00	Depr. Exp. – Automobiles	950.00	
000-1455-00	Accum. Depr. - Automobiles		950.00

7. The Student Name HELP, Inc received a $8,250 advance from a publisher and you recorded the cash receipt as *unearned revenue in the liability account Publisher Advances*. Recall from introductory accounting that unearned revenue is a liability account used to report advance collections from customers or clients because you have received the cash but yet owe the customer a service or product. The amount of this adjusting entry is based on the Student Name HELP, Inc's royalty statement. This is journal entry number 43.

Acct. #	Account Name	Debit	Credit
000-2310-00	Publisher Advances	4,000.00	
000-4120-00	Royalty Income		4,000.00

8. After recording and posting the end-of-quarter adjusting entries, close the Transaction Entry window. Make the selections to print the General Posting Journal. Transactions 37 through 43 are shown. These are the posted adjusting entries. Check the entries on the General Posting Journal to make sure that each one of the end-of-quarter adjusting entries are correct.

 Read me: Error Correction

What if you made a mistake? For example, let's say you notice that in transaction number 40 you credited Computer Equipment, Account No. 000-1430-00 *instead* of crediting Account No. 000-1435-00, Accum. Depr.-Computer Equipment. What should you do? The following steps assume Journal Number 40 was incorrect. If you made a mistake with another entry, use that one.

Follow these steps to Back Out of Journal Entry 40.

1. From the Financial page, link to General. Click 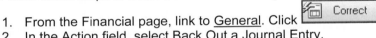 .
2. In the Action field, select Back Out a Journal Entry.
3. For this example, type **40** in the Original Journal Entry field.
4. Click ☑ **OK** .
5. Click ✗ Delete . When the window appears asking Are you sure you want to delete this transaction?, click  .
6. Now record and post the correct debits and credits. Observe that the Journal Entry field shows 44. Journal Entry 43 was the last adjusting entry.
7. Reprint the General Posting Journal report. Notice that transaction number 44 prints with the correct accounts debited and credited.

For auditing purposes, DGP shows an additional journal entry number because within the system, the entry is shown as deleted; an audit trail remains so that the accountant knows an entry was made and then deleted.

---

9. Print the summary trial balance (adjusted) to screen and file from 100120XX to 123120XX. The suggested file name is **Chapter 4_ Summary Trial Balance_Adjusted.txt**. Compare your unadjusted trial balance to the one shown on the next page.

	To: 12/31/2008 Last		Sorted By: Segment1 Include: Posting			
Description	Beginning Balance	Debit	Credit	Net Change	Ending Balance
Gainesville Checking	$0.00	$40,665.15	$12,426.22	$28,238.93	$28,238.93
Sunshine Savings	$0.00	$4,500.50	$0.00	$4,500.50	$4,500.50
FL State Retirement	$0.00	$33,222.78	$0.00	$33,222.78	$33,222.78
Prepaid Insurance	$0.00	$2,100.00	$525.00	$1,575.00	$1,575.00
Prepaid Rent	$0.00	$600.00	$600.00	$0.00	$0.00
Computer Equipment	$0.00	$7,805.35	$0.00	$7,805.35	$7,805.35
Accum. Depr.-Computer Equipment	$0.00	$0.00	$567.11	($567.11)	($567.11)
Furniture and Fixtures	$0.00	$5,000.00	$0.00	$5,000.00	$5,000.00
Accum. Depr.-Furniture and Fixtures	$0.00	$0.00	$225.00	($225.00)	($225.00)
Automobiles	$0.00	$19,000.00	$0.00	$19,000.00	$19,000.00
Accum. Depr.-Automobiles	$0.00	$0.00	$950.00	($950.00)	($950.00)
Supplies	$0.00	$2,024.88	$174.88	$1,850.00	$1,850.00
Accounts Payable	$0.00	$5,250.65	$5,250.65	$0.00	$0.00
Publisher Advances	$0.00	$4,000.00	$8,250.00	($4,250.00)	($4,250.00)
Common Stock	$0.00	$0.00	$88,444.46	($88,444.46)	($88,444.46)
Teaching Income	$0.00	$0.00	$7,965.00	($7,965.00)	($7,965.00)
Royalty Income	$0.00	$0.00	$7,750.15	($7,750.15)	($7,750.15)
Advertising and Marketing Expense	$0.00	$115.00	$0.00	$115.00	$115.00
Automobile Registration Expense	$0.00	$201.00	$0.00	$201.00	$201.00
Bank Charges Expense	$0.00	$45.00	$0.00	$45.00	$45.00
Conference Expense	$0.00	$203.60	$0.00	$203.60	$203.60
Depr. Exp.-Automobiles	$0.00	$950.00	$0.00	$950.00	$950.00
Depr. Exp.-Computer Equipment	$0.00	$567.11	$0.00	$567.11	$567.11
Depr. Exp.-Furniture and Fixtures	$0.00	$225.00	$0.00	$225.00	$225.00
Dues and Subscriptions Expense	$0.00	$340.00	$0.00	$340.00	$340.00
Insurance Expense	$0.00	$525.00	$0.00	$525.00	$525.00
Internet Service Provider Expense	$0.00	$89.70	$0.00	$89.70	$89.70
Maintenance and Repairs Expense	$0.00	$210.00	$0.00	$210.00	$210.00
Postage and Delivery Expense	$0.00	$74.00	$0.00	$74.00	$74.00
Printing and Reproduction Expense	$0.00	$170.39	$0.00	$170.39	$170.39
Rent Expense	$0.00	$4,350.00	$0.00	$4,350.00	$4,350.00
Supplies Expense	$0.00	$174.88	$0.00	$174.88	$174.88
Telephone Expense	$0.00	$278.94	$0.00	$278.94	$278.94
Utilities Expense	$0.00	$439.54	$0.00	$439.54	$439.54

	Accounts	Beginning Balance	Debit	Credit	Net Change	Ending Balance
Grand Totals:	34	**$0.00**	**$133,128.47**	**$133,128.47**	**$0.00**	**$0.00**

PRINTING FINANCIAL STATEMENTS

Before printing the end-of-quarter financial statements, let's make sure the layout will reflect current period balances for December, and year to date balances for October through December.

1. From the Financial page's Reports area, link to <u>Advanced Financial</u>.

2. Open the Income Statement. Click Layout .

3. Double-click C2. Compare your Financial Column Definition window to the one shown on the next page.

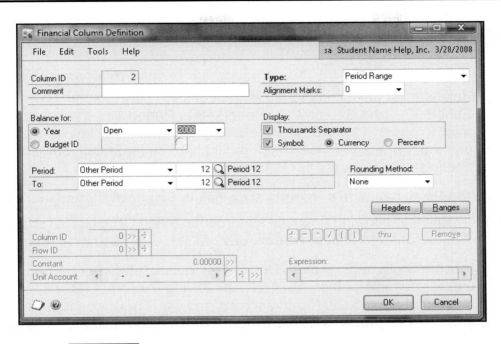

4.   Click [OK].

5.   Double-click on C3, the Current YTD column. Compare your
     definitions to the one shown below.

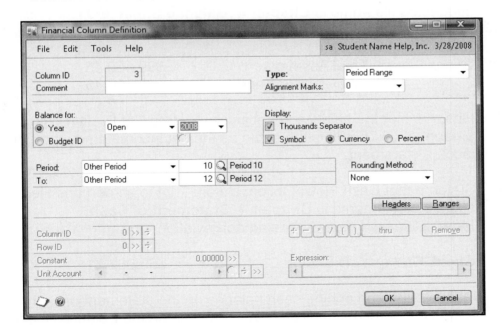

6. Click [OK]; close the Advanced Financial Report Layout window, click [Save].

7. Make similar selections for statement of cash flow (column C2—Period 12—and column C3—Period 10 to Period 12). If necessary, refer to pages 117-118 for the statement of cash flow layout and printing, For the balance sheet and income statement layout and printing refer to pages 114-115.

From the Financial page's Reports area, link to <u>Financial Statements</u> to print or view the following financial statements. (*Hint:* Click [Destination] to make selections to print to screen, save to file, or print to the printer.)

1. Income Statement; Option, Detail. The income statement reports a current period Net Income of $1,796.21 and Current YTD net income of $6,755.99. Print to screen and file. The suggested file name is **Chapter 4_Income Statement_EOY.txt**. (*Hint:* EOY is an abbreviation for End of Year.)

   Check Figure: Current Period Net Income $1,796.21
   Current YTD $6,755.99

2. Balance Sheet; Option, Detail. Print to screen and file. The suggested file name is **Chapter 4_Balance Sheet_EOY.txt**. (*Hint:* EOY is an abbreviation for End of Year.)

   Check Figure: Total Assets: $99,450.45
   Total liabilities and equity: $99,450.45

   Observe that the balance sheet's year-to-date Net Profit/(Loss) amount of $6,755.99 is the same as the net income amount on the income statement.

3. Statement of Cash Flow; Option, Detail. Print to screen and file. The suggested file name is **Chapter 4_Statement of Cash Flow_EOY.txt**. (*Hint:* EOY is an abbreviation for End of Year.)

   Check Figure: YTD Ending Cash: $65,962.21

   Observe that the ending cash balance on the statement of cash flow is the same as the Total Cash balance on the Balance Sheet.

CLOSING THE FISCAL YEAR

At the end of the year, DGP automatically completes the closing procedure. Follow these steps to close the Student Name HELP, Inc's fiscal year:

In accounting, you learn that ***closing entries*** clear temporary accounts, such as the revenue and expense accounts. The effect of a closing entry is a net increase or a net decrease to the Retained Earnings account. In addition, the revenue and expense accounts are adjusted to zero so you can accumulate the next year's revenues and expenses.

Period Close

When using DGP, the closing procedure has two levels. First, you close the period. This is called a ***soft close***. Second, you complete year-end closing. This is called a ***hard close.*** To close each period, follow these steps.

1.   From the Microsoft Dynamics GP menu, select Tools; Setup, Company, Fiscal Periods to open the Fiscal Periods Setup window. You may want to enlarge the window to see Periods 1 through 12. Notice that the boxes in the Financial column are blank.

2.   Click on each box in the Financial column. Compare your Fiscal Periods Setup window with the one shown here.

		Last Day	12/31/2008					Open All		Close All
Number of Periods		12								
							Series Closed			
Period	Period Name	Date		Financial	Sales	Purchasing	Inventory	Payroll	Project	
1	Period 1	1/1/2008		✓						
2	Period 2	2/1/2008		✓						
3	Period 3	3/1/2008		✓						
4	Period 4	4/1/2008		✓						
5	Period 5	5/1/2008		✓						
6	Period 6	6/1/2008		✓						
7	Period 7	7/1/2008		✓						
8	Period 8	8/1/2008		✓						
9	Period 9	9/1/2008		✓						
10	Period 10	10/1/2008		✓						
11	Period 11	11/1/2008		✓						
12	Period 12	12/1/2008		✓						

3.   Click [✓ OK] to close the window and save your entries.

Year-End Close

Before you can perform the year-end closing routine, you need to setup the next fiscal year by going to the Fiscal Periods Setup window.

1.   From the Microsoft Dynamics menu, select Tools; Setup, Company, Fiscal Periods. The Fiscal Periods Setup window appears.

2.   Type **20XY (the year following your current year, i.e. 2009 if current year is 2008)** in the Year field. Click [Calculate]. Periods 1-12 for 20XY appear.

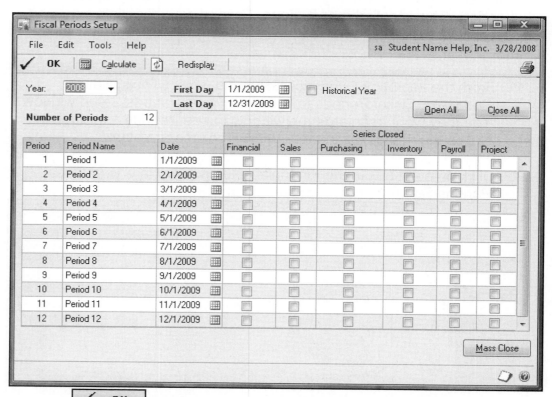

3.   Click [✓ OK] to close the window and save your entries.

Follow these steps to close two fiscal years – the year prior to your current year and the current year.

1. On the Navigation pane, select [Financial]. In the Routines area, link to <u>Year-End Closing</u>. If necessary, select Account No. 000-3000-00 as the Retained Earnings Account. Compare your Year-End Closing window to the one shown here.

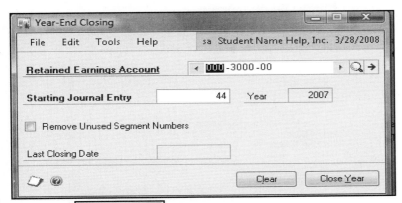

2.

3. Click [Close Year].

4. When you print to screen, a blank report appears. This closes the prior year. Close the Screen Output – Year End Closing Journal. You are returned to the Year-End Closing window. Observe that 20XX is shown in the Year field and the Last Closing Date field shows 12/31/20WX (the prior year).

5. Click [Close Year] to close 20XX, your current year.

6. Print to screen and file. The suggested file name is **Chapter 4_Closing Entries.txt**. The Year End Closing Report appears showing the closing entries.

```
                                    Year End Closing Report

Journal      Transaction      Source            Transaction          Audit Trail
Entry        Date             Document          Reference            Code

       44    12/31/2008       ADJ               Closing Entry        GLTRX00000009

       Account                     Description                        Debit          Credit

       000-3000-00                 Retained Earnings                                 $6,755.99
       000-4110-00                 Teaching Income                    $7,965.00
       000-4120-00                 Royalty Income                     $7,750.15
       000-5110-00                 Advertising and Marketing Expense                 $115.00
       000-5120-00                 Automobile Registration Expense                   $201.00
       000-5130-00                 Bank Charges Expense                              $45.00
       000-5135-00                 Conference Expense                                $203.60
       000-5145-00                 Depr. Exp.-Automobiles                            $950.00
       000-5147-00                 Depr. Exp.-Computer Equipment                     $567.11
       000-5149-00                 Depr. Exp.-Furniture and Fixtures                 $225.00
       000-5150-00                 Dues and Subscriptions Expense                    $340.00
       000-5175-00                 Insurance Expense                                 $525.00
       000-5180-00                 Internet Service Provider Expense                 $89.70
       000-5185-00                 Maintenance and Repairs Expense                   $210.00
       000-5190-00                 Postage and Delivery Expense                      $74.00
       000-5195-00                 Printing and Reproduction Expense                 $170.39
       000-5235-00                 Rent Expense                                      $4,350.00
       000-5245-00                 Supplies Expense                                  $174.88
       000-5250-00                 Telephone Expense                                 $278.94
       000-5255-00                 Utilities Expense                                 $439.54

                                                          Totals:    $15,715.15      $15,715.15
```

6.   Close the Year End Closing Report and the Year-End Closing window.

PRINT THE POST-CLOSING TRIAL BALANCE

After the fiscal year is closed, a post-closing trial balance is printed. Only permanent accounts appear on the post-closing trial balance. All temporary accounts (revenues and expenses) should have zero balances after closing is completed. This completes DGP's accounting cycle.

1.   From the Financial page's Reports area, link to Trial Balance.
2.   In the Reports list, select Summary. Click New .
3.   In the Option field, select Trial Balance.
4.   In the Year field, select 20XY, the year after the current year.
5.   Type **010120XY** in the From field. Observe that the To field shows 1/1/20XY (the year after current year, i.e. if you were in 2008, From field shows 1/1/2009)
6.   Print to screen and file. (*Hint:* Click Destination to make selections to print to screen, save to file, or print to the printer.) The suggested

file name is **Chapter 4_Postclosing Trial Balance.txt**.
Check Figure: Retained Earnings shows an account balance of
$6,755.99 – that is the net income from the December 31, 20XX
income statement. All the revenue and expense accounts are
closed.

Student Name Help, Inc.
General Ledger

To:
12/31/2009
Last

Sorted By: Segment1
Include: Posting

Description	Beginning Balance	Debit	Credit	Net Change	Ending Balance
Gainesville Checking	$28,238.93	$0.00	$0.00	$0.00	$28,238.93
Sunshine Savings	$4,500.50	$0.00	$0.00	$0.00	$4,500.50
FL State Retirement	$33,222.78	$0.00	$0.00	$0.00	$33,222.78
Prepaid Insurance	$1,575.00	$0.00	$0.00	$0.00	$1,575.00
Computer Equipment	$7,805.35	$0.00	$0.00	$0.00	$7,805.35
Accum. Depr.-Computer Equipment	($567.11)	$0.00	$0.00	$0.00	($567.11)
Furniture and Fixtures	$5,000.00	$0.00	$0.00	$0.00	$5,000.00
Accum. Depr.-Furniture and Fixtures	($225.00)	$0.00	$0.00	$0.00	($225.00)
Automobiles	$19,000.00	$0.00	$0.00	$0.00	$19,000.00
Accum. Depr.-Automobiles	($950.00)	$0.00	$0.00	$0.00	($950.00)
Supplies	$1,850.00	$0.00	$0.00	$0.00	$1,850.00
Publisher Advances	($4,250.00)	$0.00	$0.00	$0.00	($4,250.00)
Retained Earnings	($6,755.99)	$0.00	$0.00	$0.00	($6,755.99)
Common Stock	($88,444.46)	$0.00	$0.00	$0.00	($88,444.46)

	Accounts	Beginning Balance	Debit	Credit	Net Change	Ending Balance
Grand Totals:	14	$0.00	$0.00	$0.00	$0.00	$0.00

7. Save your report settings.
8. Close all windows.

SMARTLIST

To verify which accounts have balances after closing the current year, a
user could search for accounts that are still open. Using the SmartList,
complete the following activities.

1. Using the SmartList [Search], do a search that lists accounts
with balances still open after the close of 20XX (your current year).
(*Hint:* SmartList; Financial, Account Summary.)

Column Name: Period ID
Filter: is equal to
Value: 0
2. Export to Excel.

3. Save. The suggested file name is **Your Name Post Closing EOY.xls**. (*Hint:* Excel 2007 files end in the extension, .xlsx. Excel 2003 files end in the extension, .xls.).

Your printout will include a listing of all accounts still open after yearend. Compare this list with your post closing trial balance printed on the previous page.

Account Number	Account Description	Credit Amount	Debit Amount
000-1110-00	Gainesville Checking	$12,426.22	$40,665.15
000-1120-00	Sunshine Savings	$0.00	$4,500.50
000-1130-00	FL State Retirement	$0.00	$33,222.78
000-1200-00	Prepaid Insurance	$525.00	$2,100.00
000-1430-00	Computer Equipment	$0.00	$7,805.35
000-1435-00	Accum. Depr.-Computer ...	$567.11	$0.00
000-1440-00	Furniture and Fixtures	$0.00	$5,000.00
000-1445-00	Accum. Depr.-Furniture a...	$225.00	$0.00
000-1450-00	Automobiles	$0.00	$19,000.00
000-1455-00	Accum. Depr.-Automobil...	$950.00	$0.00
000-1720-00	Supplies	$174.88	$2,024.88
000-2310-00	Publisher Advances	$8,250.00	$4,000.00
000-3000-00	Retained Earnings	$6,755.99	$0.00
000-3100-00	Common Stock	$88,444.46	$0.00

SARBANES-OXLEY COMPLIANCE (SOX Box)

SOX Box
As discussed in previous SOX boxes, compliance emphasizes internal controls within accounting systems. Businesses must ensure that effective internal controls exist within the information technology environment. Characteristics of systems include: **Completeness:** The user can record transactions once and the system only accepts the one transaction. The system rejects duplicate transactions or data. **Validity:** Authorization is required from an accepted source. **Accuracy:** Data entered is the correct information. **Restricted Access:** Responsibilities and tasks are segregated by roles to protect against unauthorized activity or securing access of data outside the area of responsibility.

Software system features that can enhance these characteristics include:
1) Regular backup of information
2) Tracking changes through the use of logs
3) Role based security and access of information
4) Access restrictions through the use of passwords and limited access to windows
5) Data validation that checks data with master tables
6) Application controls that prevent, detect, and correct transaction errors
7) Automated controls such as checking that debits and credits match
8) Reconciliation
9) Defined roles and task
10) Electronic approvals to process transaction
11) Date and time stamps
12) E-mail alerts to prompt users of workflow tasks or available reports

As companies perform their internal control analysis for the Section 404 report, systems with these characteristics and features will strengthen their internal controls. In addition, understanding the system will assist the accountant's role in providing documentation of the internal controls.

INTERNAL CONTROL ACTIVITY	
An important internal control within a system is the accounting period. Once an accounting period is closed, you cannot post an entry to a previous period. Systems include this control so that once financial statements are printed and issued, you cannot record another entry that would alter the past results.	
1.	From the Microsoft, Dynamics GP menu, select Transactions; Financial; General.
2.	Change the transaction date to 123120XX (the current year you just closed) and enter. You will receive the following error message: 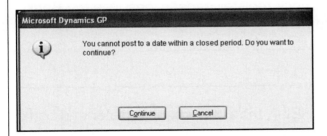 This will mitigate recording or posting entries to periods that are closed. This screen will occur whether the date is entered on a batch or a transaction.

SUMMARY AND REVIEW

OBJECTIVES: In Chapter 4, you completed the following activities.

1. If necessary, load Exercise 3-4 data.
2. Record and post deposits and checks for December.
3. Complete bank reconciliation.
4. Complete an inquiry for the checkbook register.
5. Print the trial balance (unadjusted).
6. Journalize and post quarterly adjusting entries in the general journal.
7. Print financial statements.
8. Close the fiscal year.
9. Print a Post-Closing Trial Balance.
10. Use the SmartList.
11. Review Sarbanes-Oxley compliance (SOX Box).
12. Complete an internal control activity.

True/Make True: Write the word True in the space provided if the statement is true. If the statement is not true, write the correct answer.

1. You can complete the activities in Chapter 4 without completing Chapter 3.

2. Step 4 of DGP's Accounting Cycle is reconciling the bank statement.

3. To record and post check register transactions, use the Bank Deposits Entry window.

4. The Student Name HELP, Inc's checkbook register and bank statement are used as source documents for recording entries.

5.   The bank reconciliation feature can reconcile the cash account only.

_____

_____

6.   In Chapter 4, data is recorded and posted for December 20XX (Your current year).

_____

_____

7.   DGP includes an editing feature so that general journal entries can be corrected.

_____

_____

8.   The Student Name HELP, Inc's current year-to-date net income is $6,755.99.

_____

_____

9.   At the end of the quarter, the Student Name HELP, Inc's total assets are $99,450.45.

_____

_____

10.   On the post-closing trial balance, the Student Name HELP, Inc's retained earnings are $78,444.46.

_____

_____

Exercise 4-1: Answer the following questions in the space provided.

1. What is the Accum. Depr.-Computer Equipment
    balance on December 31?   _____

2. What is the Prepaid Insurance balance on
    December 31?   _____

3. What is the Supplies Expense balance on
    December 31?   _____

4. What is the Postage and Delivery Expense
    balance on December 31?   _____

5. What is the Retained Earnings balance on
    December 31?   _____

Exercise 4-2: Answer the following questions in the space provided.

1. What is the date of the post-closing
    trial balance?   _____

2. What is the Common Stock balance on
    the post-closing trial balance?   _____

3. What is the Retained Earnings balance on
    the post-closing trial balance?   _____

4. What financial statements show the net
    income earned by the Student Name HELP, Inc?_____

5. What is the Gainesville Checking balance
    after closing entries have been made?   _____

Exercise 4-3: Internal Control

Access the Public Company Accounting Oversight Board Standard No. 5 at
http://www.pcaobus.org/Rules/Rules_of_the_Board/Auditing_Standard_5.pdf

Answer the following questions:

1. How does this standard define the period-end financial reporting process? That is, what does it include?

    _____

    _____

2. How would an auditor assess the period-end reporting process?

    _____

    _____

3. Review paragraph 34. Consider the tools and skills that an accountant develops and the internal controls available within DGP. How can the auditor better understand the system and the likely sources of misstatement?

    _____

    _____

    _____

Exercise 4-4: SmartList

Once you have completed the adjusting entries, you may want to review the entries to verify that you recorded all adjusting entries. Using the

SmartList , complete the following activities.

1.   Using the SmartList ![Search], do a search that lists journal entries recorded on December 31, 20XX. (*Hint:* SmartList; Financial, Accounting Transactions, History Financials Journal.)

>   Column Name: TRX Date
>   Filter: is equal to
>   Value: 123120XX (your current year)

2.   Export to Excel.

3.   Save. The suggested file name is **Your Name Exercise 4-4 Entries.xls**. (*Hint:* Excel 2007 files end in the extension, .xlsx. Excel 2003 files end in the extension, .xls.).

4.   Print your Excel file so it fits on one page. Your printout will include a listing of all journal entries recorded on December 31, 20XX. A review of these entries could assist your determination that you have recorded all necessary adjusting entries.

5.   *Before* exiting Dynamics GP, review the information in the Read me box.   Select "Yes" to unload data to your external media. If you are working on your own computer, select "No."

Read me: Create a Chapter 4 EOY folder

Periodically unload data to external media. For instance, create a Chapter 4 EOY folder. Then, exit Dynamics GP and unload data to the Chapter 4 EOY folder.

Chapter

5

Acquisitions and Payments

OBJECTIVES: In Chapter 5, you will complete the following activities:

1. If necessary, load data. [1]
2. Change user date.
3. Record and post deposits and checks for January.
4. Enter vendor defaults and preferences.
5. Print the vendor list.
6. Complete purchase order processing.
7. Set up posting for purchasing transactions.
8. Record and post vendor purchases on account.
9. Record and post vendor payments.
10. Complete series posting.
11. Complete bank reconciliation.
12. Print reports.
13. Use the SmartList.
14. Review Sarbanes-Oxley compliance (SOX Box).
15. Complete an internal control activity.

The textbook website at www.mhhe.com/dynamicsgp10essentials contains many learning resources and textbook updates. Check it out!

In Chapter 4, you used the Dynamics GP Financial module to record the cash receipts and payments for the month of December, completed adjusting entries, printed financial statements, and closed the fiscal year. Chapters 5 and 6 work together to record cash transactions for January and February 20XY (the year after your current year XX) and improve internal controls over vendor and customer activities. In Chapter 5, you will set up and use the Dynamics GP Payables Management module to implement controls over your business' buying and paying processes. You will set up your vendors, acquire supplies and services, and make

---

[1] All activities in Chapter 4, including the exercises, must be completed before starting Chapter 5.

The McGraw-Hill Companies, Inc., *Computer Accounting Essentials with Microsoft Dynamics GP 10.0, 2e*

vendor payments. Then in Chapter 6, you will implement controls over your business' selling and collection processes by setting up and using the Dynamics GP Receivables Management module.

Chapter 5 focuses on the ***acquisition and payment process*** that includes the activities associated with maintaining, buying, and paying for the goods and services needed by the business. For a service business, this process includes acquiring and paying for supplies, insurance, property and equipment, utilities, and other services.

In Dynamics GP acquisition and payments take place in the accounts payables module, also known as Payables Management.
The flowchart below illustrated how vendors are paid.

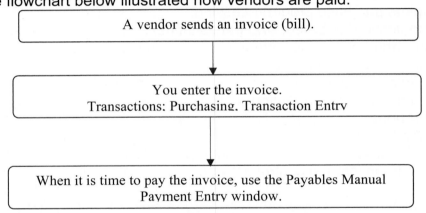

GETTING STARTED

Follow these steps to continue using Student Name HELP Inc. data.

1. Start Dynamics GP and open the Student Name HELP, Inc. company.

2. Click [OK].

3. To make sure you are starting in the right place, display or print the Trial Balance Summary report from 01/01/20XY to 01/01/20XY (the year after the year you closed in Chapter 4). Compare the trial balance summary report to the one on page 151.

4. Close all windows to return to the desktop.

USER DATE

The user date is the date that is displayed on the toolbar. For example, in the lower left corner of your DGP desktop, the current date is shown on the toolbar:

7/13/2008   Student Name HELP, Inc.   sa

User date shows current date.

In DGP, The current date is the default. You can modify the user date in two ways:

- Change the operating system date. See your operating system documentation for information about how to change the operating system date.
- Change the user date. Follow the steps below to change the user date.

1. Click the User Date field on the toolbar to open the User Date window.

2. Type **010120XY** in the date field, i.e., 2009.

3. Click ⬜ OK .

4. Observe that the user date on the toolbar changes to 1/1/20XY.

1/1/2009   Student Name HELP, Inc.   sa   User date is 1/1/2009

You have changed the user date so that when you do reports the dates will display correctly. Modifying the user date in this way is a *temporary* change. Each time you exit DGP, the user date will revert to the current date.

CHECKBOOK REGISTER: JANUARY 20XY

Use your checkbook register to record and post this receipt for the month of January of the new year (year XY). (*HINT:* See Chapter 3.)

Check No.	Date	Description of Transaction	Payment	Deposit	Balance
	12/31/XX	*Year-End Closing*			*28,238.93*
	1/6	000-4110-00 Gainesville College (teaching income)		2,655.00	30,893.93
	1/6	000-4110-00 Gainesville College (teaching bonus)		2,655.00	

1. Record and post bank transaction entries using the check register shown above. (*HINT:* Financial page; Financial, Transactions area, Bank Transactions)

2. Close Bank Transaction window. Display/Print the Bank Transaction Posting Journal and the General Posting Journal appear. Review and close.

3. Post the bank deposit entry on 01/07/20XY. (*Hint:* Financial page; Financial, Transactions area, Bank Deposits.)

4. Close the Bank Deposits Entry window. Display/Print the Bank Deposit Posting Journal. Review and close.

VENDOR PREFERENCES AND DEFAULTS

Before you can use the Dynamics GP Payables Management module, you must setup Payables Management.

 Read me

As you know from using other Windows programs, there is usually more than one way to do the same thing. This is also true with Dynamics GP. For example, you can use Microsoft Dynamics GP; Tools; Setup, Purchasing, Payables to setup Payable Management; *or* you can use Purchasing; on the Purchasing desktop scroll down to the Setup section and pick Payables. Using either method, the same Payables Maintenance Setup window appears.

Follow these steps to use the setup routine.

1. From your Navigation pane, select 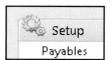; click on ⊞ Purchasing. Scroll to the Setup area and pick Payables to open the Payables Management Setup window.

2. The Payables Management Setup window appears. Use the Payables Management Setup window to set the default entries that appear throughout the accounts payable module.

3. In the Aging Periods area, select Due Date.

4. Select CHECKBOOK for the <u>Checkbook ID</u>.

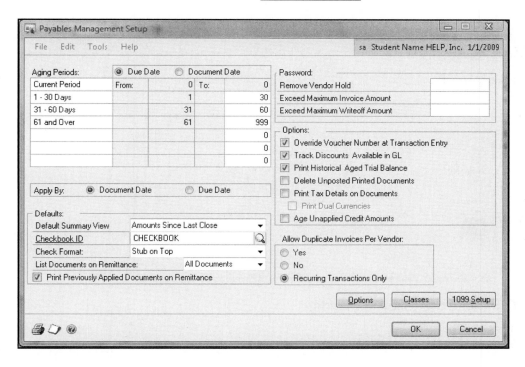

5. Compare your screen with above screenshot. When satisfied, click OK. You are returned to the Purchasing page.

Vendor Maintenance

Use the Vendor Maintenance window to create new vendor records. All vendor IDs should have the same number of characters. Student Name

HELP, Inc. uses 3 character vendor IDs.
Follow these steps to add a vendor.

1. The Purchasing pane should be displayed. (*Hint:* If not, on your
    Navigation bar, select ![Purchasing]; then click on
    [Purchasing].) Scroll to the Cards section and pick
    Vendor.

2. The Vendor Maintenance window appears.

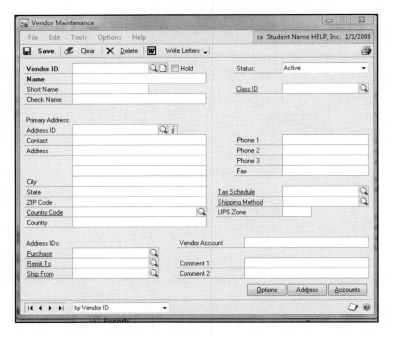

Complete the following fields.

Vendor ID:	BUG
Name:	Business Gallery (The Short Name and Check Name fields are automatically completed.)
Address ID:	PRIMARY
Contact:	Brent Courtney
Address:	32 Gaines St.
City:	Millhopper
State:	FL
ZIP Code:	35206
Phone 1:	800 545-1212, Ext 4210

Click [<u>O</u>ptions]. The Vendor Maintenance Options window appears.

3.   Type **Net 30** in the <u>Payment Terms</u> field. Press <Tab>. When the window appears asking if you want to add this payment term, click [<u>A</u>dd].

4.   The Payment Terms Setup window appears. Complete the following fields: Due: Net Days: 30. Compare your Payments Terms Setup window to the one shown here.

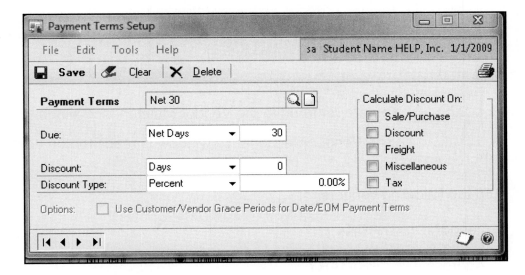

5.   Click [💾 **Save**]. Close the Payment Terms Setup window. You are returned to the Vendor Maintenance Options window.

6.   Click [OK]. You are returned to the Vendor Maintenance window.

7.   Click [Accounts]. The Vendor Account Maintenance window appears. Complete the following fields.

> Accounts Payable: 000-2110-00, Accounts Payable
> Miscellaneous: 000-1720-00, Supplies

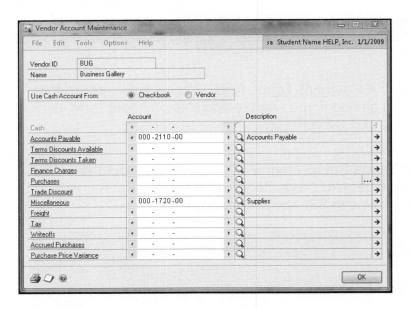

Click [OK]. You are returned to the Vendor Maintenance window.

Click [Save]. The Vendor Maintenance window is ready for the next vendor record.

Add the following vendors.

Vendor ID:	ADK
Name:	AD King
Address ID:	PRIMARY
Contact:	Lucy White
Address:	42 Alachua Sink St.
City:	Micanopy
State:	FL
ZIP Code:	33208
Phone 1:	800 555-9033

Options: Payment Terms, Net 30; <u>Checkbook ID</u>, CHECKBOOK

Accounts:

Accounts Payable:	000-2110-00, Accounts Payable
Miscellaneous:	000-5195-00, Printing and Reproduction Expense

Vendor ID: MGC
Name: Midwest Gas Co.
Address ID: PRIMARY
Contact: Clay Woods
Address: 82 Melrose Avenue
City: Starke
State: FL
ZIP Code: 35246
Phone 1:   800 545-7808, Ext 9010

Options: Payment Terms, Net 30; <u>Checkbook ID</u>, CHECKBOOK

Accounts:

  Accounts Payable: 000-2110-00, Accounts Payable
  Miscellaneous: 000-5255-00, Utilities Expense

Vendor ID: GRR
Name: Greene Rentals
Address ID: PRIMARY
Contact: Bubba Autry
Address: 123 43 St.
City: Mill Hammock
State: FL
ZIP Code: 34567
Phone 1:   800 544-1233

Options: Payment Terms, Net 30; <u>Checkbook ID</u>, CHECKBOOK

Accounts:

  Accounts Payable: 000-2110-00, Accounts Payable
  Miscellaneous: 000-5235-00, Rent Expense

Vendor ID:	ISP
Name:	Internet Service Provider
Address ID:	PRIMARY
Contact:	Scooter Yates
Address:	1982 48 Avenue
City:	Sunshine
State:	FL
ZIP Code:	31246
Phone 1:	800 445-2808

Options: Payment Terms, Net 30; Checkbook ID, CHECKBOOK

Accounts:

Accounts Payable:	000-2110-00, Accounts Payable
Miscellaneous:	000-5180-00, Internet Service Provider Expense

Vendor ID:	RAD
Name:	Richards Advertising, Inc.
Address ID:	PRIMARY
Contact:	Yancy Richards
Address:	1948 Avenue Q
City:	Sunset
State:	FL
ZIP Code:	31200
Phone 1:	800 445-2700

Options: Payment Terms, Net 30; Checkbook ID, CHECKBOOK

Accounts:

Accounts Payable:	000-2110-00, Accounts Payable
Miscellaneous:	000-5110-00, Advertising and Marketing Expense

Vendor ID:	MCA
Name:	MCA Bell
Address ID:	PRIMARY
Contact:	Customer Service
Address:	567 State Street
City:	Commerce
State:	FL
ZIP Code:	31460
Phone 1:	800 555-1234

Options: Payment Terms, Net 30; Checkbook ID, CHECKBOOK

Accounts:

Accounts Payable:	000-2110-00, Accounts Payable
Miscellaneous:	000-5250-00, Telephone Expense

When you have completed recording and saving the 7 vendors, close to return to Purchasing page.

Printing the Vendor List

Follow these steps to print the Vendor List.

1. From the Purchasing page's Reports area, link to Setup/Lists.

2. The Purchasing Setup Reports window appears. In the Reports list, select Vendor List. Click New .

3. Type **Vendor List** in the Option field.

4. Click Destination to make the selections to print to your screen and file. The suggested file name is Chapter 5_Vendor List.txt.

5. The Vendor Summary List appears. Compare yours to the one on the next page.

The McGraw-Hill Companies, Inc., *Computer Accounting Essentials with Microsoft Dynamics GP 10.0, 2e*

```
System:      7/13/2008    3:04:01 PM          Student Name HELP, Inc.              Page:      1
User Date:   1/1/2009                         VENDOR SUMMARY LIST                  User ID:   sa
                                              Payables Management


Ranges:
  Vendor ID:          First - Last                              Short Name:   First - Last
  Vendor Name:        First - Last                              ZIP Code:     First - Last
  Vendor Class:       First - Last                              State:        First - Last
  User-Defined 1:     First - Last                              Telephone:    First - Last
  Vendor Status:      First - Last                              Contact:      First - Last
  1099 Type:          First - Last

Sorted By:  Vendor ID


Vendor ID      Name                          Class ID       Phone 1                      Contact Person
---------------------------------------------------------------------------------------------------------
  Address
---------------------------------------------------------------------------------------------------------
    City                      State                         ZIP Code     Country
---------------------------------------------------------------------------------------------------------
ADK            AD King                                       (800) 555-9033  Ext. 0000    Lucy White
  42 Alachua Sink St.
    Micanopy                  FL                            33208

BUG            Business Gallery                              (800) 545-1212  Ext. 4210    Brent Courtney
  32 Gaines St.
    Millhopper                FL                            35206

GRR            Greene Rentals                                (800) 544-1233  Ext. 0000    Bubba Autry
  123 43 St.
    Mill Hammock              FL                            34567

ISP            Internet Service Provider                     (800) 445-2808  Ext. 0000    Scooter Yates
  1982 48 Avenue
    Sunshine                  FL                            31246
```

```
MCA            MCA Bell                                      (800) 555-1234  Ext. 0000    Customer Service
  567 State Street
    Commerce                  FL                            31460

MGC            Midwest Gas Co.                               (800) 545-7808  Ext. 9010    Clay Woods
  82 Melrose Avenue
    Starke                    FL                            35246

RAD            Richards Advertising, Inc.                    (800) 445-2700  Ext. 0000    Yancy Richards
  1948 Avenue Q
    Sunset                    FL                            31200

Total Vendors:        7
```

5. Close all windows. Save the report settings.

PURCHASE ORDER PROCESSING

You use the Purchase Order Processing Setup window to set preferences and default entries that appear throughout Dynamics GP. In the work that follows you want to make sure that you can record and post purchases from vendors *without* having to create a purchase order first. For example, a business will use utilities monthly and would not issue a purchase order to the utility company requesting utilities before using them. By checking the defaults that follow, you can process transactions without a purchase order.

1. From the navigation pane, select 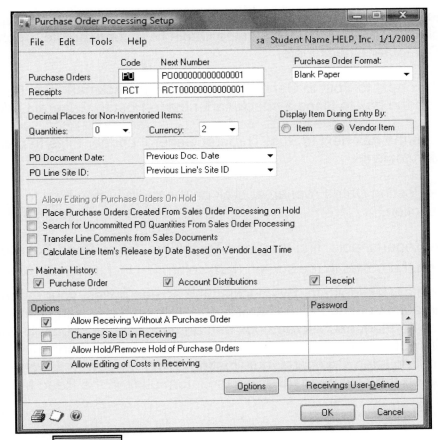**Purchasing**. From the Purchasing page's Setup area, link to <u>Purchase Order Processing</u>. The Purchase Order Processing Setup window appears.

2. Accept the defaults for Purchase Orders and Receipts numbers. Make sure the Display Item During Entry By shows Vendor Item is selected. Also, make sure that the Option area shows a checkmark next to Allow Receiving Without A Purchase Order.

    Check that the Options section matches the Purchase Order Processing Setup window shown here.

3. Click OK.

POSTING SETUP

Before you record transactions, you need to set up posting in Dynamics GP. Use the Posting Setup window to determine how transactions are posted for each entry in Dynamics GP's accounts payable module.

Posting Setup: Purchasing

To specify posting settings, follow these steps.

1. From the Microsoft Dynamics GP menu, select Tools; Setup, Posting, Posting. The Posting Setup window appears.

2. In the Series field, select Purchasing.

3. In the Origin field, select All. Selecting All in the Origin field sets up a template for all the selections in the Origin field; for example, Apply To, Computer Checks, etc.

4. The box next to Post to General Ledger has a checkmark in it. If *not*, click on the box to place a checkmark next to Post to General Ledger.

5. Click on the box next to Post Through General Ledger Files to place a checkmark in it.

6. In the Posting Date From area, click on the radio button next to Transaction.

7. In the Reports table, find the Send To column. In the Send To column, click on the boxes in the screen ( ) column. Uncheck the boxes in the printer ( ) column. By checking the screen boxes, your reports will default to printing to the screen. Scroll down the Posting Setup window to mark each screen box and unmark each print box. If want to print out a hard-copy of a report, you can change the printer destination later. Compare your Posting Setup window to the one shown on the next page. (Review the information in the Read Me box.)

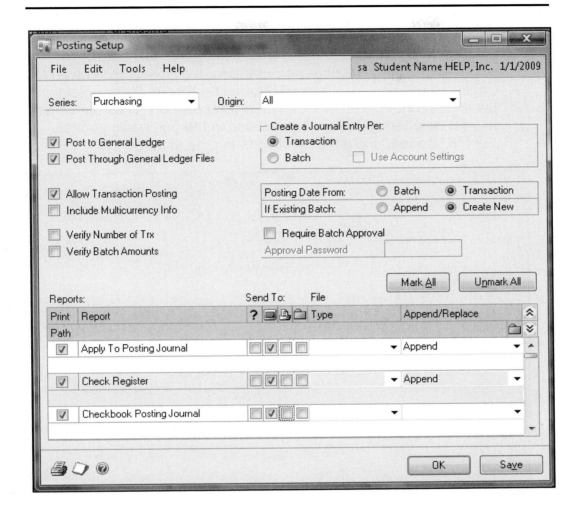

Read me

When setting up print destinations, you have options. In the Send To column, you can specify one or more print destinations—screen, printer, file, etc. You can also uncheck reports in the Path column so that the report does *not* print. In this example, you select the screen icon so that reports print to your screen. Scroll up and down the Posting Setup window to make sure the Screen is selected for each report. The Posting Setup window on the next page shows the last seven reports.

---

8. Click [Save]. The Posting Setup window is cleared.

9. To check that Purchasing posting is set up correctly, in the Series field, select Purchasing. In the Origin field, select Payables Trx

---

Entry (Trx is an abbreviation for transaction). Compare your Posting Setup window to the one shown on the next page. Observe that the selections you made for the Series, Purchasing; Origin, All are shown. If you select another Origin, these selections will appear again. Remember, when you selected All as the Origin, you set up a template for all selections in the purchasing series. *(Hint:* If needed, make the selections to print to screen.)

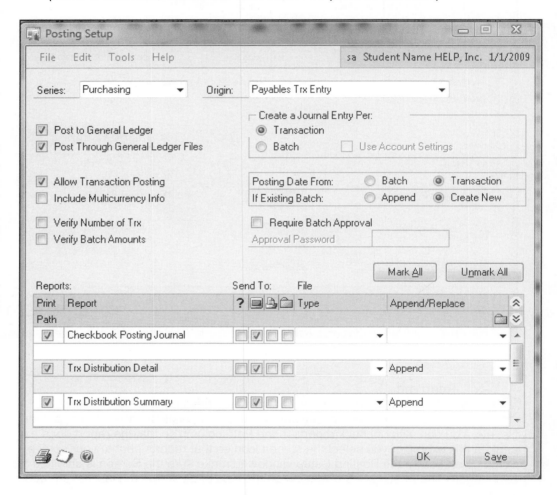

10. Click ⬚ OK ⬚.

RECORDING TRANSACTIONS

Invoices, credit memos, finance charges, and miscellaneous charges are the document types that you can enter in Payables Management.

An invoice is a bill for goods or services that you receive from a vendor. When you receive an invoice from the vendor, you enter it into Dynamics GP to track the invoice and make payment on it.

Earlier in this chapter you used Dynamics GP's Vendor Maintenance window to set up vendor records. This included payment terms of Net 30 and account distributions. Here is a listing of your vendors and their account distributions:

Vendor	Account Distribution
ADK AD King	000-5195-00 Printing and Reproduction Expense
BUG Business Gallery	000-1720-00 Supplies
GRR Greene Rentals	000-5235-00 Rent Expense
ISP Internet Service Provider	000-5180-00 Internet Expense
MCA MCA Bell	000-5250-00 Telephone Expense
MGC Midwest Gas Co.	000-5255-00 Utilities Expense
RAD Richards Advertising, Inc.	000-5110-00 Advertising Expense

You are now ready to receive vendor invoices, enter them into Dynamics GP to track and make payments on them.

PURCHASING MISCELLANEOUS FROM A VENDOR

In the transactions that follow, your service business purchases miscellaneous items, i.e., supplies, advertising, and utilities on account from vendors. Since service-based businesses acquire only non-inventory items, the steps they use for recording and posting purchases differs from how retailers record the purchase of merchandise inventory.

The transaction you are going to record and post is:

Voucher No.	Date	Transaction Description
1	1/08	Purchase office supplies on account from Business Gallery, $300.00, Invoice No. 10601, Net 30.

Follow these steps to open the Payables Transaction entry window.

1.   From the Purchasing page's Transactions area, link to <u>Transaction Entry</u>. The Payables Transaction Entry window appears. Observe that the Voucher No. is 1 (with zeroes in front of the 1).

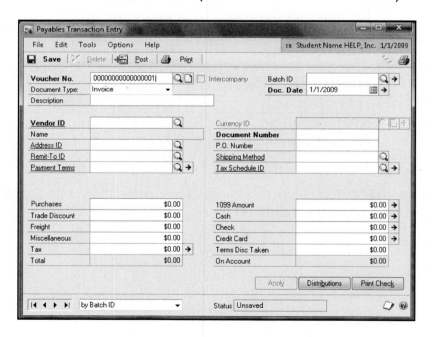

2. If necessary, select Invoice as the Document Type.

3. Type **Office supplies** as the Description.

4. Type **010820XY** as the date.

5. Select **Business Gallery** as the vendor.

6. Type **10601** as the Document Number.

7. Type **300.00** in the **Miscellaneous** field. Observe that the On Account field is automatically completed with the Miscellaneous amount, $300.00. (*HINT:* Do not enter 300.00 in the Purchases field!)

8. Click [Distributions]. Observe that the Distribution Reference column shows the accounts set up previously. (The Supplies account, 000-1720-00, is debited and the Accounts Payable account, 000-2110-00, is credited.)

9. Click [OK]. You are returned to the Payables Transaction Entry window.

10. Click [Post].

11. When you close the Payables Transaction Entry window, the Payables Transaction Posting Journal report appears showing the detail of this entry. Observe that the Audit Trail Code is PMTRX000001. PMTRX is an abbreviation of Payables Management Transaction. When you close the Payables Transaction Posting Journal, the Distribution Breakdown Register appears, followed by the GL Distribution Summary, Transaction Check Register, and Checkbook Posting Journal also display.

Audit Trail Code PMTRX00000001		
Invoice No.	**Vendor**	**Amount**
10601	Business Gallery	$300.00
	TOTAL	**$300.00**

Additional Transactions

The following transactions need to be entered on the Payables Transaction Entry window (Purchasing page; Purchasing, Transactions area; Transaction Entry). Click [Post] after each entry is recorded.

Voucher No.	Date	Miscellaneous Transaction Description
2	1/ 01	Invoice LL106 for this month rent received from Greene Rentals, $1,250.00, Net 30.
3	1/08	Invoice 46GN for $29.90 was received from Internet Service Provider for monthly Internet service, Net 30.
4	1/13	Invoice CU25 for $135.10 received from Midwest Gas Co. for this month's utilities bill, Net 30.
5	1/16	Invoice 11606 for $97.55 received from MCA Bell for the purchase of monthly telephone service; Net 30.

When you close the Payables Transaction Entry window, the Payables Transaction Posting Journal report appears showing the details of these entries. Observe that the Audit Trail Code is PMTRX000002. PMTRX is an abbreviation of Payables Management Transaction. When you close the Payables Transaction Posting Journal, the Distribution Breakdown Register appears, followed by the GL Distribution Summary, Transaction Check Register, and Checkbook Posting Journal also display.

Audit Trail Code PMTRX00000002		
Invoice No.	**Vendor**	**Amount**
LL106	Greene Rentals	$1,250.00
46GN	Internet Service Provider	29.90
CU25	Midwest Gas Co.	135.10
11606	MCA Bell	97.55
	TOTAL	**$1,512.55**

If you made a mistake with one of your entries, you need to make a reversing entry, then record the correct entry again. This will add a voucher number to the transaction entries.

Payables Inquiry

To see the transactions that have been recorded, follow these steps.

1. On the Purchasing page; Payables, in the Inquiry area link to <u>Transaction by Document</u>. (Observe that you could also select other criteria—Transaction by Vendor, Payables Summary, etc.) The Payables Transaction Inquiry – Document window appears. Compare your window to the one shown here.

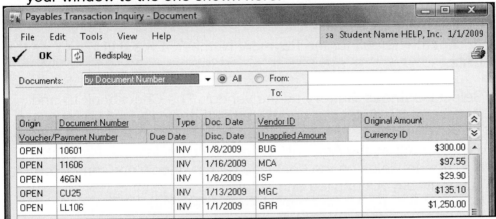

The table shows the information about each purchase transaction that was recorded.

Voucher column:	Shows that the invoice is open. (Vendor has *not* been paid.)
Payment Number:	Invoice number of each transaction.
Due Date:	INV (for invoice)
Unapplied Amount:	Vendor ID number; for example, MCA is for MCA Bell.
Currency ID:	Dollar amount owed to the vendor.

2. Click ✓ **OK** to close the Payables Transaction Inquiry – Document window.

ENTERING VENDOR PAYMENTS

Let's make a vendor payment. This is the transaction that you are going to record and post.

Payment No.	Date	Transaction Description
1	1/15	Issued Check 4027 to Business Gallery in payment of Invoice 10601, $300.00.

1. From the Purchasing page's Transactions area, link to <u>Manual Payments</u>. The Payables Manual Payment Entry window appears.

2. Accept the default for the Payment Number. Type **011520XY** as the Date.

3. Select **Business Gallery** as the vendor. The Checkbook ID and Document No. fields are completed automatically.

4. Type **300.00** as the Amount. When you complete the Amount field, the Amount fields on the right side of the window are completed automatically (Unapplied and Total).

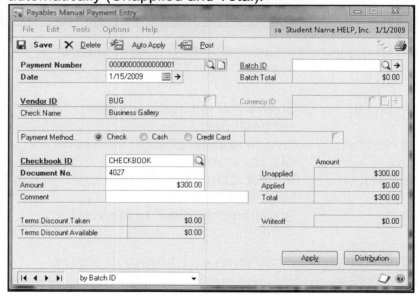

5. Click [Apply]. The Apply Payables Documents window appears. Click on the box next to 10601 to place a checkmark in it. Expand the table. Compare your Apply Payables Documents window to the one shown here. Observe that the INV (invoice) is shown as $300.00.

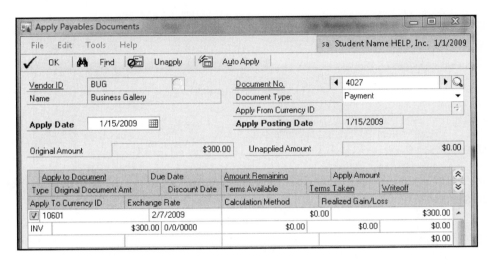

6. Click [Auto Apply], then [✔ OK]. The Payables Manual Payment Entry window appears.

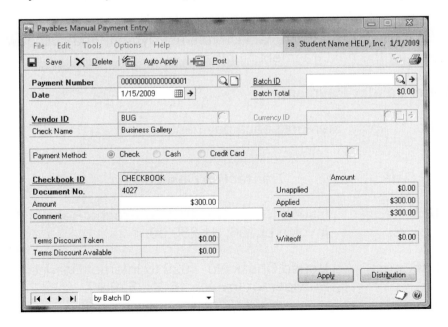

7. Click | Distribution |. Expand the table.

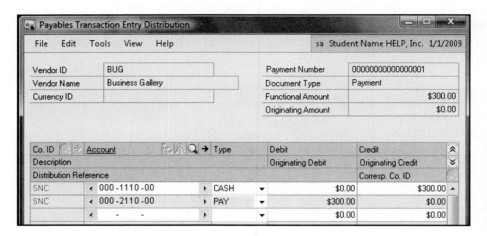

FYI: When payment is made, the following entry is journalized in the system.

Account No.	Account	Debit	Credit
000-1110-00	Cash		300.00
000-2110-00	Accounts Payable	300.00	

8. Click | OK |. You are returned to the Payables Manual Payment Entry window.

9. Click | Post |. The Payables Manual Payment Entry window is ready for the next Payment Number 2.

Additional Vendor Payments

Remember to apply, then post each payment.

Payment No.	Date	Transaction Description
2	1/15	Issued Check No. 4028 to Greene Rentals. for Invoice LL106; $1,250.00.
3	1/26	Issued Check No. 4029 to Internet Service Provider for Invoice 46GN; $29.90.

| 4 | 1/28 | Issued Check No. 4030 to Midwest Gas Co. for Invoice CU25; $135.10. |
| 5 | 1/29 | Issued Check No. 4031 to MCA Bell for Invoice 12100; $97.55. |

When you close the Payables Manual Payment Entry window, the following reports appear: Manual Payments Posting Journal shows total payments of $1,812.55; Distribution Breakdown Register also shows a total of $1,812.55; GL Distribution Summary; and the Checkbook Posting Journal shows a total of 5 transactions.

SERIES POSTING

Student Name HELP, Inc. is set up to do transaction-level posting into the vendor records or ledger. In accounting terms, this means that each time you journalize or enter a transaction you also post it to the subsidiary accounts payable ledger. Because you are using transaction-level posting, Dynamics GP automatically sets up a batch for you so that you can also post to the General Ledger. This batch posting of transactions is called a **Series Posting**.

Follow these steps to complete the series posting of the batch that Dynamics GP automatically set up. Once series posting is completed, the payables transactions post to the general ledger.

1. Go to the Financial page. (*Hint:* From the navigation pane, select ![Financial].)

2. In the Transactions list, link to Series Post. The Series Posting window appears.

3. Click Mark All .

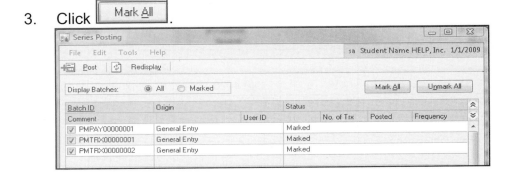

The number of batches DGP sets up automatically may differ on your Series Posting window depending on when you did your work. PMPAY is an abbreviation of Payables Management Payment. The other comment abbreviations are: PMPAY: Payables Management Payment and PMTRX: Payables Management Transaction.

4. Click [Post]. Then, make the selections to print the General Posting Journal that shows the transactions that you recorded and posted.

5. Close the Series Posting window.

RECONCILING BANK STATEMENT: JANUARY 20XY

1. Use your bank statement to reconcile the bank statement. Remember to record the bank service charge (account # 000-5130-00). (*Hint: Financial page; Financial, Transactions list, Reconcile Bank Statement.*)

Statement of Account Gainesville Bank January 1 to January 31, 20XY Account # 0908-33-5689			Student Name HELP Inc. 1235 W. 75th Street Gainesville, FL 32192	
REGULAR CHECKING				
Previous Balance	12/31/XX	$29,692.53		
1 Deposits(+)		5,310.00		
5 checks (-)		3,266.15		
Service Charges (-)	1/30/XY	15.00		
Ending Balance	1/30/XY	**$31,721.38**		
DEPOSITS				
	1/7	5,310.00		
CHECKS (Asterisk * indicates break in check number sequence)				
	1/3	4025	203.60	
	1/3	4026	1,250.00	
	1/16	4027	300.00	
	1/16	4028	1,250.00	
	1/27	4029	29.90	
	1/30	4030	135.10	
	1/30	4031	97.55	

2. Print the Reconciliation Posting Journal, Bank Adjustments Posting Journal, Cleared Transactions Journal, and the General Posting Journal. Your Adjusted Book balance is $31,721.38. (That is the ending check register balance minus the service charge.)

PRINTING REPORTS

In the steps that follow you are going to print two types of trial balance and one distribution report:

- Summary Trial Balance—Financial. This is a general ledger trial balance and represents updated account balances. Observe that Account 000-1110-00, Gainesville Checking has an account balance of $31,721.38.

- Quick Aged Trial Balance—Payables Management. This is a vendor report, which lists each vendor and the amount due.

- Distribution History-Summary—Payables Management. This report shows debit and credit balances in each account affected by the transactions recorded and posted so far.

Trial Balance: Financial

Follow these steps to print the trial balance.

1. From the Financial page's Reports area, link to <u>Trial Balance</u>.

2. In the Reports field, select Summary.

3. Click New .

4. Type or select Trial Balance in the Option field.

5. In the Include area, click on the box next to Posting accounts to place and checkmark in it.

6. Type **010120XY** in the From field.

7. Type **013120XY** in the To field.

8.   Make the selections to print to screen and file. (*Hint:* Posting Accounts must be checked in order for the Trial Balance to report account balances correctly.) The suggested file name is Chapter 5_Trial Balance.txt. Compare your trial balance to the one shown here, if errors, delete error and make appropriate entry to correct.

TRIAL BALANCE SUMMARY FOR 2009 Student Name HELP, Inc. General Ledger					Page: 1 User ID: sa
To: 12/31/2009 Last		Sorted By: Include:	Segment1 Posting		
Description	**Beginning Balance**	**Debit**	**Credit**	**Net Change**	**Ending Balance**
Gainesville Checking	$28,238.93	$5,310.00	$1,827.55	$3,482.45	$31,721.38
Sunshine Savings	$4,500.50	$0.00	$0.00	$0.00	$4,500.50
FL State Savings	$33,222.78	$0.00	$0.00	$0.00	$33,222.78
Prepaid Insurance	$1,575.00	$0.00	$0.00	$0.00	$1,575.00
Computer Equipment	$7,805.35	$0.00	$0.00	$0.00	$7,805.35
Accum. Depr.-Computer Equipment	($567.11)	$0.00	$0.00	$0.00	($567.11)
Furniture and Fixtures	$5,000.00	$0.00	$0.00	$0.00	$5,000.00
Accum. Depr.-Furniture and Fixtures	($225.00)	$0.00	$0.00	$0.00	($225.00)
Automobiles	$19,000.00	$0.00	$0.00	$0.00	$19,000.00
Accum. Depr.-Automobiles	($950.00)	$0.00	$0.00	$0.00	($950.00)
Supplies	$1,850.00	$300.00	$0.00	$300.00	$2,150.00
Accounts Payable	$0.00	$1,812.55	$1,812.55	$0.00	$0.00
Publisher Advances	($4,250.00)	$0.00	$0.00	$0.00	($4,250.00)
Retained Earnings	($6,755.99)	$0.00	$0.00	$0.00	($6,755.99)
Common Stock	($88,444.46)	$0.00	$0.00	$0.00	($88,444.46)
Teaching Income	$0.00	$0.00	$5,310.00	($5,310.00)	($5,310.00)
Bank Charges Expense	$0.00	$15.00	$0.00	$15.00	$15.00
Internet Service Provider Expense	$0.00	$29.90	$0.00	$29.90	$29.90
Rent Expense	$0.00	$1,250.00	$0.00	$1,250.00	$1,250.00
Telephone Expense	$0.00	$97.55	$0.00	$97.55	$97.55
Utilities Expense	$0.00	$135.10	$0.00	$135.10	$135.10

	Accounts	**Beginning Balance**	**Debit**	**Credit**	**Net Change**	**Ending Balance**
Grand Totals:	21	$0.00	$8,950.10	$8,950.10	$0.00	$0.00

Self-Check: The ending balance in Account No. 000-1110-00, Gainesville Checking, is $31,721.38; the ending balance in Account No. 000-2110-00, Accounts Payable, is $0.00. (*Hint:* On the trial balance, a parenthesis represents a credit balance.)

9.   Close all windows. Save your report options.

Aged Trial Balance: Payables Management

1.   From the navigation pane, select Purchasing. From the Pruchasing page's Reports area link to <u>Trial Balance</u>.

2.   In the Reports field, select Quick Aged Trial Balance.

3. Click .

4. Type **Quick Aged TB** in the Option field.

5. Type **013120XY** in the Print/Age as of field.

6. Make the selections to print to screen and file. The suggested file name is Chapter 5_Quick Aged Trial Balance.txt. Compare your Quick Aged Trial Balance to the one shown here.

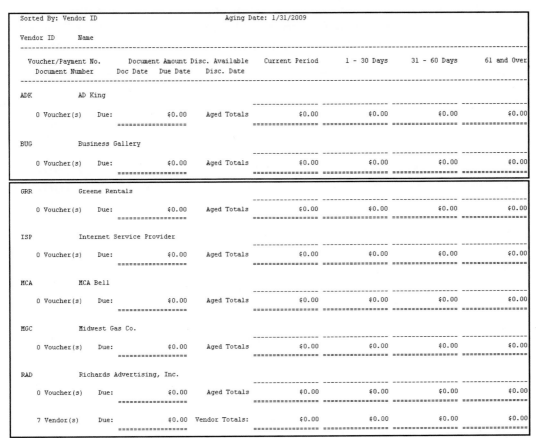

Self-Check: The amount due to vendors is $0.00.

7. Save your report changes.

8. Close the Payables Trial Balance Reports window.

SMARTLIST

1. You can print journals using SmartList. From the Microsoft Dynamics GP menu, select SmartList; click the plus sign next Financial. Click + next to Account Transactions. Then link to Current Purchasing Journal. (If a Search Account Transactions window appears, click O<u>K</u> to close it. *Or,* you may need to change the user date to 013120XY. Close the SmartList.

2. The right pane shows Account Transactions. These are the purchase transactions recorded in the purchase journal for Student Name HELP, Inc. The Account Transactions window is shown here.

Account Transactions

TRX Date	Account Number	Account Description	Debit Amo...	Credit Am...	Source Document
1/8/2009	000-1720-00	Supplies	$300.00	$0.00	PMTRX
1/8/2009	000-2110-00	Accounts Payable	$0.00	$300.00	PMTRX
1/1/2009	000-2110-00	Accounts Payable	$0.00	$1,250.00	PMTRX
1/1/2009	000-5235-00	Rent Expense	$1,250.00	$0.00	PMTRX
1/8/2009	000-2110-00	Accounts Payable	$0.00	$29.90	PMTRX
1/8/2009	000-5180-00	Internet Service Provid...	$29.90	$0.00	PMTRX
1/13/2009	000-2110-00	Accounts Payable	$0.00	$135.10	PMTRX
1/13/2009	000-5255-00	Utilities Expense	$135.10	$0.00	PMTRX
1/16/2009	000-2110-00	Accounts Payable	$0.00	$97.55	PMTRX
1/16/2009	000-5250-00	Telephone Expense	$97.55	$0.00	PMTRX
1/15/2009	000-1110-00	Gainesville Checking	$0.00	$300.00	PMPAY
1/15/2009	000-2110-00	Accounts Payable	$300.00	$0.00	PMPAY
1/15/2009	000-1110-00	Gainesville Checking	$0.00	$1,250.00	PMPAY
1/15/2009	000-2110-00	Accounts Payable	$1,250.00	$0.00	PMPAY
1/26/2009	000-1110-00	Gainesville Checking	$0.00	$29.90	PMPAY
1/26/2009	000-2110-00	Accounts Payable	$29.90	$0.00	PMPAY
1/28/2009	000-1110-00	Gainesville Checking	$0.00	$135.10	PMPAY
1/28/2009	000-2110-00	Accounts Payable	$135.10	$0.00	PMPAY
1/29/2009	000-1110-00	Gainesville Checking	$0.00	$97.55	PMPAY
1/29/2009	000-2110-00	Accounts Payable	$97.55	$0.00	PMPAY

3. You can also access other journals and reports by accessing the links listed under Purchasing.

4. Close all windows.

SARBANES-OXLEY COMPLIANCE (SOX Box)

Companies need to set up internal controls in the purchasing and accounts payable departments that meet SOX standards. As a company purchases various items from vendors, a high potential for fraud exists. Strong internal controls will reduce risk and protect the company assets. Internal controls need to address the areas of inventory purchasing, supplier payments, appropriate approvals, and audit trails.
A focus on segregation of duties reduces risks. A company must implement procedures that remove conflicts that have an adverse impact on operational performance and introduce delays or errors in the process by involving multiple people.

The SOX Box below lists ways to reduce risk.

SOX Box

A company can reduce risk by:
 	
 1. Separating custody of assets and accounting responsibilities.
 2. Separating authorization of transactions and custody of related assets.
 3. Separating operations and recordkeeping responsibilities such as:
    i. Receiving from purchasing and supplier master data.
    ii. Requisition from purchasing.
    iii. Purchasing from accounts payable and supplier master tables.
    iv. Inventory control from accounts payable.
    v. Purchasing from returns and debit memos
 4. Establishing approvals.
 5. Limiting the approval amount for purchasing or paying invoices.

In addition, a company needs strong general controls relating to its systems as well as application controls to ensure complete and accurate processing of authorized business transactions. Application controls deal with large numbers of users on a daily basis and can directly affect accurate financial reporting, a primary objective of SOX.

This type of compliance is not a onetime procedure but an ongoing process that addresses evolving standards. Strong internal controls will prevent fraudulent activities and detect potentially fraudulent activities as well as identify and prevent unintentional errors by employees.

INTERNAL CONTROL ACTIVITY: TRACE THE AUDIT TRAIL

The audit trail is a collection of records that allows you to trace a transaction from any point in Dynamics GP back to the location of its original entry. With the information you've entered about the transactions, you can trace transactions from their originating point in Dynamics GP to the actual source documents—such as purchase invoices, vouchers, checks, or receipts—that provided the basis for the transactions.

When you trace the audit trail using posting journals, you'll use two tools: source document codes and audit trail codes. These tools allow you to track a transaction to its origin by two separate paths:

- The source document code typically identifies the entry or document that serves as the basis for the transaction.
- The audit trail code identifies the posting journal the transaction appears on.

INTERNAL CONTROL ACTIVITY	
In this activity, use the Audit Trail Codes Setup window to display the purchasing module's prefix, next sequence number, and source document codes.	
1.	From the Dynamics GP menu, select Tools; Setup, Posting, Audit Trail Codes.
2.	In the Series list, select Purchasing.
3.	The Audit Trail Codes Setup for Purchasing displays.
4.	To make sure you have the appropriate window displayed, the Prefix for a Payment Entry, the Prefix is PMPAY; Next Sequence Number, 2; Source Document, PMPAY. Notice the Payables Transaction Entry audit code information too.
5.	Close the Screen Output – Transaction Source window. Close the Audit Trail Codes Setup; Purchasing series window.

In step 4, the following table is shown:

Payment Entry	PMPAY	2	PMPAY
Currency Revaluation	PMRVL	1	MC
Payables Trx Entry	PMTRX	3	PMTRX

SUMMARY AND REVIEW

OBJECTIVES: In Chapter 5, you completed the following activities:

1. If necessary, load data. [2]
2. Change user date.
3. Record and post deposits and checks for January.
4. Enter vendor defaults and preferences.
5. Print the vendor list.
6. Complete purchase order processing.
7. Set up posting for purchasing transactions.
8. Record and post vendor purchases on account.
9. Record and post vendor payments.
10. Complete series posting.
11. Complete bank reconciliation.
12. Print reports.
13. Use the SmartList.
14. Review Sarbanes-Oxley compliance (SOX Box).
15. Complete an internal control activity.

The textbook website at www.mhhe.com/dynamicsgp10essentials contains many learning resources and textbook updates. Check it out!

Multiple Choice Questions: In the space provided, write the letter that best answers each question.

_____1.   Activities associated with maintaining, buying, and paying for the goods and services needed by the business are called:

     a. Acquisitions and payments.
     b. Customers and clients.
     c. Vendors and suppliers.
     d. Receivables management.
     e. All of the above.

---

[2]All activities in Chapter 4, including the exercises, must be completed before starting Chapter 5.

_____2.   Activities associated with accounts payables are part what Dynamics GP module?

    a. Receivables management.
    b. Payables management.
    c. Human Resources.
    d. Customer credit and terms.
    e. All of the above.

_____3.   Purchase invoices are entered using which of the following windows?

    a. Posting setup.
    b. Vendor maintenance.
    c. Payables transaction entry distribution.
    d. Payables transaction entry.
    e. All of the above.

_____4.   Each transaction for a purchase on account is identified by a/an:

    a. Payment number.
    b. Document.
    c. Voucher number.
    d. Origin number.
    e. All of the above.

_____5.   The default purchases account for Business Gallery is:

    a. 000-2110-00, Accounts Payable.
    b. 000-1720-00, Supplies.
    c. 000-5110-00, Advertising Expense.
    d. 000-5180-00, Internet Expense.
    e. None of the above.

_____6.   For items purchased from AD King, which account is used?

a. 000-5130-00, Bank Charge Expense.
b. 000-5195-00, Printing and Reproduction Expense.
c. 000-5180-00, Internet Service Provider Expense.
d. 000-5255-00, Utilities Expense.
e. None of the above.

_____7.   The following report shows the total amount paid to vendors:

a. PR detail.
b. AP report.
c. GL distribution summary.
d. AP distribution report.
e. All of the above.

_____8.   In order to post accounts to the general ledger, you need to complete which Dynamics GP feature?

a. Posting setup.
b. Inventory posting.
c. Payables management.
d. Series posting.
e. None of the above.

_____9.   Which feature needs to be selected when setting up a template for posting in Dynamics GP?

a. Series Posting.
b. Series Inventory.
c. Origin, Apply To.
d. Origin, All.
e. None of the above.

___10. In Chapter 5, which of the following abbreviations was used as an audit trail code?

    a. FATRB.
    b. ITTRA.
    c. HQTRT.
    d. PMTRX.
    e. All of the above.

Exercise 5-1: Follow the instructions below to complete Exercise 5-1.

1. Record and post each of the following transactions.

Date	Transaction Description (Miscellaneous)
	Miscellaneous Purchases: (*HINT:* Purchasing page; Purchasing, Transactions area, link to <u>Transaction Entry</u>.)
2/1	Invoice LL206 for this month rent received from Greene Rentals, $1,250.00, Net 30.
2/2	Invoice 97GN for Internet services was received from Internet Service Providers, $29.90, Net 30.
2/8	Invoice 356PNM for printing, $300.00, was received from AD King., Net 30.
2/8	Invoice GN409 for advertising from Richards Advertising, $500.00, Net 30.
2/13	Invoice 13750 for this month's telephone service, $88.25, was received from MCA Bell, Net 30.
2/16	Invoice CU 63 for monthly utilities, $240.20, was received from Midwest Gas Co., Net 30.

Payments:
(*HINT:* Purchasing page; Purchasing, Transactions area, link to <u>Manual Payments</u>.)

2/5	Issued Check No. 4032 to Internet Service Providers in payment of Invoice 97GN $29.90.
2/6	Issued Check No. 4033 to Greene Rentals in payment of Invoice LL206, $1,250.00.
2/15	Issued Check No. 4034 to MCA Bell in payment of Invoice 13750, $88.25.
2/19	Issued Check No. 4035 to AD King in payment of Invoice 356PNM, $300.00.
2/27	Issued Check No. 4036 to Richards Advertising in payment of Invoice GN409, $500.00.
2/28	Issued Check No. 4037 to Midwest Gas Co. in payment of Invoice CU63 $240.20.

2. When you close all windows, display or print reports.

3. Complete series posting. Print the General Posting Journal. On page 1, the Payment Entry, Batch Total Actual is $4,816.70 (that's the debits plus the credits); on page 3, the Payable Trx Entry, Batch Total Actual is $4,816.70 (each debit plus each credit).

4. Print the Summary Trial Balance (Financial) for 2/28/20XY to printer and file. Suggested file name is Your Name Exercise 5-1 Trial Balance. **Self-Check**: The ending balance in Account No. 2110, Accounts Payable is a credit balance of $0.00.

5. Print to screen the Quick Aged Trial Balance (Purchasing) (Print/Age as of 2/28/20XY). **Self-Check:** The Vendor Totals are $0.00.

Exercise 5-2: Answer the following questions in the space provided.

1. What is the ending balance in Gainesville Checking?_____

2. What is the net change in Accounts Payable?   _____

3. What amount is owed to Business Gallery?   _____

4. What is the total amount owed to vendors?   _____

5. What is the Supplies account balance?   _____

Exercise 5-3: Internal Control Activity

This exercise emphasizes how the design of accounting software facilitates the segregation of duties. Go online to http://www.microsoft.com/dynamics/product/familiartoyourpeople.mspx. The right hand side of the website displays a link to a whitepaper titled Microsoft Dynamics Role Tailored Business Productivity. Use the website and the whitepaper to answer the following questions

1. What is the Microsoft Dynamics Customer model?

2. Review the Customer model. How many job positions are listed within the finance function?

3. Beginning on page 10 of the whitepaper, an explanation is provided on how the customer model is used to design user experience that directly supports the specific work a person does. What are a user's three primary roles?

4. Choose one of three positions. Review the various models within DGP software and indicate screens and modules that this person should access.

5. Use the same position. Review the various models within DGP software and indicate screens and modules that this person should NOT access.

Exercise 5-4: SmartList

Using the SmartList, create a list of the invoices by vendor. Complete the following activities:

1. Using the SmartList, do a search that lists all vendors. (*Hint:* SmartList; Purchasing, Payables Transactions, Invoices by Vendor.)

    Search Definition:
    Column Name: Document Date
    Filter: is between
    Value: 01/01/20XY
                    01/31/20XY

2. Export to Excel.

3. Save. The suggested file name is **Your Name Exercise5-4 Vendors.xls**. (*Hint:* Excel 2007 files end in the extension, .xlsx. Excel 2003 files end in the extension, .xls.).

4. Compare these vendors and invoice amounts with the vendors and amounts listed on the Quick Aged Trial Balance earlier this chapter.

5. *Before* exiting Dynamics GP, review the information in the Read me box. Select "Yes" to unload data to your external media. If you are working on your own computer, select "No."

Read me: Create a Chapter 5 End folder

Periodically unload data to external media. For instance, create a Chapter 5 End folder. Then, exit Dynamics GP and unload data, and then back it up in to the Chapter 5 End folder.

Follow these steps to exit DGP, unload data, and back up your work to external media.

1. From DGP's menu bar, select File; Exit.
2. Window appears which asks Do you want to unload data? Select Yes. (Data will detach and the DYNAMICS.mdf file is updated.)
3. Data files can now be copied to create a backup.
4. Set up a new folder location on your external media named Your Name [Your first and last name] Chapter 5 End. (i.e., Susan Crosson Chapter 5 End) *Hint:* Each time you back up a chapter or exercise use a different folder and folder name.
5. Remember that the DGP files unload into the folder that they loaded from the last time you started DGP and loaded data. Browse to that folder.
6. Copy/Paste or Drag/Drop the six data files from that folder, i.e., Chapter 4 EOY folder, into the newly created Your Name Chapter 5 End folder.
7. Your files are now backed up.

Chapter

6   Sales and Collections

OBJECTIVES: In Chapter 6, you will complete the following activities:

1. If necessary, load data.[1]
2. Change user date.
3. Enter customer defaults and preferences.
4. Complete sales order processing.
5. Display the client list.
6. Record and post service transactions.
7. Record and post client collections.
8. Complete series posting.
9. Record and post other cash transactions.
10. Complete bank reconciliation.
11. Print trial balance reports.
12. Use the SmartList.
13. Review Sarbanes-Oxley compliance (SOX Box).
14. Complete an internal control activity.

The textbook website at www.mhhe.com/dynamicsDGP10essentials contains many learning resources and textbook updates. Check it out!

Chapter 5 and 6 work together to improve controls over vendor and client activities. In Chapter 5, you learned how to use Dynamics GP's Payables Management module to record and post purchases of services and resources on account and make vendor payments. Now that you have implemented the payable management module for greater internal control over vendor activities, you are ready to tighten internal controls over your client or customer activities. To do that, you need to set up and use Dynamics GP's Receivables Management module. In this chapter, you set up clients or customers using Dynamics GP's Receivables Management module. Then, you record sales and collections transactions. Before you can use DGP's Receivables Management module, you need to set up customer or client defaults. After you set up

---

[1] All activities in Chapter 5, including Exercises, must be completed before starting Chapter 6.

these defaults, Dynamics GP will use this information when you record sales.

In Chapter 6, you will see how DGP's accounts receivable system works. *Accounts receivable* are what customers or clients owe your business. Credit transactions from customers or clients are called *accounts receivable transactions*. The payment terms for Student Name HELP Inc. clients are Net 15. This means that clients pay for the services sold on account within 15 days.

Client receipts work similarly to vendor payments. When a client pays an existing invoice there are two steps:

1. Enter the client's ID code so that a list of existing invoices available for payment for the client displays.

2. Select the invoice that applies to the client's check. Then apply the payment to that invoice.

To set up the Receivables Management module in DGP, you use the Receivables Management Setup window. Then you set up preferences, default entries, and options. You can also set up checkbooks using the Checkbook Maintenance window.

GETTING STARTED

Follow these steps to continue using Student Name HELP Inc.'s company data.

1. Start Dynamics GP. Type your password. If necessary, load data.

2. The Company Login window appears. In the Company field, select Student Name HELP Inc.

3. Click ⬚ OK ⬚.

4. To make sure you are starting in the right place, display or print the Trial Balance Summary report from 01/01/20XY to 02/28/20XY. The ending credit balance in Account No. 2110, Accounts Payable is $0.00; debits equal credits of $13,766.80. If you printed Exercise 5-1's summary trial balance in step 4, compare it to the one just printed. Close all windows to return to the menu bar.

USER DATE

The user date is the date that is displayed on the toolbar. For example, in the lower left corner of your DGP desktop, the current date is shown on the toolbar:

| User date shows current date. | ⟶ | 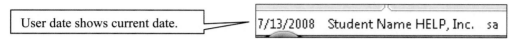 |

Follow the steps below to change the user date.

1. Double click the User Date field on the toolbar to open the User Date window.

2. Type **020120XY** in the date field, i.e., 2009.

3. Click [OK].

4. Observe that the user date on the toolbar changes to 2/1/20XY.

You have changed the user date so that when you do reports the dates will display correctly. Modifying the user date in this way is a *temporary* change. Each time you exit DGP, the user date will revert to the current date.

CLIENT PREFERENCES AND DEFAULTS

To get started, follow the setup routine in Receivables Management.

Follow these steps to use the setup routine.

1. From the navigation pane, select [Sales]. From the Sales page's Setup area, link to <u>Receivables</u>. The Receivables Management Setup window appears.

2. In the Aging Periods area, select Document Date.

3. In the Apply by area, select Document Number.
4. Type **15.00** in the NSF charge field.

5. In the <u>Checkbook ID</u> field, select CHECKBOOK.

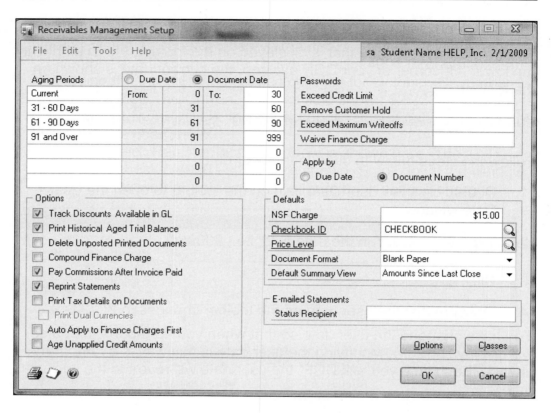

6.   In the <u>Price Level</u> field, click on the lookup icon (🔍). The Price Levels window appears. Click New. The Price Level Setup window appears.

7.   Type **RETAIL** in the Price Level field.

8.   Type **Retail Customer Price** in the Description field.

9. Click **Save**. Close the Price Level Setup window. You are returned to the Receivables Management Setup window.

10. In the <u>Price Level</u> field, select RETAIL.

11. Click **Options**. The Receivables Setup Options window appears. Observe the default numbers for Sales/Invoices, Scheduled Payments, Debits Memos, etc.

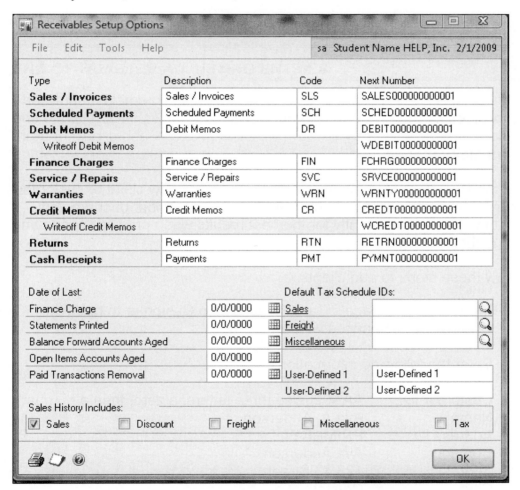

12. After reviewing the information on the Receivables Setup Options window, Click **OK**. You are returned to the Receivables Management Setup window.

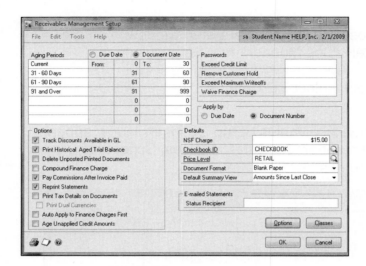

13. Click [OK] to return to the Sales page.

Client Maintenance

Use the Customer Maintenance window to create new client or customer records. All customer IDs should have the same number of characters. Use the system consistently for the best results when printing reports and using other windows.

Follow these steps to add clients.

1. From the Sales page's Cards area, link to <u>Customer</u> to open the Customer Maintenance window.

2. Enter the following information:

Customer ID:	AAA02 (Use three letters, a zero, then a number.)
Name:	Ava A. Anderson
Address ID:	PRIMARY
Contact:	Ava Anderson
Address:	123 43 Street
City:	Crystal Lake
State:	FL
ZIP Code:	32601
Phone 1:	(352) 221-2211
Payment Terms:	Net 15

Compare your Customer Maintenance window to the one shown below.

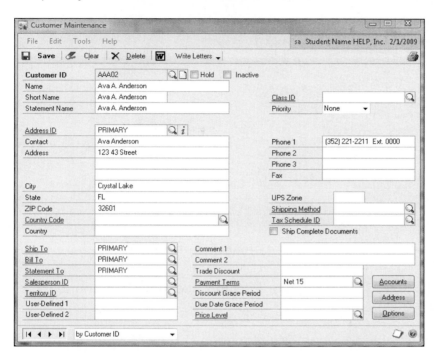

3. Click ⌐Accounts⌐. The Customer Account Maintenance screen appears.

4. In the <u>Checkbook ID</u> field, select CHECKBOOK. Complete the following fields.

    Accounts Receivable: 000-1160-00, Accounts Receivable
    (*HINT:* You must to add Accounts Receivable to your chart of accounts)

    a. A window appears and asks "Do you want to add this account?" Select "Add."

    b. "What type of account do you want to add?" Select "Posting."

    c. Account Maintenance screen appears. Complete using the screenshot on the next page as your guide:

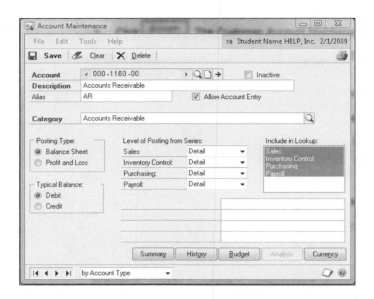

d. Click ☐ **Save** . Close ☒ the Account Maintenance screen.

5. The Customer Account Maintenance screen re-appears.
Add Sales: 000-4100-00, Professional Fees
Then, compare your Customer Account Maintenance window with the one shown below.

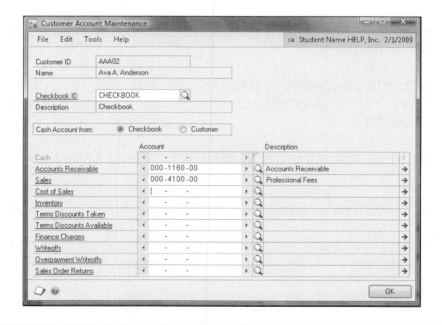

6.   Click [OK]. You are returned to the Customer Maintenance window.

7.   Click [Options]. The Customer Maintenance Options window appears.

8.   In the Credit Limit area, select Amount.

9.   Type **1000.00** in the Amount field.

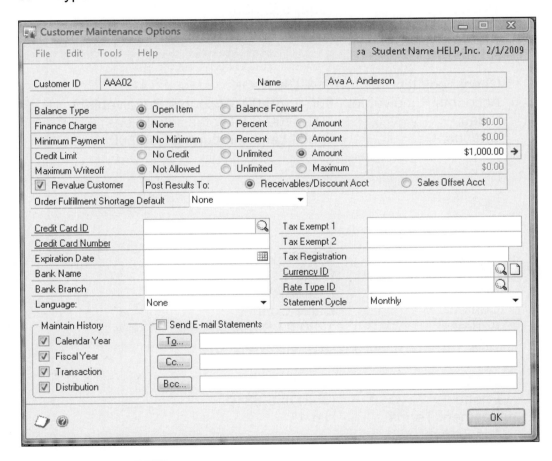

10.   Click [OK]. You are returned to the Customer Maintenance window.

11.   Click [Save].

Add the following customers.

Customer ID:	**BBB02** (Use 3 letters and 2 numbers)
Name:	Betty B. Brown
Address:	PRIMARY
Contact:	Betty Brown
Address:	1342 34 Avenue
City:	Keystone
State:	FL
ZIP Code:	32602
Phone 1:	(352) 555-3350
Payment Terms:	Net 15

Accounts:

<u>Checkbook ID</u>**:**	CHECKBOOK
Accounts Receivable:	000-1160-00, Accounts Receivable
Sales:	000-4100-00, Professional Fees
Options:	Credit Limit: Amount, $1,000.00

Customer ID:	**CCC02**
Name:	Callie C. Conner
Address:	PRIMARY
Contact:	Callie Conner
Address:	1280 23 Street
City:	Crystal River
State:	FL
ZIP Code:	32611
Phone 1:	(352) 555-8810
Payment Terms:	Net 15
Accounts:	

<u>Checkbook ID</u>**:**	CHECKBOOK
Accounts Receivable:	000-1160-00, Accounts Receivable
Sales:	000-4100-00, Professional Fees
Options:	Credit Limit; Amount, $1,000.00

Use the chart to make sure that the customer accounts have been set up correctly.

Customer	Account Numbers
AAA02 Ava A. Anderson	000-1160-00 Accounts Receivable 000-4100-00 Professional Fees
BBB02 Betty B. Brown	000-1160-00 Accounts Receivable 000-4100-00 Professional Fees
CCC02 Callie C. Conner	000-1160-00 Accounts Receivable 000-4100-00 Professional Fees

Display the Client List

Follow these steps to print the Client List.

1. From the Sales list, select Customers.

2. The Customers list appears showing 3 records.

	Customer Name	Customer ID	Phone Number	Contact
☐	Ava A. Anderson	AAA02	(352) 221-2211 Ext. 0000	Ava Anderson
☐	Betty B. Brown	BBB02	(352) 555-3350 Ext. 0000	Betty Brown
☐	Callie C. Conner	CCC02	(352) 555-8810 Ext. 0000	Callie Conner

3. Close all windows.

POSTING SETUP

Before you record service transactions, you need to set up Dynamics GP's transaction posting. The Posting Setup window defines how each entry of a transaction is posted in DGP's accounts receivable module.

Posting Setup: Sales

To specify posting settings, follow these steps.

1. From the Microsoft Dynamics GP menu, select Tools; Setup, Posting, Posting. The Posting Setup window appears.

2. In the Series field, select Sales.

3. In the Origin field, select All. When All is selected in the Origin field, you are setting up a template for all the selections in the Origin field.

4. The box next to Post to General Ledger has a checkmark in it. If *not*, click on the box to place a checkmark next to Post to General Ledger.

5. Click on the box next to Post Through General Ledger Files to place a checkmark in it.

6. In the Posting Date From area, click on the radio button next to Transaction.

7. In the Reports table, click on the boxes in the screen (▣) column. Uncheck the boxes in the printer (▤) column. By checking the screen boxes, your reports will default to printing to your monitor. Scroll down the Posting Setup window to mark each screen box and unmark each print box. If want to print out a hard-copy of a report, you can change the printer destination later. Compare your Posting Setup window to the one shown below.

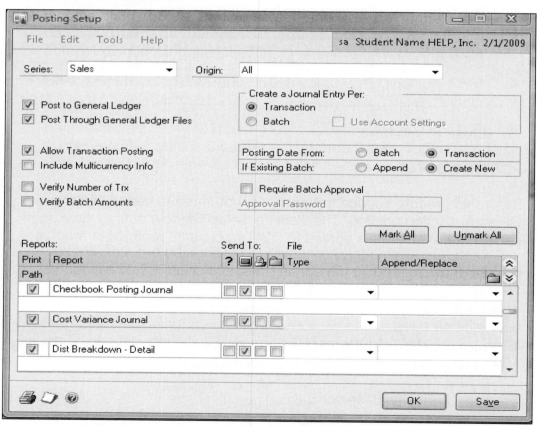

8. Click [OK].

ENTERING SALES TRANSACTIONS

In Dynamics GP, information about a sale is recorded on the Receivables Transaction Entry window. On the Receivables Transaction Entry window, you enter sales invoices for the clients or customers stored in DGP's customer file. You have entered three credit clients for Student Name HELP Inc.

You can record several different types of transactions in Receivables Management. These include sales invoices, debit memos, finance charges, service/repairs, warranties, credit memos, and return transactions. When you post transactions, posting journals are printed. Student Name HELP Inc. sells private consultations to clients (also known as customers). You will use the Receivables Transaction Entry window to record these sales of services made to your clients.

ENTERING SALE OF SERVICES TRANSACTIONS

Student Name HELP Inc. sells private consultations to clients or customers. The service transaction that you are going to work with is:

Number	Date	Transaction Description
SRVCE000000000001	02/1/20XY	Send invoice to AAA02 for February consulting $500.00, Net 15.

Follow these steps to enter the service transaction.

1. From the navigation pane, select

    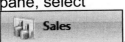.

    From the Sales page's Transactions area, <u>Transaction Entry</u>. The Receivables Transaction Entry window appears.

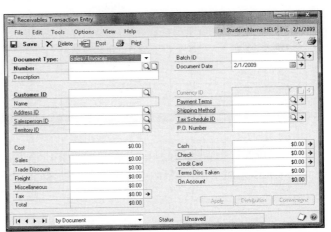

---

2. In the Document Type field, select Service/Repairs. Observe that SRVCE000000000001 is completed automatically in the Number field.

3. Type **Consultation** in the Description field.

4. Type **020120XY** in the Document Date field.

5. Select AAA02, in the Customer ID field.

6. Type **500.00** in the Sales field.

7. Compare your Receivables Transaction Entry window to the one shown here.

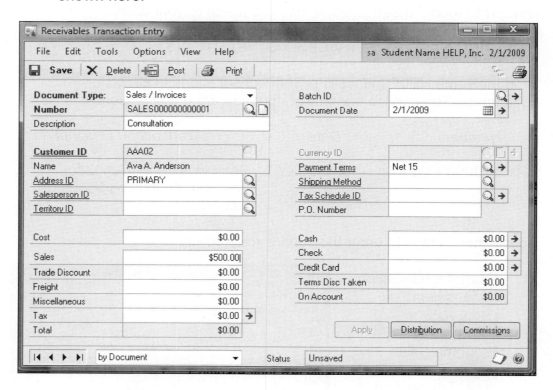

8. Click Distribution . In the Distribution Reference table, confirm the account 000-4100-00 for Professional Fees is selected for Sales.

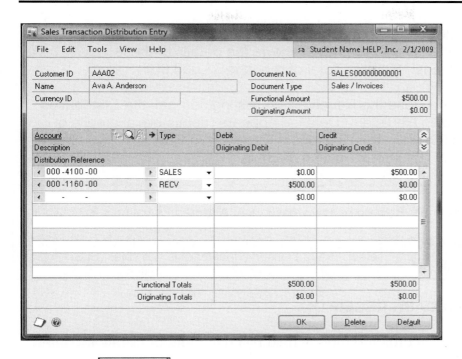

9.   Click [OK]. You are returned to the Receivables Transaction Entry window.

10.   Click [Post]. A new Receivables Transaction Entry window appears.

Additional Transactions

Number	Date	Transaction Description
SRVCE000000000002	02/1	Send invoice to BBB02 for February consulting $1,500.00, Net 15, Distribution 000-4100-00. (Click "Yes" when asked about sale exceeding customer credit limit.)
SRVCE000000000003	02/1	Send invoice to CCC02 for February consulting $1,000.00, Net 15, Distribution 000-4100-00.

11.   Close the Receivables Transaction Entry window, the Receivables Posting Journal prints which shows the details of these transactions. (Check: Total of report is $3,000.00)

12.   When you close the Receivables Posting Journal, the Distribution Breakdown Register – Detailed appears (debits equal credits of $3,000.00); then the Distribution Breakdown Register – Summary; then the Checkbook Posting Journal.

 Read me: How do I know what Ava A. Anderson's balance is?

Do a Transaction by Customer Inquiry. (*Hint:* From the Sales page's Inquiry area, link to Transaction by Customer; select AAA02.) Observe that there is one sales (SLS) amount: $500.00. Close the Receivables Transaction Inquiry – Customer window.

RECORDING CASH RECEIPTS

A cash receipt records the money paid by customers or clients for sales transactions that were made on account. To accurately update the client or customer's account, you apply the payment to the appropriate sales invoice.

Here is the transaction that you will work with:

Receipt No.	Date	Transaction Description
PYMNT00000000001	02/5/20XY	Received payment from AAA02 for February consulting.

1.   From the Sales page's Transactions area, link to Cash Receipts to open the Cash Receipts Entry window. PYMNT00000000001 automatically appears in the Receipt field.

2.   Type **020520XY** as the Date.

3.   Select AAA02 as the customer.

4.   Type **500.00** as the Amount. Compare your Cash Receipts Entry

window to the one shown here.

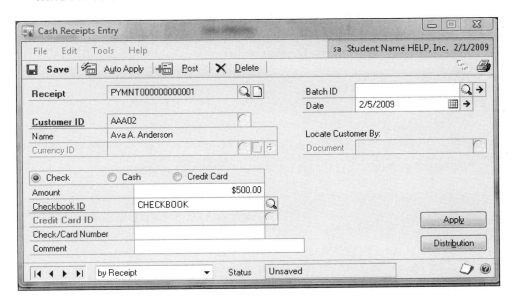

5.   Click <u>Apply</u> . The Apply Sales Documents window appears.

6.   In the Apply to column, click on a box to place a checkmark in it.
     Expand the table.

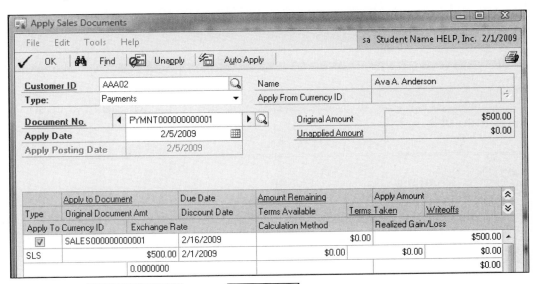

7.   Click <u>Auto Apply</u> ; then ✔ **OK** . You are returned to the Cash
     Receipts Entry window.

8. Click 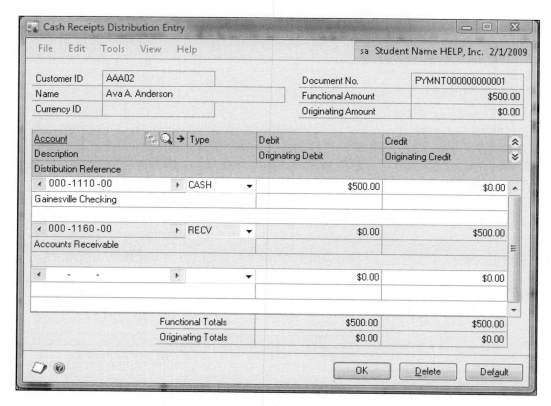. The Cash Receipts Distribution Entry window appears. Expand the table. Observe the distribution accounts: Account No. 000-1110-00, Gainesville Checking; and Account No. 000-1160-00, Accounts Receivable.

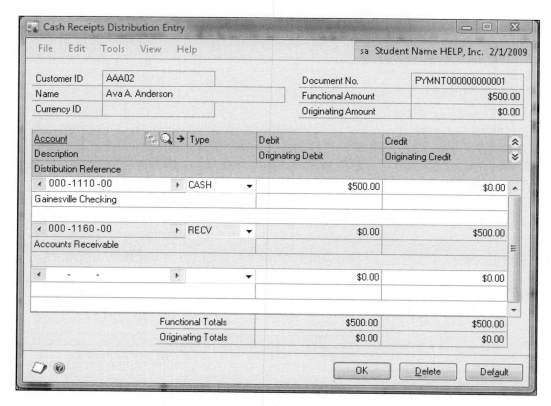

9. Click OK. then Post. You are ready for the next cash receipt.

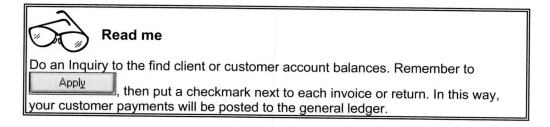

Read me

Do an Inquiry to the find client or customer account balances. Remember to Apply, then put a checkmark next to each invoice or return. In this way, your customer payments will be posted to the general ledger.

Additional Transactions

Record and post the following transactions.

Receipt No.	Date	Transaction Description
PYMNT00000000002	02/5	Received $1,500.00 payment from BBB02 for February consulting.
PYMNT00000000003	02/5	Received $1,000.00 payment from CCC02 for February consulting.

.
When you close the Cash Receipts Entry window, the following reports appear: Cash Receipts Posting Journal ($3,000.00 as the total); Distribution Breakdown Register – Detail; Distribution Breakdown Register – Summary; and the Checkbook Posting Journal.

SERIES POSTING

Student Name HELP Inc. is set up to do transaction-level posting. Each time you entered a sales transaction, you selected post to the specific customer account in the accounts receivable subsidiary ledger. Because you are using transaction-level posting, DGP automatically set up a batch so that you can also post this activity in to the general ledger. This type of posting is called a series posting.

Follow these steps to complete the series posting of the batch that DGP automatically set up. Once series posting is completed, the receivables transactions will be posted to the general ledger account, Accounts Receivable.

1. On the navigation pane, select [Financial]. From the Financial page's Transactions area, link to <u>Series Post</u>. The Series Posting window appears.

2. Click [Mark All] to place a checkmark in each box in the table.

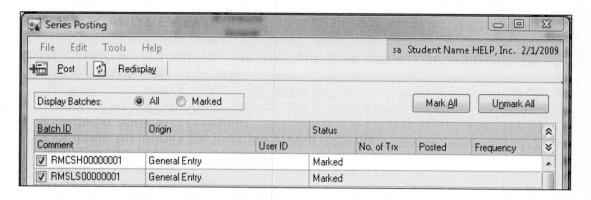

3. Click . Then, make the selections to print/display the General Posting Journal which shows each of the transactions that you recorded and posted.

4. Close the Series Posting window.

ENTERING OTHER CASH TRANSACTIONS

1. Use the check register to journalize and post other types of cash transactions for February. (*HINT:* See Chapter 3)

Check No.	Date	Description of Transaction	Payment	Deposit
	2/7	Receive from Gainesville College teaching income (000-4110-00)		$2,655.00
4038	2/28	Pay U.S. Post Office for postage(account 000-5190-00)	$38.00	
	2/28	Deposit from sale of 1,000 shares of $1 par value common stock to investors. (000-3100-00)		$1,000.00

2. Print the Bank Transaction Posting Journal and the General Journal Posting Journal.

3. Post the bank deposit entry on 2/28. (*Hint:* Financial page; Financial, Transactions list, Bank Deposits. Deposit date: 022820XY; Description: February deposits; Mark All, Post.) Self-Check: Total Deposits $6,655.00.

4. Print the Bank Deposit Posting Journal.

RECONCILING BANK STATEMENT: FEBRUARY 20XY

1. Use your bank statement to reconcile the bank statement. Remember
    to record the bank service charge (account # 000-5130-00). (*Hint:*
    Financial page; Financial, Transactions list, <u>Reconcile Bank Statement.</u>)

Statement of Account			Student Name HELP Inc.	
Gainesville Bank			1235 W. 75th Street	
February 1 to February 28, 20XY		Account # 0908-33-5689	Gainesville, FL 32192	
REGULAR CHECKING				
Previous Balance	1/31/XY	$31,721.38		
1 Deposits(+)		6,655.00		
7 checks (-)		2,446.35		
Service Charges (-)	2/28	15.00		
Ending Balance	2/28	**$35,915.03**		
DEPOSITS				
	2/28	6,655.00		
CHECKS (Asterisk * indicates break in check number sequence)				
	2/3/06	4032	29.90	
	2/10/06	4033	1,250.00	
	2/10/06	4034	88.25	
	2/20/06	4035	300.00	
	2/22/06	4036	500.00	
	2/25/06	4037	240.20	
	2/28/06	4037	38.00	

2. Print the Reconciliation Posting Journal, Bank Adjustments
    Posting Journal, Cleared Transactions Journal, and the General
    Posting Journal. Your Adjusted Book balance is $35,915.03. (That
    is the ending check register balance minus the service charge.)

PRINTING REPORTS

Follow these steps to print the trial balance.

1. From the Financial page's Reports area, select <u>Trial Balance</u>.

2. In the Reports field, select Summary.
3. Click [New].
4. Type or select Trial Balance in the Option field.
5. In the Include area, click on the box next to Posting accounts to place and checkmark in it.
6. Type **010120XY** in the From field.
7. Type **022820XY** in the To field.
8. Make the selections to print to screen and file. Suggested file name is **Chapter 6_Trial Balance.txt**. Compare your Trial Balance Summary to the one shown below.

	TRIAL BALANCE SUMMARY FOR 2009 Student Name HELP, Inc. General Ledger				Page: 1 User ID: sa	

Description	Beginning Balance	Debit	Credit	Net Change	Ending Balance
Gainesville Checking	$28,238.93	$11,965.00	$4,288.90	$7,676.10	$35,915.03
Sunshine Savings	$4,500.50	$0.00	$0.00	$0.00	$4,500.50
FL State Savings	$33,222.78	$0.00	$0.00	$0.00	$33,222.78
Accounts Receivable	$0.00	$3,000.00	$3,000.00	$0.00	$0.00
Prepaid Insurance	$1,575.00	$0.00	$0.00	$0.00	$1,575.00
Computer Equipment	$7,805.35	$0.00	$0.00	$0.00	$7,805.35
Accum. Depr.-Computer Equipment	($567.11)	$0.00	$0.00	$0.00	($567.11)
Furniture and Fixtures	$5,000.00	$0.00	$0.00	$0.00	$5,000.00
Accum. Depr.-Furniture and Fixtures	($225.00)	$0.00	$0.00	$0.00	($225.00)
Automobiles	$19,000.00	$0.00	$0.00	$0.00	$19,000.00
Accum. Depr.-Automobiles	($950.00)	$0.00	$0.00	$0.00	($950.00)
Supplies	$1,850.00	$300.00	$0.00	$300.00	$2,150.00
Accounts Payable	$0.00	$4,220.90	$4,220.90	$0.00	$0.00
Publisher Advances	($4,250.00)	$0.00	$0.00	$0.00	($4,250.00)
Retained Earnings	($6,755.99)	$0.00	$0.00	$0.00	($6,755.99)
Common Stock	($88,444.46)	$0.00	$1,000.00	($1,000.00)	($89,444.46)
Professional Fees	$0.00	$0.00	$3,000.00	($3,000.00)	($3,000.00)
Teaching Income	$0.00	$0.00	$7,965.00	($7,965.00)	($7,965.00)
Advertising and Marketing Expense	$0.00	$500.00	$0.00	$500.00	$500.00
Bank Charges Expense	$0.00	$30.00	$0.00	$30.00	$30.00
Internet Service Provider Expense	$0.00	$59.80	$0.00	$59.80	$59.80
Postage and Delivery Expense	$0.00	$38.00	$0.00	$38.00	$38.00
Printing and Reproduction Expense	$0.00	$300.00	$0.00	$300.00	$300.00
Rent Expense	$0.00	$2,500.00	$0.00	$2,500.00	$2,500.00
Telephone Expense	$0.00	$185.80	$0.00	$185.80	$185.80
Utilities Expense	$0.00	$375.30	$0.00	$375.30	$375.30

	Accounts	Beginning Balance	Debit	Credit	Net Change	Ending Balance
Grand Totals:	26	$0.00	$23,474.80	$23,474.80	$0.00	$0.00

9. Observe that there is a zero (0.00) ending balance in Account No. 000-1160-00, Accounts Receivable. All customers have paid their account balances for sales made on account. Close all windows. Save your report options.

Quick Aged Trial Balance

Follow these steps to see your client or customer accounts in the Quick Aged Trial Balance report.

1. From the navigation pane, select Sales. From the Sales page's Report area, link to <u>Trial Balance</u>.

2. In the Reports field, select Quick Aged Trial Balance.

3. Click [New].

4. Type **Quick Aged TB** in the Option field.

5. In the From field, select the customer AAA02.

6. In the To field, select the customer CCC02.

7. Make the selections to print to screen and file. Suggested file name is Chapter 6_QuickAged Trial Balance. Observe that each customer has a zero balance.

```
System:       7/14/2008  8:26:08 AM           Student Name HELP, Inc.                      Page:     1
User Date:  2/1/2009                          QUICK AGED TRIAL BALANCE                     User ID: sa
                                              Receivables Management

Ranges:          From:                        To:
  Customer ID    First                        Last
  Customer Name  First                        Last

Sorted By: Customer ID

Customer       Name                    Account Type
-----------------------------------------------------------------------------------------------------

  Document Number    Type    Date      Amount   Discount  Writeoff     Current   31 - 60 Days  61 - 90 Days   91 and Over
-----------------------------------------------------------------------------------------------------

AAA02          Ava A. Anderson            Open Item          Aged as of 0/0/0000
  SALES000000000001 SLS  2/1/2009     $500.00
  PYMNT000000000001 PMT  2/5/2009     $500.00
                                                         ---------------  ---------------  ---------------  ---------------
                         Totals:        $0.00              $0.00          $0.00            $0.00            $0.00
                                                         ===============  ===============  ===============  ===============

BBB02          Betty B. Brown             Open Item          Aged as of 0/0/0000
  SALES000000000002 SLS  2/1/2009   $1,500.00
  PYMNT000000000002 PMT  2/5/2009   $1,500.00
                                                         ---------------  ---------------  ---------------  ---------------
                         Totals:        $0.00              $0.00          $0.00            $0.00            $0.00
                                                         ===============  ===============  ===============  ===============

CCC02          Callie C. Conner           Open Item          Aged as of 0/0/0000
  SALES000000000003 SLS  2/1/2009   $1,000.00
  PYMNT000000000003 PMT  2/5/2009   $1,000.00
                                                         ---------------  ---------------  ---------------  ---------------
                         Totals:        $0.00              $0.00          $0.00            $0.00            $0.00
                                                         ===============  ===============  ===============  ===============

            3 Customers    Grand Totals:   $0.00              $0.00          $0.00            $0.00            $0.00
                                                         ===============  ===============  ===============  ===============
```

SMARTLIST

Use the SmartList to see the Account Summary. The SmartList's Account Summary shows the same account balances as the Trial Balance Summary. The steps that follow show you how to compare the SmartList's account balance for Account No. 000-1110-00, Gainesville Checking – Operating Account to the Trial Balance Summary.

SmartList favorites include predefined searches, called *favorites*. You can view search results for favorites or modify them. You also can create additional favorites.

When you select a favorite, the system displays search results in the SmartList window; the system can sort the results by any of the columns included in the favorite. You can select a favorite and choose Search in the SmartList window to open a window where you can modify the search criteria for the favorite.

1. Previously, the SmartList was accessed from the Microsoft Dynamics DGP menu. You can also access the SmartList from the navigation pane's Administration module. Click 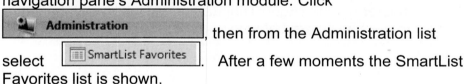, then from the Administration list select [SmartList Favorites]. After a few moments the SmartList Favorites list is shown.

2. How many SmartList favorites are listed?
   Answer: 119

SARBANES-OXLEY COMPLIANCE (SOX Box)

SOX Box
SOX compliance requires accurate financial reporting. Internal controls for accounts receivables, one of the largest assets on companies' balance sheets, are very critical. Any weakness in the financial controls for accounts receivable can seriously impact the financial operations and financial statements for a company. Several risks exist in the credit sales transactions that general and application controls can address. Systems provide the integration of modules such as sales, accounts receivable, and cash to assure that account balances are current and up to date. As invoices or cash collections are processed, the accounts receivable balance is updated real time or through batch processing. A company needs to establish and maintain strong internal controls in the accounts receivable department. This includes segregation of duties, cash application controls, aging accounts receivable, appropriate credit policy, sales invoice accuracy, and appropriate approval processes. Controls can increase the accuracy and completeness of invoices. A system can define pricing for a given customer or require approval before distributing to the customer. Customers need proper evaluation and assignment of credit limits. A system can require entering customer credit limits to assure credit sales are within the credit limits. Technology allows the automatically routing of possible problem accounts. Sales and customer service personnel can access customer balances and payment history in real time. The customer master table codes invoices and cash receipts. This assures correct application of cash receipts to the appropriate customers. Strong general controls relating to its systems as well as application controls ensure complete and accurate processing of authorized business transactions. Application controls deal with large numbers of users on a daily basis and can directly affect accurate financial reporting, a primary objective of SOX. The evaluation of internal controls is an ongoing process that addresses evolving standards. Strong internal controls will prevent fraudulent activities and detect potentially fraudulent activities as well as identify and prevent unintentional errors by employees.

	INTERNAL CONTROL ACTIVITY
	Information processing goals include input accuracy, validity, and completeness as well as update completeness and accuracy. Update goals apply when a delay exists between the input of data and its processing. Accurate reporting results only when the user enters all required data accurately for valid transactions. Some system internal controls assist with input accuracy, validity, and completeness. As a user enters transactions, the user can receive online prompting. This internal control requires the user to answer requests for the input or questions about the data. Different systems use prompts such as accept, edit, or reject a completed screen.
1.	From the Sales page's Transactions area, link to <u>Invoice Entry</u>. A window appears that says Sales Order Processing and Invoicing modules are both installed, click ⌗ OK ⌗. Now, you can record an invoice.
2.	The Document Type field shows Invoice. Press <Tab> and the Document No. appears automatically.
3.	In the <u>Customer ID</u> field, select AAA02I.
4.	Click ✕ <u>D</u>elete . You receive the following prompt asking if you are sure you want to delete the record. This increases the input accuracy and completeness. Microsoft Dynamics GP ⓘ Are you sure you want to delete this record? [<u>D</u>elete] [<u>C</u>ancel]
5.	Click <u>D</u>elete. Close the Invoice Entry window.

SUMMARY AND REVIEW

OBJECTIVES: In Chapter 6 you completed the following activities:

1.   If necessary, load data.
2.   Change user date.
3.   Enter customer defaults and preferences.
4.   Complete sales order processing.
5.   Display the client list.
6.   Record and post service transactions.
7.   Record and post client collections.
8.   Complete series posting.
9.   Record and post other cash transactions.
10.   Complete bank reconciliation.
11.   Print trial balance reports.
12.   Use the SmartList.
13.   Review Sarbanes-Oxley compliance (SOX Box).
14.   Complete an internal control activity.

The textbook website at www.mhhe.com/dynamicsDGP10essentials contains many learning resources and textbook updates. Check it out!

True/Make True: Write the word True in the space provided if the statement is true. If the statement is not true, write the correct answer.

1. In Chapter 6 you set up customers using DGP's payables management module.

   _____

   _____

2. Accounts receivable are what customers owe to Student Name HELP Inc.

   _____

   _____

3. The payment terms for Student Name HELP Inc. customers are Net 30.

_____

_____

4. You completed the receivables management setup to set customer preferences, default entries and options.

_____

_____

5. Student Name HELP Inc. charges sales tax on services.

_____

_____

6. Use customer maintenance window to set up customer information.

_____

_____

7. The credit limit for clients or customers is $5,000.00

_____

_____

8. Student Name HELP Inc. sells consultations to clients.

_____

_____

9.   Student Name HELP Inc. reconciles their bank statement monthly.

_____

_____

10.   DGP automatically creates a batch for each invoice and customer
      receipt.

_____

_____

Exercise 6-1: Follow the instructions below to complete Exercise 6-1.

Record and post the following service transactions. (*HINT:* Sales page;
Sales, Transactions area, <u>Transaction Entry</u>.)

Date	Transaction Description
02/28	Send invoice to AAA02 for February 16-28 consultations $100.00, Net 15.
02/28	Send invoice to BBB02 for February 16-28 consultations $150.00, Net 15.
02/28	Send invoice to CCC02 for February 16-28 consultations $150.00, Net 15.

1. Remember to click [⊞ Post] .

2. Complete series posting.

Exercise 6-2: Follow the instructions below to complete Exercise 6-2. Exercise 6-1 *must* be completed before starting Exercise 6-2.

1. Print to screen and file the Trial Balance – Summary (Financial). (Enter Date: From 010120XY, To 022820XY) Suggested file name **Your Name Exercise 6-2_Trial Balance**.

2. Print to screen and file the Quick Aged Trial Balance (Sales). (Customer AAA02 to CCC02) Suggested file name **Your Name Exercise 6-2_Quick Aged Trial Balance**.

Exercise 6-3: Internal Control Activity

Print the Audit Trail code for the Sales series. (*Hint:* Microsoft Dynamics DGP menu; Tools, Setup, Posting, Audit Trail Codes. Select the Sales series.

Answer the following questions for Receivables Sales Entry:

1. What is the Prefix for a Receivables Sales entry?

2. What is the Next Sequence Number?

3. How is the Source Document identified?

Answer the following questions for the Receivables Cash Receipts:

4. What is the Prefix for the Receivables Cash Receipts?

5. What is the Next Sequence Number?

6. How is the Source Document identified?

Exercise 6-4: SmartList

A search can provide detail of how long it takes customers to pay their invoices. To access this SmartList Favorites report, follow these steps:

1. From the Administration page, select SmartList Favorites, Customers, Average Days to Pay.

2. How long on average does it take customers to pay?

3. Export to Excel.

4. Save. The suggested file name is **Your Name Exercise 6-4_Average Days to Pay.xls**. (*Hint:* Excel 2007 files end in the extension, .xlsx. Excel 2003 files end in the extension, .xls.).

5. *Before* exiting Dynamics GP, review the information in the Read me box.   Select "Yes" to unload data to your external media. If you are working on your own computer, select "No."

Read me: Create a Chapter 6 End folder

Periodically unload data to external media. For instance, create a Chapter 6 End folder. Then, exit Dynamics GP and unload data, and then back it up in to the Chapter 6 End folder.

Follow these steps to exit DGP, unload data, and back up your work to external media.

1. From DGP's menu bar, select File; Exit.
2. Window appears which asks Do you want to unload data? Select Yes. (Data will detach and the DYNAMICS.mdf file is updated.)
3. Data files can now be copied to create a backup.
4. Set up a new folder location on your external media named Your Name [Your first and last name] Chapter 6 End. (i.e., Susan Crosson Chapter 6 End) *Hint:* Each time you back up a chapter or exercise use a different folder and folder name.
5. Remember that the DGP files unload into the folder that they loaded from the last time you started DGP and loaded data. Browse to that folder.
6. Copy/Paste or Drag/Drop the six data files from that folder, i.e., Chapter 5 End folder, into the newly created Your Name Chapter 6 End folder.
7. Your files are now backed up.

Chapter 7 — End of Quarter Activities

OBJECTIVES: In Chapter 7, you will complete the following activities:

1. If necessary, load data.[1]
2. Reset the user date.
3. Sell services to clients.
4. Record and post client collections.
5. Purchase from vendors.
6. Record and post vendor payments.
7. Enter other cash transactions.
8. Complete bank reconciliation.
9. Print trial balance (unadjusted).
10. Journalize and post quarterly adjusting entries.
11. Print adjusted trial balance.
12. Print financial statements.
13. Use the SmartList.
14. Review Sarbanes-Oxley compliance (SOX Box).
15. Complete an internal control activity.

The textbook website at www.mhhe.com/dynamicsDGP10essentials contains many learning resources and textbook updates. Check it out!

In Chapters 5 and 6 you worked with Dynamics GP's payables or receivables management modules along with the Dynamics GP's financial management module. In this chapter, you will use all three modules to record March's transactions for Student Name HELP Inc., complete the end of quarter tasks of recording adjusting entries, preparing trial balances and financial statements.

GETTING STARTED

Follow these steps to continue using Student Name HELP Inc.'s company data.

---

[1] All activities in Chapter 6, including Exercises, must be completed before starting Chapter 7.

1. Start Dynamics GP. Type your password. If necessary, load data.

2. The Company Login window appears. In the Company field, select Student Name HELP Inc.

3. Click OK.

4. To make sure you are starting in the right place, display/print the Trial Balance Summary report from 01/01/20XY to 02/28/20XY. The ending debit balance in Accounts Receivable is $0.00; debits equal credits of $23,874.80. If you printed Exercise 6-2's summary trial balance in step 1, compare the one just printed to that one. Close all windows to return to the menu bar.

USER DATE

Follow the steps below to change the user date.

1. Click the User Date field on the toolbar to open the User Date window.

2. Type **030120XY** in the date field.

3. Click OK.

4. Observe that the user date on the toolbar changes to 3/1/20XY.

You have changed the user date so that when you do reports the dates will display correctly. Modifying the user date in this way is a *temporary* change. Each time you exit DGP, the user date will revert to the current date.

SELLING SERVICES TO CLIENTS

For the month of March, record and post the following service transactions. Remember Professional Fees account number is 000-4100-00. Click Post after every transaction. If transaction exceeds credit limit of customer, click Yes to continue. (*HINT:* Sales page; Sales, Transactions list, Transaction Entry.)

Date	Transaction Description
3/1	Send invoice to AAA02 for March consulting $500.00, Net 15.
3/1	Send invoice to BBB02 for March consulting $500.00, Net 15.
3/1	Send invoice to CCC02 for March consulting $500.00, Net 15

1. When you close the Receivables Transaction window, reports print.

2. Complete series posting. (*Hint:* Financial page; Financial, Transactions list, <u>Series Post</u>.) Reports print.

RECORDING CASH RECEIPTS

Record and post the following transactions. (*HINT:* Sales page; Sales, Transactions list, <u>Cash Receipts</u>.)

Date	Transaction Description
3/4	Received $100.00 payment from AAA02 for February 16-28 consultations.
3/4	Received $150.00 payment from BBB2 for February 16-28 consultations.
3/4	Received $150.00 payment from CCC02 for February 16-28 consultations.
3/5	Received $500.00 payment from AAA02 for March consulting.
3/5	Received $500.00 payment from BBB02 for March consulting.
3/5	Received $500.00 payment from CCC02 for March consulting.

1. When you close the Cash Receipts Entry window, reports print.

2. Complete series posting on 3/5. Print reports.

PURCHASING MISCELLANEOUS FROM VENDORS

Record and post each of the following transactions. (*HINT:* Purchasing page; Purchasing, Transactions list; <u>Transaction Entry</u>)

Date   *Transaction Description (Miscellaneous)*

03/1   Invoice LL306 for this month rent received from Greene Rentals, $1,250.00, Net 30.

03/2   Invoice 307GN for Internet services was received from Internet Service Provider, $29.90, Net 30.

03/8   Invoice1163 for office supplies, $60.00, was received from Business Gallery, Net 30.

03/8   Invoice GN333 for this month's telephone from MCA Bell, $110.00, Net 30.

03/13   Invoice CU413 for this month's utilities, $302.00, was received from Midwest Gas Co., Net 30.

1. When you close the Payables Transaction Entry window, reports print.

2. Complete series posting on 03/13. Print reports.

ENTERING VENDOR PAYMENTS

Record and post each of the following transactions. (*HINT:* Purchasing page; Purchasing, Transactions list; <u>Manual Payment</u>.)

Date   *Transaction Description*

03/6   Issued Check No. 4039 to Greene Rentals in payment of Invoice LL306, $1,250.00.

03/15   Issued Check No. 4040 to Internet Service Providers in payment of Invoice 307GN, $29.90.

03/19 Issued Check No. 4041 to Business Gallery in payment of Invoice 1163, $60.00.

03/27 Issued Check No. 4042 to MCA Bell in payment of Invoice GN333, $110.00.

03/28 Issued Check No. 4043 to Midwest Gas Co. in payment of Invoice CU413 $302.00.

1.   When you close all windows, display or print reports.

2.   Complete series posting on 03/28. Print reports.

ENTERING OTHER CASH TRANSACTIONS

1.   Use the check register to journalize and post other types of cash transactions for March. (*Hint:* Financial page; Financial, Transactions list, Bank Transactions.)

2.

Check No.	Date	Description of Transaction	Payment	Deposit
	3/8	Receive from Gainesville College teaching income (000-4110-00).		$2,655.00
4044	3/28	Pay Victor Albert for repairs (000-5185-00).	$400.00	
4045	3/28	Pay The Courier for a newspaper subscription (000-5150-00).	$145.00	

3.   Close Bank Transaction Entry window, reports print.

4.   Post the bank deposit entry on 3/28. (*Hint:* Financial page; Financial, Transactions list, Bank Deposits.) Reports print.

RECONCILING BANK STATEMENT: MARCH 20XY

1.   Use your bank statement to reconcile the bank statement. Remember to record the bank service charge (account # 000-5130-00). Enlarge window to view all the deposits and checks for March.

Statement of Account			Student Name HELP Inc.	
Gainesville Bank			1235 W. 75th Street	
March 1 to March 31, 20XY Account # 0908-33-5689			Gainesville, FL 32192	
REGULAR CHECKING				
Previous Balance	2/28/XY	$35,915.03		
1 Deposits(+)		4,555.00		
7 checks (-)		2,296.90		
Service Charges (-)	3/31	15.00		
Ending Balance	3/31	**$38,158.13**		
DEPOSITS				
	3/28	4,555.00		
CHECKS (Asterisk * indicates break in check number sequence)				
	3/20	4039	480.00	
	3/20	4040	930.00	
	3/20	4041	900.00	
	3/31	4042	2,500.00	
	3/31	4043	60.00	
	3/31	4044	500.00	
	3/31	4045	2,000.00	

2. Print the Reconciliation Posting Journal, Bank Adjustments Posting Journal, Cleared Transactions Journal, and the General Posting Journal. Your Adjusted Book balance is $38,158.13. (That is the ending check register balance minus the service charge.)

PRINTING TRIAL BALANCE (UNADJUSTED)

Follow these steps to print the trial balance.

1. From the Financial page's Reports area, select <u>Trial Balance</u>.
2. In the Reports field, select Summary.
3. Click New .
4. Type or select Trial Balance in the Option field.
5. In the Include area, click on the box next to Posting accounts to place and checkmark in it.
6. Type **010120XY** in the From field.

7. Type **0033120XY** in the To field.
8. Make the selections to print to screen and file. Suggested file name is **Chapter 7_Unadjusted Trial Balance.txt**. Compare your Trial Balance Summary to the one shown below.

Description	Beginning Balance	Debit	Credit	Net Change	Ending Balance
Gainesville Checking	$28,238.93	$16,520.00	$6,600.80	$9,919.20	$38,158.13
Sunshine Savings	$4,500.50	$0.00	$0.00	$0.00	$4,500.50
FL State Savings	$33,222.78	$0.00	$0.00	$0.00	$33,222.78
Accounts Receivable	$0.00	$4,900.00	$4,900.00	$0.00	$0.00
Prepaid Insurance	$1,575.00	$0.00	$0.00	$0.00	$1,575.00
Computer Equipment	$7,805.35	$0.00	$0.00	$0.00	$7,805.35
Accum. Depr.-Computer Equipment	($567.11)	$0.00	$0.00	$0.00	($567.11)
Furniture and Fixtures	$5,000.00	$0.00	$0.00	$0.00	$5,000.00
Accum. Depr.-Furniture and Fixtures	($225.00)	$0.00	$0.00	$0.00	($225.00)
Automobiles	$19,000.00	$0.00	$0.00	$0.00	$19,000.00
Accum. Depr.-Automobiles	($950.00)	$0.00	$0.00	$0.00	($950.00)
Supplies	$1,850.00	$360.00	$0.00	$360.00	$2,210.00
Accounts Payable	$0.00	$5,972.80	$5,972.80	$0.00	$0.00
Publisher Advances	($4,250.00)	$0.00	$0.00	$0.00	($4,250.00)
Retained Earnings	($6,755.99)	$0.00	$0.00	$0.00	($6,755.99)
Common Stock	($88,444.46)	$0.00	$1,000.00	($1,000.00)	($89,444.46)
Professional Fees	$0.00	$0.00	$4,900.00	($4,900.00)	($4,900.00)
Teaching Income	$0.00	$0.00	$10,620.00	($10,620.00)	($10,620.00)
Advertising and Marketing Expense	$0.00	$500.00	$0.00	$500.00	$500.00
Bank Charges Expense	$0.00	$45.00	$0.00	$45.00	$45.00
Dues and Subscriptions Expense	$0.00	$145.00	$0.00	$145.00	$145.00
Internet Service Provider Expense	$0.00	$89.70	$0.00	$89.70	$89.70
Maintenance and Repairs Expense	$0.00	$400.00	$0.00	$400.00	$400.00
Postage and Delivery Expense	$0.00	$38.00	$0.00	$38.00	$38.00
Printing and Reproduction Expense	$0.00	$300.00	$0.00	$300.00	$300.00
Rent Expense	$0.00	$3,750.00	$0.00	$3,750.00	$3,750.00
Telephone Expense	$0.00	$295.80	$0.00	$295.80	$295.80
Utilities Expense	$0.00	$677.30	$0.00	$677.30	$677.30

	Accounts	Beginning Balance	Debit	Credit	Net Change	Ending Balance
Grand Totals:	28	$0.00	$33,993.60	$33,993.60	$0.00	$0.00

9. Observe that there is a zero (0.00) ending balance in Account No. 000-2110-00, Accounts Payable. All vendors have been paid their account balances for purchases made on account. Close all windows. Save your report options.

END-OF-QUARTER ADJUSTING ENTRIES

Record and save the following March 31, 20XY adjusting entries: Record and post each of the following transactions. (*Hint:* Financial page; Financial, Transactions list, General. Reference field is Adjusting entry)

1. Office supplies on hand in the supply cabinet are $750.00. The Supplies account currently shows $2,210.00. Thus, $1,460.00 of supplies has been used this quarter.

Acct. #	Account Name	Debit	Credit
000-5245-00	Supplies Expense	1460.00	
000-1720-00	Supplies		1,460.00

Hint: Click [Post] *after each transaction entry.*

2. Three months of prepaid insurance has expired $525.00.

Acct. #	Account Name	Debit	Credit
000-5175-00	Insurance Expense	525.00	
000-1200-00	Prepaid Insurance		525.00

3. Depreciate computer equipment for the first quarter, use this calculation: $7,805.35-$1,000.00 ÷ 3 years X (3 months ÷ 12 months) = $567.11.

Acct. #	Account Name	Debit	Credit
000-5147-00	Depreciation Expense - Computer equipment	567.11	
000-1435-00	Accumulated Depreciation - Computer equipment		567.11

4. Depreciate furniture and fixtures for the first quarter, use this calculation: $5,000 - $500 ÷ 5 years X (3 months ÷ 12 months) = $225.00.

Acct. #	Account Name	Debit	Credit
000-5149-00	Depreciation Expense – Furniture and Fixtures	225.00	
000-1445-00	Accumulated Depreciation - Furniture and Fixtures		225.00

5. Depreciate automobile for the first quarter, use this calculation: $19,000 ÷ 5 years X (3 months ÷ 12 months) = $950.00.

Acct. #	Account Name	Debit	Credit
000-5145-00	Depreciation Expense – Automobile	950.00	
000-1455-00	Accumulated Depreciation - Automobile		950.00

6. You received an advance from a publisher last year. This was recorded as *unearned revenue* in the liability account, Publisher Advances and appeared on your beginning Balance Sheet. The balance in the Publisher Advances account has been earned this quarter.

Acct. #	Account Name	Debit	Credit
000-2310-00	Publisher Advances	4,250.00	
000-4120-00	Royalty Income		4,250.00

7. Check to make sure that each one of your adjusting entries is correct by reviewing the printed or displayed General Ledger Posting Journal.

8. Then close all open windows to return to the desktop.

> **Read me**
>
> **What if you made a mistake?** The following steps assume a Journal entry was incorrect.
> Follow these steps to Back Out of the incorrect Journal Entry.
> Select Transaction; Financial, General. Click [Correct].
> In the Action field, select Back Out a Journal Entry.
> Type the number of the incorrect Journal Entry (i.e., **40)** in the Original Journal Entry field.
> Click [✓ OK]. Click [X Delete]. When the screen appears asking Are you sure you want to delete this transaction?, click [Delete].
> Now record and post the correct debits and credits. Observe that the Journal Entry field shows a new Journal Entry number.
> If you reprint the General Posting Journal report, notice that an extra transaction number prints with the correct accounts debited and credited. For auditing purposes, GP shows an additional journal entry number so that the accounting records show that an entry was deleted.
> **What if you make too many mistakes?**
> If you want to start over from the last time you unloaded and backed up your data, exit DGP. Unload your faulty data and drag the folder to Trash. Using the last backup on your external media restart DGP and load DYNAMICS.mdf from this prior backup.

PRINTING ADJUSTED TRIAL BALANCE

Follow these steps to print the adjusted trial balance.

1. From the Financial page's Reports area, select <u>Trial Balance</u>.
2. In the <u>Reports</u> field, select Summary.
3. Click [New].
4. Type or select Trial Balance in the Option field.
5. In the Include area, click on the box next to Posting accounts to place and checkmark in it.
6. Type **010120XY** in the From field.
7. Type **0033120XY** in the To field.
8. Make the selections to print to screen and file. Suggested file name is **Chapter 7_Adjusted Trial Balance.txt.** Compare your Trial Balance Summary to the one shown on the next page.

Description	Beginning Balance	Debit	Credit	Net Change	Ending Balance
Gainesville Checking	$28,238.93	$16,520.00	$6,600.80	$9,919.20	$38,158.13
Sunshine Savings	$4,500.50	$0.00	$0.00	$0.00	$4,500.50
FL State Savings	$33,222.78	$0.00	$0.00	$0.00	$33,222.78
Accounts Receivable	$0.00	$4,900.00	$4,900.00	$0.00	$0.00
Prepaid Insurance	$1,575.00	$0.00	$525.00	($525.00)	$1,050.00
Computer Equipment	$7,805.35	$0.00	$0.00	$0.00	$7,805.35
Accum. Depr.-Computer Equipment	($567.11)	$0.00	$567.11	($567.11)	($1,134.22)
Furniture and Fixtures	$5,000.00	$0.00	$0.00	$0.00	$5,000.00
Accum. Depr.-Furniture and Fixtures	($225.00)	$0.00	$225.00	($225.00)	($450.00)
Automobiles	$19,000.00	$0.00	$0.00	$0.00	$19,000.00
Accum. Depr.-Automobiles	($950.00)	$0.00	$950.00	($950.00)	($1,900.00)
Supplies	$1,850.00	$360.00	$1,460.00	($1,100.00)	$750.00
Accounts Payable	$0.00	$5,972.80	$5,972.80	$0.00	$0.00
Publisher Advances	($4,250.00)	$4,250.00	$0.00	$4,250.00	$0.00
Retained Earnings	($6,755.99)	$0.00	$0.00	$0.00	($6,755.99)
Common Stock	($88,444.46)	$0.00	$1,000.00	($1,000.00)	($89,444.46)
Professional Fees	$0.00	$0.00	$4,900.00	($4,900.00)	($4,900.00)
Teaching Income	$0.00	$0.00	$10,620.00	($10,620.00)	($10,620.00)
Royalty Income	$0.00	$0.00	$4,250.00	($4,250.00)	($4,250.00)
Advertising and Marketing Expense	$0.00	$500.00	$0.00	$500.00	$500.00
Bank Charges Expense	$0.00	$45.00	$0.00	$45.00	$45.00
Depr. Exp.-Automobiles	$0.00	$950.00	$0.00	$950.00	$950.00
Depr. Exp.-Computer Equipment	$0.00	$567.11	$0.00	$567.11	$567.11
Depr. Exp.-Furniture and Fixtures	$0.00	$225.00	$0.00	$225.00	$225.00
Dues and Subscriptions Expense	$0.00	$145.00	$0.00	$145.00	$145.00
Insurance Expense	$0.00	$525.00	$0.00	$525.00	$525.00
Internet Service Provider Expense	$0.00	$89.70	$0.00	$89.70	$89.70
Maintenance and Repairs Expense	$0.00	$400.00	$0.00	$400.00	$400.00
Postage and Delivery Expense	$0.00	$38.00	$0.00	$38.00	$38.00
Printing and Reproduction Expense	$0.00	$300.00	$0.00	$300.00	$300.00
Rent Expense	$0.00	$3,750.00	$0.00	$3,750.00	$3,750.00
Supplies Expense	$0.00	$1,460.00	$0.00	$1,460.00	$1,460.00
Telephone Expense	$0.00	$295.80	$0.00	$295.80	$295.80
Utilities Expense	$0.00	$677.30	$0.00	$677.30	$677.30

	Accounts	Beginning Balance	Debit	Credit	Net Change	Ending Balance
Grand Totals:	34	$0.00	$41,970.71	$41,970.71	$0.00	$0.00

PRINTING FINANCIAL STATEMENTS

Before printing the end-of-quarter financial statements, let's make sure the layout will reflect current period balances for March, and year to date balances for January through March.

1. From the Financial page's Reports area, link to <u>Advanced Financial</u>.

2. Open the Income Statement. Click Layout .

3. Double-click C2. Select **20XY** (i.e., 2009) for the "Balance For: Year Open." Type **3** for the "Period: Other Period" and "To: Other Period." Compare your Financial Column Definition window to the one shown on the next page.

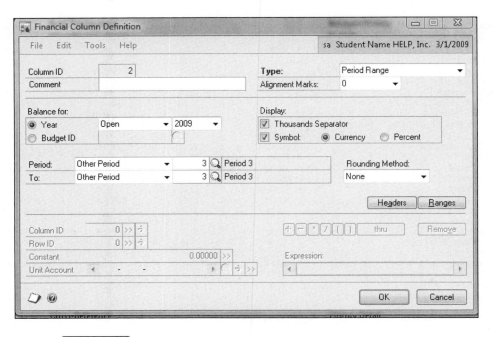

4. Click ⎣ OK ⎦.

5. Double-click on C3, the Current YTD column. Compare your definitions to the one shown below. Notice Balance for the current year 20XY and periods are 1 and 3 (i.e., January-March).

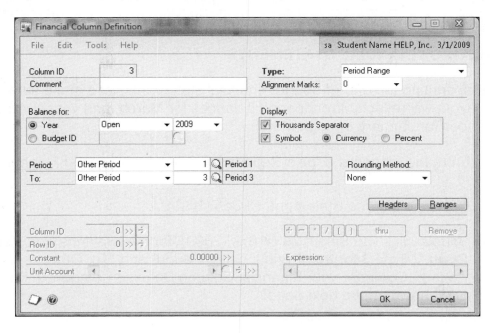

6. Click [OK]; close the Advanced Financial Report Layout
    window, click [Save].

7. Make similar selections for the Statement of Cash Flow.

8. For Balance Sheet layout, double-click C2. Compare your Financial
    Column Definition window to the one shown here. If necessary,
    refer to Chapter 2 page 72 for the balance sheet layout and printing
    the balance sheet. Notice Balance for the current year 20XY (i.e.,
    2009) and periods are 0 to 3 (i.e., Beginning of year-March).

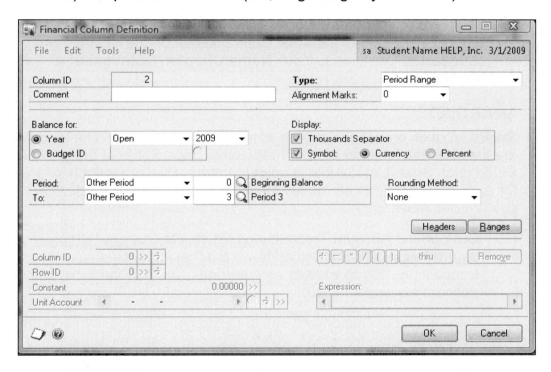

9. Click [OK].

10. Close all windows and return to Desktop.

From the Financial page's Reports area, link to <u>Financial Statements</u> to
print to screen and file the following financial statements.

1. Income Statement; Option, Income Statement. The income
    statement reports a current period Net Income of $2,425.99 and

Current YTD Net Income of $9,802.09. Suggested file name is **Your Name Chapter 7 IncomeStatement.txt.**

2. Balance Sheet; Option, Balance Sheet. The balance shows total assets of $106,002.54 and total liabilities and equity of $106,002.54. Observe that the balance sheet's year-to-date Net Profit/(Loss) amount is the same as the amount on the income statement. Suggested file name is **Your Name Chapter 7 Balance Sheet.txt.**

3. Statement of Cash Flow; Option, Cash Flow. The statement of cash flow shows a year-to-date ending cash balance of $75,881.41. Observe that the ending cash balance on the statement of cash flow is the same as the Total Cash balance on the Balance Sheet. Suggested file name is **Your Name Chapter 7 Statement of Cash Flows.txt.**

SMARTLIST

SmartList uses predefined search criteria called *favorites.* The favorites are listed on the left side of the SmartList window. Some of the criteria within each SmartList favorite is used to create a default search, or view, for each favorite. You can modify the view to create a variety of customized views.

1. Click on the Account Transactions list, link to Current Purchasing Journal. Now the right pane shows purchasing account transactions. If you want to view journals, you use the SmartList's account transactions links.

2. Click + next to Customers; link to Customer Balance. Observe that the outstanding March 31, 20XY customer balances appear.

3. Go to Vendors; link to Vendor Balance in the Vendors SmartList favorites list. These account balances agree with the March 31, 20XY adjusted trial balance and financial statements.

4. Each time you select a SmartList favorite, you can convert this information to Excel or Word by selecting either Excel Word.

5. Close all windows.

SARBANES-OXLEY COMPLIANCE (SOX Box)

SOX Box
Section 302 increases corporate responsibility and requires the CEO and CFO to personally certify quarterly and annual reports. This certification indicates that they have reviewed the financial reports; the reports do not contain any materially misleading or untruthful statements or material omission; the financial statements fairly present the financial condition of the company in all material respects; and management is responsible for establishing, maintaining, and reporting on the effectiveness of internal controls. The CEO and CFO are responsible for reporting on the effectiveness of internal controls. Disclosure is required for any significant deficiencies in the internal controls and information on any fraud that involves employees involved with internal activities. In addition, Section 302 must disclose any significant changes in internal controls or related factors that could have a negative impact on the internal controls. Corporate officers who provide false certifications, material misstatements or material omissions are liable. An officer providing a false certification can face severe penalties including fines and/or imprisonment up to 20 years.

INTERNAL CONTROL ACTIVITY	
The system accesses information and automatically calculates values for fields. This increases the accuracy of information and provides more useful information. To observe one of these calculated totals, perform the steps listed below.	
1.	To look at net changes in accounts information, you use the Financial page's Inquiry selections.
2.	Go to the Financial page's Inquiry area and link to <u>Net Change</u>.
3.	Complete a Net Change Inquiry. Select account 000-1110-00 Gainesville checking. Observe the beginning balance, ending balance, total debits, total credits, net change in the account balance, and the total entries made during the period. The system has accessed information and automatically calculated all this information about the activity in the account during the period.
4.	Close the screen.

SUMMARY AND REVIEW

OBJECTIVES: In Chapter 7 you completed the following activities:

1. If necessary, load data.[2]
2. Reset the user date.
3. Sell services to clients.
4. Record and post client collections.
5. Purchase from vendors.
6. Record and post vendor payments.
7. Enter other cash transactions.
8. Complete bank reconciliation.
9. Print trial balance (unadjusted).
10. Journalize and post quarterly adjusting entries.
11. Print adjusted trial balance.
12. Print financial statements.
13. Use the SmartList.
14. Review Sarbanes-Oxley compliance (SOX Box).
15. Complete an internal control activity.

The textbook website at www.mhhe.com/dynamicsDGP10essentials contains many learning resources and textbook updates. Check it out!

Multiple Choice Questions: In the space provided, write the letter that best answers each question.

_____1. The date displayed on the toolbar *before* any changes are made is called the:

    a. System date.
    b. Monthly period.
    c. Yearly period.
    d. User date.
    e. All of the above.

---

[2] All activities in Chapter 6, including Exercises, must be completed before starting Chapter 7.

_____2. When you restart Dynamics GP, the date that appears on the toolbar next the company name is the:

    a. Current date.
    b. Monthly period.
    c. Yearly period.
    d. None of the above.

_____3. When you change to user date it is:
    a. a permanent change.
    b. a temporary change.
    c. occurs only on the screen.
    d. occurs only on reports.
    e. None of the above.

_____4. Series posting must be done for:

    a. Sales transactions.
    b. Cash receipts.
    c. Purchase transactions.
    d. Cash payments.
    e. All of the above.

_____5. To record and post vendor payments:
    a. Transaction entry.
    b. Manual payment.
    c. Transaction payment.
    d. Vendor voucher.
    e. All of the above.

_____6.   To record and post customer payments:

    a. Transaction entry.
    b. Sales Transaction entry.
    c. Cash receipts.
    d. Customer payment.
    e. All of the above.

_____7.   To record and post adjusting entries:

      a. Bank transaction.
      b. General.
      c. Quick journal.
      d. Transaction entry.
      e. All of the above.

_____8.   Vendor transactions that are identified as open, need to be:

      a. Paid by the due date.
      b. Printed before the due date.
      c. Reported to the manager.
      d. Recorded and posted.
      e. None of the above.

_____9.   The left pane on the SmartList window is called:

      a. Search.
      b. Content.
      c. Favorites.
      d. Columns.
      e. None of the above.

_____10.   You can use SmartList to export to:

      a. Peachtree.
      b. QuickBooks.
      c. Excel.
      d. Word.
      e. Both c. and d.

Exercise 7-1: Use SmartList to answer the following questions:

1. What is the Accumulated Depreciation-Computer Equipment balance on March 31?   _____

2. What is the Prepaid Insurance balance on March 31?   _____

3. How much does Betty B. Baker owe us on March 31?   _____

4. How much do we owe Richards Advertising on March 31?

    _____

5. What is the Retained Earnings balance on March 31?   _____

Exercise 7-2: Use the March 31, 20XY adjusted trial balance, income statement, balance sheet, and statement of cash flows to answer the following questions. Submit your reports along with your answers to this exercise.

1. What is the Accounts Receivable account balance?   _____

2. What is the Common Stock account balance?   _____

3. What is the Publisher Advances account balance?   _____

4. What is the Professional Fees account balance?   _____

5. What is the Accounts Payable account balance?   _____

Exercise 7-3: Internal Control

This exercise will familiarize you with the required Section 302 certifications. You can obtain an example of Section 302 certification by accessing a company's annual report at the Securities and Exchange Commission website. Follow the following steps:

1) Go to: http://www.sec.gov/edgar/searchedgar/webusers.htm and click on Companies & Other Filers under General-Purpose Searches.
2) Enter a company's name that you want to learn more about into the text box and click on Find Companies, or
3) Your next screen may provide you with a list of several companies. Select a company.
4) Under Form Type, type 10-K (the annual report that publicly traded companies must file with the SEC) and click on Retrieve All Filings.
5) Browse through the list until you find Form 10-K and click on the report.
6) Click on the 10-K htm file. When the file opens, notice the description lists certification by various financial officers. Select one of these certifications of the officer pursuant to Section 302.
7) Copy and paste this section of the report to a Word document.
8) Also, copy and paste the Edgar website of the 10-K report into your Word document. Save the file and submit to your instructor.

Answer the following questions:

1) How does the report address internal controls?

2) To whom did these certifying officers disclose or report the evaluation of internal control?

3) How do the officers address fraud?

4) How many financial officers provided 302 certifications and what are their positions?

Exercise 7-4: SmartList

Once you have completed the recording various transactions, you may create a listing of specific types of entries. Using the SmartList, complete the following activities.

1.   Do a search that lists all cash receipts recorded for the accounting period. (Hint: SmartList; Financial, Accounting Transactions, Current Sales Journal.) For Search Definition 3 use:

     Column Name: Source Document
     Filter: CRJ

2.   Export to Excel.

3.   Save. The suggested file name is **Your Name Exercise 7-4 CashReceipt.xls.** (Hint: Excel 2007 files end in the extension, .xlsx. Excel 2003 files end in the extension, .xls.).

Exercise 7-5: TURN IN DATA FILES TO YOUR PROFESSOR: How to backup unloaded data files to external media.

Follow these steps to exit DGP, unload data, and back up your work to external media. Turn in your external media to your professor. Remember to label your external media with your name and course section.

1.   From DGP's menu bar, select File; Exit.

2.   Window appears which asks Do you want to unload data? Select Yes. (Data will detach and the DYNAMICS.mdf file is updated.)

3.   Data can now be copied for backup to external media.

4.   Set up a new folder location on your external media named Your Name [Your first and last name] Chapter 7. (i.e., Susan Crosson Chapter 7) *Hint:* Each time you back up a chapter or exercise use a different folder and folder name.

5. Remember that the DGP files unload into the folder that they loaded from the last time you started DGP and loaded data. Browse to that folder.

6. Copy/Paste or Drag/Drop the six data files from that folder, i.e., Chapter 6 End folder, into the newly created Your Name Chapter 7 folder.

7. Your files are now backed up and ready to be turned in to your professor. **(Remember to label your external media with your name and course section.)**

Appendix A
Troubleshooting

Periodically, the Troubleshooting appendix at
www.mhhe.com/dynamicsgp10 essentials is updated.

1. Installation Failed
2. Login Failed
3. Microsoft Outlook Not Set Up
4. Get Change/Operation Message
5. Home Page Metrics
6. Script Error
7. Permissions: Windows Vista
8. Error when Loading and Unloading Data
9. USB Drive Does <u>Not</u> Need Permissions
10. User Date
11. Uninstall Dynamics GP 10.0-Education
12. Reserved Keywords
13. Checking User Account Control (UAC)
14. Required Software Configuration
15. Windows Management Instrumentation (WMI)
16. Remove SQL Support File

INSTALLATION FAILED

When you try to install DGP, one or more of the components are *not* checked. A Component Installation window similar to the one below appears.

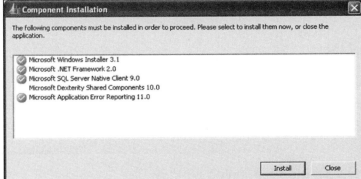

Another window appears that says the .NET Framework 2.0 is not installed.

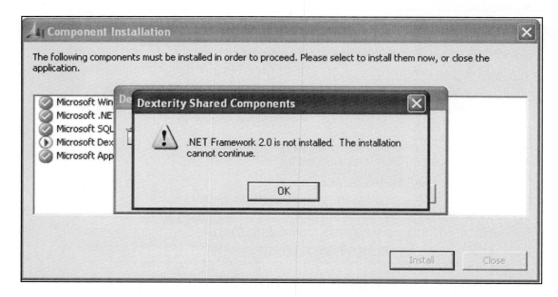

1. Click OK.
2. Go to Control Panel's Programs and Features (*or* Add/Remove Programs in XP), and uninstall the Microsoft .Net Framework 2.0 Service Pack 1.
3. After removing .Net, reinstall Dynamics GP.

LOGIN FAILED

First, make sure you are entering the appropriate password. Complete the steps below if the password entered is correct but the log in fails.

A login failed window may appear if the DGP software and the SQL database are still in use. Try these steps and then log in again.

1. Click OK on the login failed window.

2. Shut down your computer. (Click Start; select Shut Down.)
3. Wait about a minute. Start the computer again. If using Vista, right-click on GP-Education; left click Run as Administrator.
4. Type your password. Load data. Open a company.

MICROSOFT OUTLOOK NOT SET UP

If you do not have Microsoft Outlook set up on your computer, you will receive the following error message. (Your User ID field will differ.)

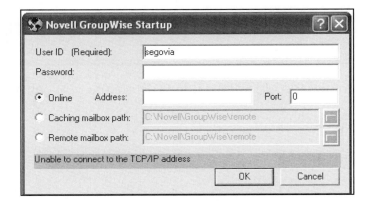

Click on Cancel and the software continues to open. This occurs each time you log into DGP.

GET/CHANGE OPERATION MESSAGE

If the Microsoft Dynamics GP windows shown below and on the next page appear, follow steps 1-8, on the next page to log in.

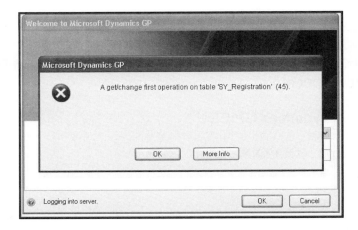

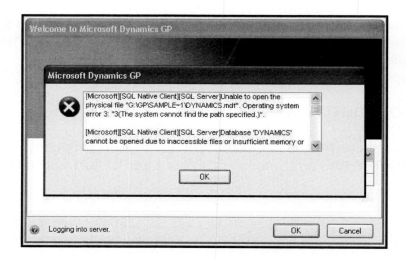

You need to unload the old data within DGP before you can load data.

Follow these steps to log in.

1. Click Start; GP-Education.

2. The Welcome to Microsoft Dynamics-GP window appears.

   Server: Dynamics GP EDU
   User ID: sa
   Password: XXXXXX

3. Click CANCEL.

4. The window prompts "Do you want to unload data?

5. Click YES

6. Start GP-Education again. The Welcome to Microsoft Dynamics-GP window appears.

   Server: Dynamics GP EDU
   User ID: sa
   Password: XXXXXX

7. Click Yes. A window prompts There isn't any data loaded, Do you want to load your data? Click YES.

8. Browse to Student Data location on hard drive or their USB and select the Dynamics.mdf file.

Remember unload data and copy to a USB drive often.

HOME PAGE METRICS

The metrics area of your home page displays graphical representations of Microsoft Dynamics GP data. For the metrics to be displayed on your home page, you must have Office Web Components installed on your computer. Office Web Components can be installed as a single product or as part of a Microsoft Office 2003 edition or a Microsoft Office XP edition. If you are using Microsoft Office 2007, you must use the Office Web Components for Microsoft Office 2003. To download Microsoft Office 2003 Web Components, go online to http://www.microsoft.com/downloads/details.aspx?FamilyID=7287252C-402E-4F72-97A5-E0FD290D4B76&displaylang=en.

SCRIPT ERROR

If you receive an Internet Explorer Script Error like the one shown below, you probably do *not* have Microsoft Office 2003 Web Components installed.

You do *not* need web components to use Dynamics GP. Click Yes at this window to continue.

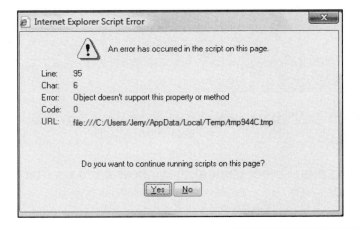

To see if web components are installed, follow these steps.

1. Go to Control Panel. In Windows Vista, select Programs and Features. (In Windows XP, select Add/Remove Programs).

2. Once the list populates, check to see if you have Microsoft Office 2003 Web Components installed. Web components allow the Metrics area to appear on your home page.

 Microsoft Office 2003 Web Components   Microsoft Corporation   1/2/2008   20.4 MB

3. If necessary, install web components from the download site shown on the previous page.

PERMISSIONS: WINDOWS VISTA

> **Read Me**
>
> Information is periodically updated online at www.mhhe.com/dynamicsgp10essentials. Please link to Troubleshooting for the most recent information regarding Permissions and other troubleshooting information.

These directions are specific to the Windows Vista operating system.

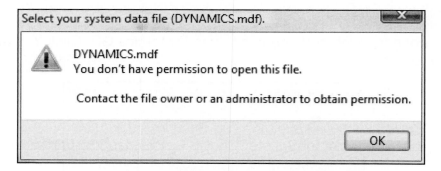

If a window prompts that You don't have permission to open this file, follow these steps.

1. Click OK; then select Cancel. A window appears that says No data is loaded.

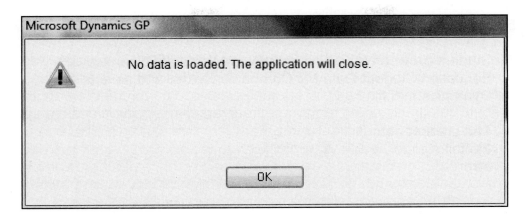

2. Click OK. The program closes and you are returned to the desktop.

3. Right-click on the desktop GP-Education desktop icon. Left-click Run as administrator. Click Continue. The Welcome to Microsoft Dynamics GP window appears. Type your password and load data. Select the appropriate company.

ERROR WHEN LOADING AND UNLOADING DATA

The scenario that would result in an error on Windows Vista with UAC enabled is:

1. Student copies the data from USB media to the C:\Program Files\Microsoft Dynamics\GP-Education\Student Data folder.

2. Student launches Dynamics GP and selects Yes to load data.

3. Student browses to C:\Program Files\Microsoft Dynamics\GP-Education\Student Data\My Companies folder and selects Dynamics.mdf file.

4. The data is attached.

5. Student exits Dynamics GP and says Yes to unload the data. (Student leaves the mdf and ldf files in the C:\Program Files\Microsoft Dynamics\GP-Education\Student Data\My Companies folder.)

6. Student launches Dynamics GP and says Yes to load data.

7. Student browses to C:\Program Files\Microsoft Dynamics\GP-Education\Student Data\My Companies folder and selects Dynamics.mdf file.

8. The student gets the following error.

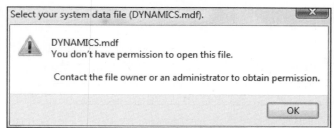

The reason for the error is because the permissions on the Dynamics.mdf file were changed by SQL. If the student would have copied the data from the C:\Program Files\Microsoft Dynamics\GP-Education\Student Data\My Companies folder to another folder and then back into the C:\Program Files\Microsoft Dynamics\GP-Education\Student Data\My Companies folder the permissions on the .mdf and .ldf files would have reset to the values needed.

USB DRIVE DOES <u>NOT</u> NEED PERMISSIONS

Data can be loaded from a USB drive. Since the USB drive uses a file format without permissions, you will not get permissions errors. **When using Windows Vista or Windows XP, a recommended option is to load data from a USB drive**

 Read Me

Files unload to the same location where you loaded files from during login. Refer to Chapter 1, pages 23-24, Unloading Data; and pages 25, Loading Data for detailed steps.

USER DATE

I am trying to print a report and receive this message: "The user date falls within a fiscal year that hasn't been set up."

Each time you start DGP and login to a company, the user date defaults to the current date (today's date). To change the User Date, go to the Microsoft Dynamics GP menu, select User Date. The User Date window appears. Type the appropriate date in the date field. For example, if you want to print a balance sheet for the period ending 12/31/2008, change the User Date to 12312008. Then, print the balance sheet. Remember, when you start Great Plains again, the user date will be the current date. When appropriate, change the user date. Another example of needing to change the user date is when you try to print a balance sheet for 10/31/2008, and the user date shows a different year.

UNINSTALL DYNAMICS GP 10.0-EDUCATION

1. Click on the Start button [ ]; select Control Panel. In Windows Vista, use Control Panel's Classic View. Select Programs and Features. The Uninstall or change a program window appears.

    > Uninstall or change a program
    >
    > To uninstall a program, select it from the list and then click "Uninstall", "Change", or "Repair".

    Or, If you are using *Windows XP,* go to My Computer; Control Panel, Add Remove Programs.

2. Select Microsoft Dynamics GP-Education 10.0 from the list. Click Uninstall to remove it. (In *Windows XP,* select Change; Remove.)

3. Go to Windows Explorer (right-click Start; left-click Explore). Delete the C:\Progam Files\Microsoft Dynamcis folder.

4. Drag any DGP data folders on the desktop into the Recycle bin.

5. Empty the Recycle Bin.

6. You are now ready to reinstall DGP from the DVD.

RESERVED KEYWORDS

Microsoft SQL Server 2005 uses reserved keywords for defining, manipulating, and accessing databases. Reserved keywords are part of the grammar of the Transact-SQL language used by SQL Server to parse and understand Transact-SQL statements and batches.

This means that the words shown in the table below *cannot* be used when creating additional companies in Dynamics GP 10.0.

ADD	EXCEPT	PERCENT
ALL	EXEC	PLAN
ALTER	EXECUTE	PRECISION
AND	EXISTS	PRIMARY
ANY	EXIT	PRINT
AS	FETCH	PROC
ASC	FILE	PROCEDURE
AUTHORIZATION	FILLFACTOR	PUBLIC
BACKUP	FOR	RAISERROR
BEGIN	FOREIGN	READ
BETWEEN	FREETEXT	READTEXT
BREAK	FREETEXTTABLE	RECONFIGURE
BROWSE	FROM	REFERENCES
BULK	FULL	REPLICATION
BY	FUNCTION	RESTORE
CASCADE	GOTO	RESTRICT
CASE	GRANT	RETURN

CHECK	GROUP	REVOKE
CHECKPOINT	HAVING	RIGHT
CLOSE	HOLDLOCK	ROLLBACK
CLUSTERED	IDENTITY	ROWCOUNT
COALESCE	IDENTITY_INSERT	ROWGUIDCOL
COLLATE	IDENTITYCOL	RULE
COLUMN	IF	SAVE
COMMIT	IN	SCHEMA
COMPUTE	INDEX	SELECT
CONSTRAINT	INNER	SESSION_USER
CONTAINS	INSERT	SET
CONTAINSTABLE	INTERSECT	SETUSER
CONTINUE	INTO	SHUTDOWN
CONVERT	IS	SOME
CREATE	JOIN	STATISTICS
CROSS	KEY	SYSTEM_USER
CURRENT	KILL	TABLE
CURRENT_DATE	LEFT	TEXTSIZE
CURRENT_TIME	LIKE	THEN
CURRENT_TIMESTAMP	LINENO	TO
CURRENT_USER	LOAD	TOP
CURSOR	NATIONAL	TRAN
DATABASE	NOCHECK	TRANSACTION

DBCC	NONCLUSTERED	TRIGGER
DEALLOCATE	NOT	TRUNCATE
DECLARE	NULL	TSEQUAL
DEFAULT	NULLIF	UNION
DELETE	OF	UNIQUE
DENY	OFF	UPDATE
DESC	OFFSETS	UPDATETEXT
DISK	ON	USE
DISTINCT	OPEN	USER
DISTRIBUTED	OPENDATASOURCE	VALUES
DOUBLE	OPENQUERY	VARYING
DROP	OPENROWSET	VIEW
DUMMY	OPENXML	WAITFOR
DUMP	OPTION	WHEN
ELSE	OR	WHERE
END	ORDER	WHILE
ERRLVL	OUTER	WITH
ESCAPE	OVER	WRITETEXT

CHECKING USER ACCOUNT CONTROL

User account control needs to be on. To check UAC do the following:

1. Select the Start button, then Control Panel. Type **user** in the Search field; select User Accounts.

2. Link to <u>Turn User Account Control on or off</u>. Click Continue. The "Use User Account Control (UAC) to help protect your computer" box should be checked. Click OK.

If UAC is turned on, you are getting a dialog when running the Setup.exe asking you to run as administrator. If not, try running the setup.exe by right-clicking on it and selecting "Run as Administrator".

REQUIRED SOFTWARE CONFIGURATION

The following are the required software configuration requirements for installing SQL Express as part of the Dynamics GP Education Edition installation. If the required software requirements are not met the installation of the SQL Express part of the Dynamics GP installation will fail.

SQL Server 2005 Express Edition

The Microsoft Dynamics GP 10.0 Education Edition uses the Express Edition of SQL Server 2005. The following are the software requirements for installing this version.

1. Requires Microsoft Internet Explorer 6.0 SP1 or later. A minimal installation of Internet Explorer is sufficient, and Internet Explorer is not required to be the default browser.
2. Windows Management Instrumentation (WMI) service must be available. Verify that the WMI service is started. (Refer to Windows Management Instrumentation and SQL Support Files section in Troubleshooting appendix.)
3. A pending reboot that has files locked could cause the install to fail. Rebooting and then re-installing will be required in this situation.

4. Verify proper incrementing for installation of SQL Server perfmon counters. Set to the proper value by default. If it has been set to the non-default value it must be manually updated to the supported value, see How to: Increment the Counter Registry Key for Setup in SQL Server 2005. (Information from link follows.)

Setup Configuration Checker (SCC) in Microsoft SQL Server Setup verifies the value of the counter registry key before SQL Server installation begins. If SCC cannot verify the existing registry key, or if SCC cannot run the lodctr.exe system program, the SCC check will fail, and Setup will be blocked.

Incorrectly editing the registry can severely damage your system. Before making changes to the registry, we recommend that you back up any valued data on the computer.

To manually set the increment for the counter registry key

1. On the Microsoft Windows 2003 or Windows XP desktop, click **Start**, click **Run**, type **regedit.exe** in **Open**, and then click **OK**. On Windows 2000, use **regedt32.exe** The Registry Editor launches.

2. Navigate to the following registry key:

    [HKEY_LOCAL_MACHINE\SOFTWARE\Microsoft\Windows NT\CurrentVersion\Perflib]

    "Last Counter"=dword:00000ed4 (5276)

    "LastHelp"=dword:00000ed5 (5277)

3. The "Last Counter" value from the previous step (5276) must match the maximum value of the "Counter" key from "Perflib\009" in the following registry key, and the "Last Help" value from the previous step (5277) must match the maximum value of the "Help" key from "Perflib\009" in the following registry key:

    [HKEY_LOCAL_MACHINE\SOFTWARE\Microsoft\Windows NT\CurrentVersion\Perflib\009]

Note that 009 is an example from the English language. The "Last Counter" and "Last Help" values are dynamically assigned by Windows; they will vary from machine to machine.

4.   If necessary, modify the value for the "Last Counter" and "Last Help" values in the "\Perflib" key: right-click **Last Counter** or **Last Help** in the right-hand pane, click **Modify**, click **Base = "Decimal,"** set the value in **Value data**, and then click **OK**. Repeat for the other key, if necessary, and then close the Registry Editor.

5.   Run SQL Server Setup again.

Concepts

You may want to review the information on the two links that follow.

Preparing to Install SQL Server 2005

How to: View SQL Server 2005 Setup Log Files

6.   If the drive to install SQL to is unformatted, read-only, or compressed, the SQL Server installation will fail.

WINDOWS MANAGEMENT INSTRUMENTATION (WMI) SERVICE

Windows Management Instrumentation (WMI) service must be available. Verify that the WMI service is started.

To check WMI, go to Start; Control Panel, Administrative Tools, Services. Check for Windows Management Instrumentation to make sure it is started.

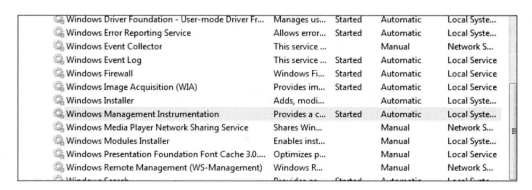

Windows Driver Foundation - User-mode Driver Fr...	Manages us...	Started	Automatic	Local Syste...
Windows Error Reporting Service	Allows error...	Started	Automatic	Local Syste...
Windows Event Collector	This service ...		Manual	Network S...
Windows Event Log	This service ...	Started	Automatic	Local Service
Windows Firewall	Windows Fi...	Started	Automatic	Local Service
Windows Image Acquisition (WIA)	Provides im...	Started	Automatic	Local Service
Windows Installer	Adds, modi...		Automatic	Local Syste...
Windows Management Instrumentation	Provides a c...	Started	Automatic	Local Syste...
Windows Media Player Network Sharing Service	Shares Win...		Manual	Network S...
Windows Modules Installer	Enables inst...		Manual	Local Syste...
Windows Presentation Foundation Font Cache 3.0....	Optimizes p...		Manual	Local Service
Windows Remote Management (WS-Management)	Windows R...		Manual	Network S...
Windows Search	Provides co...	Started	Automatic	Local Syste...

REMOVE SQL SUPPORT FILE

The other item that may cause issues with the SQL install is the Microsoft SQL Server Setup Support (English) file. Remove this file and try to install Dynamics GP 10.0-Education again.

Go to Control Panel, Programs and Features (Add/Remove Programs in XP).

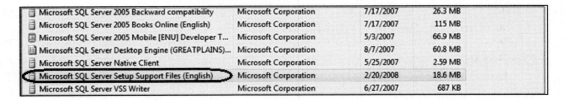

Microsoft SQL Server 2005 Backward compatibility	Microsoft Corporation	7/17/2007	26.3 MB
Microsoft SQL Server 2005 Books Online (English)	Microsoft Corporation	7/17/2007	115 MB
Microsoft SQL Server 2005 Mobile [ENU] Developer T...	Microsoft Corporation	5/3/2007	66.9 MB
Microsoft SQL Server Desktop Engine (GREATPLAINS)...	Microsoft Corporation	8/7/2007	60.8 MB
Microsoft SQL Server Native Client	Microsoft Corporation	5/25/2007	2.59 MB
Microsoft SQL Server Setup Support Files (English)	Microsoft Corporation	2/20/2008	18.6 MB
Microsoft SQL Server VSS Writer	Microsoft Corporation	6/27/2007	687 KB

Learn more about *Computer Accounting Essentials with Microsoft Dynamics GP 10.0, 2e,*
by visiting the text website at http://www.mhhe.com/dynamicsgp10essentials

Microsoft Dynamics GP 10.0 (formerly Great Plains) is the leading software used by mid to large-sized businesses including sports teams, chain stores, franchise operations, manufacturers, and medical, legal, and accounting firms. The second edition combines business process content with hands-on use of Dynamics GP software to teach the key features of Dynamics GP 10.0 using a service-based startup corporation.

Key Features:
- Includes a free copy of Microsoft Dynamics GP 10.0 software and a student data DVD
- Textbook exercises and projects support student mastery of accounting workflows and internal controls in work-authentic ways for a new service based business.
- Students set up a company dataset from scratch and explore the robust sample company, Fabrikam, Inc
- Chapters include objectives, detailed directions with numerous screen illustrations of Dynamics GP, internal control activities, SmartLists, SOX Boxes, review questions, and four exercises to explain how to:
  - set up a corporation
  - process cash receipts and payments
  - complete year end adjusting and closing procedures
  - manage vendor acquisitions and payments
  - manage customer sales and collections

Computer Accounting Essentials with Microsoft Dynamics GP 10.0, 2e, can be packaged with core accounting textbooks in Computer Accounting, Financial and Managerial Accounting, Intermediate Accounting, and Accounting Information Systems courses.

Supplements for Financial and Managerial Accounting, Intermediate Accounting, AIS, or Computer Accounting courses:

- *Computer Accounting Essentials with Microsoft Dynamics GP 10.0*, 2e, 007 811 0807

- *Computer Accounting Essentials with QuickBooks Pro 2008*, 007 337 9387

- *Computer Accounting Essentials with QuickBooks Online Plus*, 4e   978 039 018 1367

- *Computer Accounting Essentials with Microsoft Office Accounting 2007*, 007 352 7033

Semester Computer Accounting or AIS courses:

- *Computer Accounting with Microsoft Dynamics GP 10*, 2e,007 811 0793

- *Computer Accounting with Peachtree Complete 2008*, 12e, 007 337 9395

- *Computer Accounting with Microsoft Office Accounting*, 007 333 796X

For detailed information on these texts, go online to www.mhhe.com/yacht.